D1602769

Western Lands & Waters Series
XVI

SAVING CALIFORNIA'S COAST

Army Engineers at Oceanside and Humboldt Bay

by
SUSAN PRITCHARD O'HARA
and
GREGORY GRAVES

THE ARTHUR H. CLARK COMPANY
Spokane, Washington
1991

Contents

Illustrations

Foreword

In 1853, Lieutenant George H. Derby, an irrepressible, brash young Army Engineer officer who became better known for his humor than for his engineering, came to San Diego to supervise improvements to the San Diego River. The river's silt threatened to choke the city's harbor. Derby attempted to shift the river's channel back to its original bed by building a levee. A successful effort would resolve the problem of silt accumulation in the harbor, and the "two steamers that wheeze in and out once or twice a month," according to Derby, would enjoy easy access. Unfortunately, Derby had to leave before finishing the project and a storm in 1855 partially washed away the levee. Still, the project was a landmark, for it was the first federal rivers and harbors project west of the Mississippi. Army Engineers have been trying to cope with California's coastal engineering problems ever since.

In 1866, Congress established a permanent office of the Army Corps of Engineers in San Francisco to supervise rivers and harbors projects all along the Pacific coast. A handful of officers prepared surveys and investigations, improved and maintained channels, and constructed and maintained breakwaters and jetties. In California's rivers, the Army Engineers supervised snagging and dredging operations and built wing dams to maintain commercial waterways. San Francisco Harbor inevitably received much attention, and the Corps helped remove major obstacles from the bay.

In 1868, Congress authorized a Corps survey of Wilmington harbor near Los Angeles to determine its commercial needs and necessary navigation improvements. Upon completing his survey, Major R.S. Williamson recommended improving Wilmington harbor at federal expense, but his proposal called for expensive granite blocks, and Congress would not approve sufficient funds. Major G.H. Mendell was assigned to form a more acceptable plan. He utilized Williamson's general concept but substituted cheaper wood and stone for the expensive granite. Because of the failure of a contractor, an unsatisfactory original structural design, and lack of congressional appropriations, ten years passed before the project, a 6,700-foot breakwater, was completed. Further improvements were completed in 1893. In 1898, the Corps established a district office in Los Angeles, and twelve years later it completed major improvements in San Pedro Bay.

In the twentieth century, the Corps has continued to work on rivers and harbors improvements to provide safe and reliable channels for ocean-going and inland waterway traffic. Corps-built jetties and breakwaters dot the California coastline, and Corps dredges insure the navigability of the state's harbors. At the same time, Army Engineer efforts to reduce or eliminate problems of beach erosion and degradation have dramatically increased. Problems are particularly acute in California, where 86 percent of the state's coastline is receding at an average of between 0.5 and 2 feet per year. In 1930, Congress authorized the Corps to study federal property along the nation's shoreline with the study costs split with the states. Six years later, Congress provided for federal assistance for construction, but not maintenance, of shore improvement and protection projects involving federal interests. Again, federal participation was limited to no more than half of the total costs. Legislation in 1946 authorized federal financial assistance for as much as one-third of the cost of new public beach development and shore erosion prevention projects under the jurisdiction of non-federal interests. Ten years later, another law provided for cost-shared support for beach nourishment (replenishment) projects. In the 1970s and '80s, federal legislation has focused on measures to discourage development along fragile shorelines. All these laws have collectively enabled the Corps to work closely with the state of California on a number of beach erosion and shore protection projects and studies.

With over a thousand miles of shoreline, California presents a large number of coastal engineering challenges. Increasing population and conflicting economic, navigation, commercial, recreation, and environmental objectives complicate life for engineers, who already face difficult technical problems resulting from hydrological and geological phenomena. Working with engineers, political leaders and professional planners need to resolve issues that are not easily reconcilable. Compromise is essential. Federal, state, and local agencies as well as a large number of private groups, are involved. The Corps of Engineers plays an important role because of its navigation and flood control responsibilities, its large staff of coastal engineering experts, and its congressional mandate to help preserve the nation's coastal regions.

Two projects that tell us much about the evolution of the Corps' response to California coastal engineering problems, and which suggest the large number of complicated technical and political issues, are Oceanside Harbor and Humboldt Bay. The Office of History, Headquarters, U.S. Army Corps of Engineers, contracted with Gregory Graves and Susan Pritchard O'Hara to write scholarly, objective analyses of these two projects. Dr. Graves received his Ph.D. in 1987 from the University of California, Santa Barbara, where he specialized in American conservation history. He already has several publications to his credit. Mrs. O'Hara received a master's degree in public history in 1986 from the same university. A native of Humboldt County, she has long been interested in its history and development and has written several papers on the settlement of the southern portion of the country.

The Humboldt Bay jetties are a National Historical Civil Engineering Landmark in recognition of the difficulty of constructing and maintaining them in the rough waters off the rugged northern California coast. By creating a navigation channel at the bay entrance, the jetties enabled the development of many industries in Humboldt County. Mrs. O'Hara explains why the jetties were built by the Corps of Engineers in the late nineteenth century, the problems encountered during construction, the ongoing maintenance challenge, and the jetties' impact on the local communities. It is a story of major technological challenge and innovation and of close cooperation between local interests and the Corps of Engineers.

The story of Oceanside Harbor also shows the coordinated political activity that is necessary to address chronic engineering problems. It is a history of federal, state, and local efforts to establish and maintain an operational harbor, while meeting the demands of a number of diverse public interests. During the past fifty years, Oceanside officials managed, through diligence and increasing political sophistication, to acquire, maintain, and improve their valuable civilian harbor and, concurrently, to find solutions to beach erosion problems. During the same time, the Corps of Engineers steadily expanded its role at Oceanside from merely an advisory capacity to project director and design coordinator. Oceanside officials and the Corps have responded to new laws and changing public interest. While solutions have never been easily found, the city of Oceanside and the Corps have cooperated to find answers.

Both authors wish to acknowledge the help of Drs. John Greenwood and Martin Reuss of the Office of History of the Corps of Engineers. In addition, Dr. Graves wishes to thank various officials of the Los Angeles District, Corps of Engineers, who supplied information and commented on the Oceanside history: John Ferguson, Ronald Weiss, William Herron, Douglas Diemer, Donald Spencer, Carl Enson, and Anthony Turhollow. Oceanside city officials also provided helpful comments and information. Dr. Graves' wife, Francine, critiqued the text and provided moral support. Mrs. O'Hara extends her thanks to Dr. Lynwood Carranco, Dr. Carroll Pursell, Don Tuttle, and the staff of Humboldt State University Library.

PAUL K. WALKER
Chief, Office of History
U.S. Army Corps of Engineers

Humboldt Bay

by

SUSAN PRITCHARD O'HARA

Humboldt Bay has been the center of commerce for a vast interior. All of the lumber and agricultural products produced in the region were shipped through the bay from 1850 to 1914. *Courtesy D. Tuttle.*

CHAPTER I

"We're Going In"
Crossing the Humboldt Bar

Humboldt Bay, with one of the few deep-water ports along the Pacific Coast, lies 100 miles south of California's border with Oregon. Named for the noted German naturalist Alexander Von Humboldt, the bay has been the site of extensive improvement projects by the U.S. Army Corps of Engineers. The bay's mouth is blocked by a sandbar, which obstructs passage into the harbor. As early as the 1880s attempts were made to control the formation of the sandbar and to ensure a deep entrance channel into bay. As a result, two rubble-mound jetties have been constructed at the mouth of the bay. The jetties have been the focus of an intense community effort to attract congressional attention to the remote portion of California. The jetty construction also has produced several technological advances in jetty building on the Pacific Coast. In addition, the structures have influenced the economy of California's north coast and changed the topography of the bay.

Humboldt Bay forms an indentation in the California coastline some 200 miles north of San Francisco Bay. Resting in a low-lying area, the bay is approximately 14 miles long. It varies in width from 0.5 to 3.5 miles, with an average width of 0.75 mile.[1] Several small creeks empty into the bay, but "no streams of consequence are tributary to this waterway."[2] The bay does have a large tidal basin, a condition which maintains the natural channels in the bay. Separating the bay from the ocean are two sandy spits, their ends forming the entrance to the bay. Surrounding this low-lying area are the rugged coastal ranges, which in places extend to the ocean's edge. These mountains hold vast forestlands of redwood and fir, the mainstay of the region's economy. To the north and south of the bay lie the mouths of the Mad and Eel rivers. From these riparian sources come the materials that form the dangerous sandbar at the entrance to the bay.

Despite the bay's potential, the region has developed slowly because of the lack of easy access to the bay. In the late 1800s the sandbar often made the entrance impassable. Major William W. Harts, a Corps officer on the Pacific Coast, described the formation of sandbars in a paper that he presented to his colleagues in 1911. Harts explained that most bay and river entrances along the Pacific Northwest are "obstructed by a crescent-shaped encircling bar,... the distance and depth of water overlying the bars are largely dependent upon the area of the tidal prism within the bays and the exposure to storm action."[3] Access to the bay through the shifting sandbar is provided by channels carved in the sand by tidal action. At Humboldt Bay, "the channel through... [the] entrance in its natural state, was shifting and dangerous, being uncertain as to position, width, and depth, and averaging a mile in length."[4]

Adding to the dangers in the channel are the stormy conditions that prevail along the Pacific Coast. Ship masters have claimed "that nowhere else have they encountered such waves as off Humboldt."[5] In its unimproved state the entire crescent of the bar was often a field of breakers. The bar, the violent and unpredictable waves, and the shifting and often shallow channel all combined to form the hazardous entrance to Humboldt Bay.

As early as 1850, when Hans Henry Buhne first piloted the schooner *Laura Virginia* into Humboldt Bay, navigators recognized perils at the bay's entrance. The passengers and crew of the *Laura Virginia* had formed an association that was searching for the bay whose discovery by the Josiah Gregg party in 1849 had touched off a fever of land speculation in San Francisco. The newly discovered bay offered a direct route to the Trinity gold mines and many of the members of the Laura Virginia Association hoped to make their fortunes by supplying the mines. The *Laura Virginia* was not the only ship searching off the shores of northern California for the land-locked bay. The association was in competition with similar land companies aboard the *General Morgan*, the *Cameo* and the *California*. The officers and crew of the *Laura Virginia*, after having examined the mouth of the Eel River and Trinidad Bay, decided to enter a smooth stretch of water visible only from the topmast that they presumed to be the bay.

Buhne, the second officer, was sent to take soundings and to see if it was possible to guide the schooner into the bay. After crossing the bar in a small boat that was swamped twice before reaching land, Buhne returned and guided two more of the *Laura Virginia's* boats into the bay. The passengers in one of these boats became so apprehensive of the crossing that they balked, intimidated by the "terrific breakers... [that] mark... [the] line where the waves of the ocean meet the ebb tide."[6] Several days after this harrowing experience, Buhne guided the schooner itself into the bay. He later became an expert on crossing the Humboldt Bar. The pilot service Buhne established formed the basis for his fortune.

Despite the hazards encountered by Buhne and the Laura Virginia Association, early settlers at first failed to recognize the full extent of the barrier to trade and development presented by the dangerous bay entrance. There were few exports and shipping was limited. For example, after two years of settlement, only six ships arrived in San Francisco from the Humboldt region in the first half of 1852. However, shipping began to increase with the development of the lumber industry. In 1853, 143 ships sailed from Eureka to San Francisco with large loads of lumber.[7] By the late 1850s the entrance's impediment to shipping was obvious. Even with a tugboat guiding schooners in and out of the bay, by 1855 12 ships had been wrecked trying to navigate the entrance.[8] The alternative to crossing when the entrance was rough was to remain "bar-bound" for days. During the stormy winter months ships often were kept in the harbor for weeks, loaded with their valuable cargoes of redwood lumber. Other ships found it necessary to leave the bay only partially loaded so that they could make it across the shallow channels of the bar.

The burgeoning redwood lumber industry was started on the bay by the logging enterprises of James Talbot Ryan and James Duff. The pack trade to the Trinity gold mines had begun to dwindle in the mid-1850s. The bay communities of Eureka and Arcata resembled ghost towns when Ryan and Duff found that they could profitably mill the giant redwood trees that grew in abundance around the bay. Though their first three lumber shipments capsized as the burdened ships attempted to cross the Humboldt Bar, Ryan, Duff, & Company persisted because of the growing market for redwood lumber. They solved the problem of crossing the bar by purchasing a tug and hiring Hans Buhne to pilot their ships through the entrance channel. Soon other mills were built around the bay, and the logging and milling of the

Humboldt Bar after a sketch in Frank Leslie's Illustrated Newspaper, Jan. 20, 1883. Drawing by M.B. Pritchard.

redwoods began in earnest. The county's population began to swell; logging camps of more than 100 men were common. Most of the lumber was processed by large companies that had purchased vast tracts of timberland. Moreover, in order to maximize profits, the large companies ran their own timber crews. Large-scale redwood lumber production required "heavy investment of capital and operations on a massive scale if it is to yield any sizeable profit."[9]

Likewise, the only way to ensure profit was to ship lumber cheaply and in fairly large quantities. This meant shipping by steamer and schooner to San Francisco or to such distant foreign ports as those in Hawaii and Mexico. Moving the lumber by water seemed logical; the land route was mostly impassable on horseback, and the mountains to the south made the cost of building a railroad excessive. By the 1880s long wharves reached out into the bay, with ships often lying two abreast to be loaded with lumber. Many of the large timber companies owned their own fleet of vessels, most of which were built on Humboldt Bay. More than 120 were

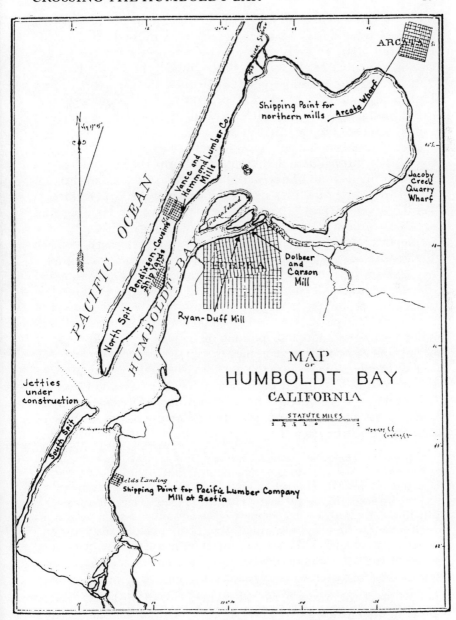

A map from *In the Redwoods Realm*, published 1893. Drawing by M.B. Pritchard.

built by the Bendixson shipyards alone. These schooners and steamers were designed to carry the maximum load over the Humboldt Bar, though they had a shallower draft than most coastal ships. In 1891 Congress recognized Humboldt Bay as a port of entry. That same year 40 cargoes moved directly from Humboldt to foreign markets, representing only about a sixth of the shipping from Humboldt. An estimated $4 million worth of lumber crossed the bay in 1891.

Lumber was not the only product being shipped from the bay in the 19th century. The rich bottomland around the bay supported a growing farming community, as did the mountainous hinterland. Sheep and cattle ranching also became part of the local economy. While never matching the timber economy, the farming and ranching products were important to the region. There were numerous reports of rich soil capable of producing any crop. In fact, the first exports from the bay in the 1850s were locally grown hay and grain products. Farmers and ranchers not only supplied the many lumber camps, but also exported some of their less perishable products. In 1890 they exported 504,450 pounds of butter; 584,250 pounds of wool; 928,000 pounds of peas; 2,840,000 pounds of oats; 5,284,000 pounds of potatoes; 7,375 pounds of barley and 25,951 boxes of apples.[10]

The problem of crossing the bar remained the crucial factor in shipping from Humboldt Bay, although U.S. Coast and Geodetic Survey maps were of some help to mariners. The earliest map, done by the agency in 1851, gave the following advice on how to find and enter the bay:

> This harbor may be easily recognized by a remarkable red bluff facing the entrance with a perpendicular front to the sea of 96 feet, and by the headland known as Table Bluff, five miles to the southard [sic]. To enter the harbor, bring Howard's House (a large four-story white house), to bear by compass S.E. and well on with a point of trees on the highland two miles back. Run in on this range until across the bar, when the breakers on either side of the channel will be sufficient guide to the anchorage.[11]

These directions were satisfactory for only a few years. The pounding of the waves had eroded the heads of the spits, greatly altering the entrance by 1858. Also, the channel had moved due west from its former northwesterly position. Recognizing the variability of the channel, the U.S. Coast and Geodetic Survey in 1858 ceased giving specific sailing directions. From then on

Crossing Humboldt Bar, Eureka, Cal.   676

This postcard illustration was sent to a man in Iowa. His brother
writes from Eureka, "...this is the entrance to the bay...and the
ships have to wait a week sometimes to get in or out, when it is
rough." *Courtesy C. Pursell.*

individuals crossing the bar depended entirely on the bar pilots.

A typical crossing was described by some of the soldiers and
their wives who came to establish Fort Humboldt in January of
1853 on board the steamer *Goliah*. When the ship reached the bay,
its captain, "Old Bully Wright," found the bar too rough to cross
and determined to wait till conditions were more favorable the
following day. He refused to signal for a pilot, believing that he
knew the entrance as well as anyone. The surgeon's wife, Mrs.
Underwood, was not as confident about passenger safety when she
saw the "masts of several wrecked vessels that were evidence of the
dangers of 'crossing the bar.'"[12] Lieutenant George Crook was also
concerned. He recalled, "we labored on the bar, the old ship nearly
breaking in two. All on board experienced great relief when we
were safely over."[13]

The increased shipping as a result of lumbering and agriculture
also brought tragedy. Between 1853 and 1880, 81 people drowned
when the vessels they were aboard attempted and failed to cross the
bar.[14] The *Humboldt Times* reported on one such disaster of 18
February 1870. The brig *Crimea*, under command of Captain

Lassen, had been towed to the entrance and was being guided over the bar channels by one of Buhne's tugboats. In the process, the brig was swept over by the heavy seas that were pounding the bar. After crossing the bar, the crew found that Captain Lassen was missing. He had last been seen "in the main rigging of his vessel, but no one saw him when he fell or was carried overboard by the sea, nor indeed does it seem that he was missed until she had cast off from the tug."[15] The crew could only conclude that Lassen had been washed overboard by the heavy seas.

The danger that the bay entrance posed was borne out by the statistics of the U.S. Life-Saving Service whose *Annual Reports* "chronicle more terrible shipwrecks at Humboldt Bay than at the great port to the south."[16] However little was done to improve the hazardous conditions of the bar in the first 40 years following settlement of the Humboldt Bay region.

The federal government's first step to improve the entrance to Humboldt Bay was the erection in 1856 of a lighthouse tower on the north peninsula, near the entrance. Although the money for building the tower was first appropriated in 1851, construction was delayed "by inadequate funding, poor transportation, and problems with contractors."[17] These problems continued to plague all future improvements on Humboldt Bay in the 19th century. Even after the tower was completed, additional construction was required to make the lighthouse serviceable. After mariners complained that the original structure was not tall enough, the tower was raised several times. In 1872, a bell boat was added to the entrance warning system to help alert ships during the dense fogs that shrouded the coastline. In one year the keepers at the Humboldt lighthouse logged "over 1,100 hours of fog."[18] The bell boat, often unreliable because of the stormy weather, was replaced in 1874 with a steam whistle.

Despite the continual improvements, mariners remained dis-satisfied with the performance of the lighthouse. In 1886, after a series of severe storms and unusually high tides had nearly destroyed the structure, the Lighthouse Board successfully peti-tioned Congress for permission to move the lighthouse to nearby Table Bluff, four miles south of the entrance. The board believed that the lighthouse's proximity to the Humboldt Bar, with its constantly breaking waves, not only cut "the sound of the fog signal, but it also obscures the light when the weather is generally clear."[19] The old lighthouse was closed officially on 31 October

1892, when the recently completed Table Bluff lighthouse began operations. The Army Corps of Engineers used the buildings of the old lighthouse as field offices while they sought other ways to improve the entrance to Humboldt Bay.

One of the first to call for more improvements at the bay entrance was William Ayres, editor of the Eureka *Democratic Standard*. Beginning in 1877, Ayres' editorials focused on getting congressional help to improve the harbor. He claimed that Humboldt Bay's potential as a shipping center needed to be developed by creating an entrance and harbor that allowed easy access for large-draft ships. Ayres believed that with as little as $300,000 the bay could become "the great initial shipping point for all foreign vessels engaged in the redwood lumber trade and for the great bulk of the shipping that is done from Humboldt County, particularly for all that portion any considerable distance inland."[20] Ayres worked diligently toward this end for the seven years that he edited the *Democratic Standard*. That the attention of Congress and the Army Corps of Engineers was drawn to this northern California bay was due largely to his efforts.

Ayres' first editorials met with little success. He was not dissuaded, however, and argued frequently and articulately about the benefits to be gained from improving the bay. Ayres believed that the harbor improvements also would aid in developing the neighboring counties of Del Norte, Siskiyou, Trinity, and Shasta. He hoped that the support of these counties would aid in gaining congressional support.

Having been involved in improving rivers and harbors since 1824, the Corps of Engineers had the experience necessary to tackle the difficult problem of securing a safe entrance to Humboldt Bay. The large amount of money required to finance such a project necessitated federal funding; even Ayres' low estimate of $300,000 was too excessive for the recently formed Humboldt County or city of Eureka. The amount was also too great a sum to be raised by the lumber barons, who stood to profit most from the proposal. The industry was recovering from the severe national depression of the 1870s and was little inclined to fund a project with unpredictable results.

Ayres and the other supporters of harbor development set about convincing Congress of the need for improvement. The congressmen then would introduce a bill, which as part of a rivers and harbors act would authorize a District Engineer to make a

In 1856 a lighthouse tower was erected, a first step toward making the rough entrance safer. The lighthouse was abandoned in 1886 after severe winter storms nearly destroyed the building. *Courtesy D. Tuttle.*

preliminary examination of the bay and its entrance. The District Engineer or a supervising Board of Engineers then would be responsible for determining the feasibility of improving the harbor. The Corps would consider such factors as the amount of trade on the bay, the population of the area, and the prospects for continued use of and need for an improved harbor entrance.[21]

Ayres believed that increasing the depth of water across the bar by six feet would greatly augment the amount of shipping on the bay. However, he had to convince such skeptics as Captain Buhne, who as late as 1881 still maintained that improving the treacherous entrance was impossible.[22] Ayres turned to economic justifications for his plans.

In a newspaper article on 27 April 1878, Ayres explained how the additional six feet of water over the bar would benefit the shippers on the bay. He cited the cost of shipping a million board feet of lumber from Eureka to San Francisco to illustrate the advantages of the deeper entrance. Under the conditions of the period, that amount of lumber had to be shipped in at least five separate cargoes, depending on the conditions of the bar. The cost for shipping the million feet at the 1878 shipping and towing charges on the bay came to $5,750. Ayres asserted that with an increased depth on the bar, ships of greater draft could use the harbor. One of these larger vessels could haul twice as much as could one of the small coastal steamers, thus lowering shipping costs on Ayres' imaginary load of a million board feet. Ayres argued that lower rates could then be charged for both the towing and shipping fees. Furthermore, because fewer men would be required to staff the ships, the shipper also would save on wages. Ayres believed that the increased depth of the bar would save the individual shipper $45,000.[23] These statistics undoubtedly impressed area lumbermen who were recovering from the devastating national depression.

Ayres also was convinced that the improved entrance to Humboldt Bay would increase the amount of shipping. For example, redwood lumber, heretofore an unprofitable item for shipment to foreign ports, could be shipped profitably once lower rates were established. Ayres thought that the additional six feet of water over the bar would immediately double the "value of every foot of redwood timber land in our county or contiguous to it. Thinking minds who are interested in the growth and development of this section should consider this proposition well."[24]

Ayres on 6 April 1878 made his first specific statement regarding ways to attain the additional six feet of depth. His recommendations were rather revolutionary; jetties had only recently been tried as a way to control the formation of channels through sandbars by directing the scouring action of the tides. Although jetties had been used for centuries to protect harbor entrances, many engineers questioned the value of using the structures to maintain a channel through a sandbar. Nonetheless, Ayres proposed that a jetty system such as the one built at the mouth of the Mississippi could provide a safer and deeper entrance channel.[25] Trade along the Mississippi had been hampered by the large sandbar of the delta, and only ships of shallow draught could make it over the bar. At the South Pass channel of the Mississippi River mouth, civil engineer James B. Eads had been able to increase the depth from 8 feet to 24 feet.[26] With the completion of the jetties at the South Pass in 1879, the "ocean-going ships of the largest size were regularly entering the Mississippi by the smallest of the major passes."[27] Though Eads' work had been done on an alluvial river, the conditions at the mouth of the Mississippi were similar to those at Humboldt Bay. The wave and storm action was less violent than at Humboldt, but Ayres was confident that the problems presented by the stormy north coast could be overcome, especially by an engineer of Eads' abilities.

Because the structures were untried, many Corps Engineers had been opposed to building jetties at the South Pass of the Mississippi River mouth. In fact, Congress had directed that Eads build his controversial jetties at the narrow, shallow South Pass channel because not only would "construction not obstruct navigation,. . . [but], if Eads failed, he would leave things no worse than they had been before."[28] Even Chief of Engineers Brigadier General Andrew Humphreys, an expert on river improvements along the Mississippi, had opposed Eads' plans. Humphreys was convinced that the only solution was to build a costly system of canals from the river mouth to where a deeper portion of the ocean could be reached.

Despite the initial skepticism regarding his proposal, Eads created what no person had before: a reliable entrance channel to the Mississippi River. As a result, Ayres heard of Eads' work through the *Democratic Standard's* exchange with such newspapers as the *St. Louis Courier.* Ayres began a two-year correspondence with Eads in the hopes of enticing him to come to Humboldt Bay to construct a similar set of jetties there. Calling Eads the "greatest civil engineer of the age," Ayres published his correspondence with Eads in the *Standard* on 22 February 1879.

In January 1879 Ayres had sent Eads a description of Humboldt Bay and the bar and requested his opinion on the feasibility of improving the entrance. After examining U.S. Coast and Geodetic Survey maps and those sent to him by Ayres, Eads stated that "the channel through the bar obstructing the entrance into the bay can be permanently deepened by the aid of jetties."[29] Eads was willing to travel to California to examine Humboldt Bay if Ayres or the community would pay him $3,000. Eads added that he was asking for only a modest sum because of his interest in the project and his awareness that a few public-minded citizens would have to raise the money. Moreover, Eads maintained that his proposal resulted "more from the desire to aid... in inaugurating and consummating an interesting and important public work."[30]

After publishing Eads' letter, Ayres energetically began raising the necessary money. Ayres saw Eads' visit to Humboldt Bay as critical to the improvement of the bay entrance for several reasons. Principal among them was Eads' political clout. Ayres thought that a favorable recommendation from Eads would convince Congress to appropriate funds for the project. Moreover, Eads' visit would attract attention to the problems of the bay entrance, stimulating more investigations into its improvement. Accordingly, Ayres called a public meeting for 19 March 1879 to raise money for Eads visit and to "discuss the subject of improving Humboldt Harbor."[31] Attending the meeting were many influential members of the community such as lumbermen John Vance, William Carson, and John Dolbeer and politicians and businessmen C.S. Ricks, E.H. Howard and Joseph Russ. Despite their interest Ayres was still unable to raise the $3,000.

The publishing of the Eads correspondence did increase public awareness of the obstacles to trade caused by the bar and its shifting channel. Eads, even without traveling to Eureka, was able to alert some congressmen to the condition of the harbor. A few weeks after the unsuccessful meeting to raise money for Eads' trip, Ayres received a letter from California Congressman J.K. Luttrell. The influential Democrat had corresponded with Eads relative to having him visit Humboldt Bay. Luttrell had recently introduced bills in Congress calling for "appropriations for the improvement of our harbors along the coast between San Francisco and Puget

Sound."[32] He also had helped pass an appropriations bill for
$250,000 to be used to develop a harbor of refuge on the Pacific
Coast north of San Francisco. The specific site was to be chosen by
the Corps of Engineers.

As a result of the congressional interest, the San Francisco
District was directed to investigate Humboldt Bay. The District
was familiar with the bay, which had been examined in 1871 and
1877 by a board of Army Engineers seeking a bay or harbor along
the Pacific Coast suitable as a harbor of refuge. The coastline
between San Francisco and the mouth of the Columbia River
lacked a safe harbor for endangered ships, and none of the few
natural bays or river mouths were of sufficient depth to allow large
naval ships to enter. Humboldt Bay had been considered a
possibility for improvement as a harbor of refuge, but had been
passed over for several reasons.

The 1871 examining board opted for not improving the bay
despite the members' opinion that once vessels entered the bay "it
is the best harbor on the Pacific Coast between San Francisco Bay
and the mouth of the Columbia River."[33] The problem, however,
was the uncertainty of the entrance. Board member Major R.S.
Williamson reported to Chief of Engineers Humphreys:

> The bar, like nearly all of the ocean bars on the Pacific Coast of the
> United States is constantly changing. Every severe storm changes
> the channel; sometimes there are two channels, and sometimes
> there is but one. In rare cases the channel is so closed that the
> steamers cannot go out.[34]

Williamson went on to relate that he had been "bar-bound" for a
fortnight in December 1865. Shortly after his arrival aboard a
passenger steamer, a storm arose and destroyed the old channel.
Only after two weeks did a new channel open sufficiently to allow
the ship to end its enforced stay. Williamson added that no vessel
"enters or leaves the bay without a pilot."[35] He felt that bar at
Humboldt Bay could "never be improved."[36]

Among the investigating Board of Engineers, Williamson was
the only one who actually had seen conditions at Humboldt Bay.
The board's report on the feasibility of improving the bay was
made without personal examination, but was based primarily on
the coast survey chart, "the well known shifting sands forming the
bar and the concurrent testimony of all persons acquainted with...
[the bar]."[37] The board presented two plans for improving the bay,
both of which included jetties. However, the board believed that

the cost of construction would far outweigh any possible benefits, which it deemed would be short-lived.

The two systems proposed by the 1871 board revealed the Army Engineers' prevailing attitudes toward jetties. The board's first proposal was for two jetties, or *pierres perdues*, of stone or masonry. These jetties would confine the channel and secure the depths necessary to allow heavily loaded ships to enter and exit the bay with ease. The board believed that the jetties would be destroyed easily and would leave "the stones or the disjointed masonry of such jettees [*sic*] scattered over the bar as so many dangerous obstructions.[38] Similarly, the board thought that jetties built of

> ...sufficiently powerful construction to withstand the force of the sea, properly located, and carried out to, say 10 fathoms of water, with their foundations laid so deep so as not to be undermined, we have no doubt but their effect would be to improve the entrance to the harbor, till such time as the resulting currents should accumulate another bar outside of the supposed entrance between such structures.[39]

The objective of the proposed jetties was to block the flow of suspended sand particles that built up the sandbar. The rubble-mound structures also would maintain a channel through the sandbar by focusing the tidal currents. Yet, in order to be effective the structures needed to be able to withstand the violent wave action at the bay's entrance. The Army Engineers thought that no matter how well built, the jetties would soon be beaten down by the wave action, leaving jetty material scattered through the channel. Moreover, the Engineers felt that the bar would only reform farther seaward beyond the jetty protected entrance. This opinion about the infeasibility of improving the entrance to Humboldt Bay was the Corps' attitude for the next ten years.

In 1877, Congress again directed the Corps to locate and improve a harbor of refuge by examining the harbors of Humboldt Bay, Mendocino, Trinidad, and Crescent City. The Corps was to study each bay, find one that could be made suitable as a harbor of refuge through the construction of a breakwater, and estimate the cost. The final criterion raised the board's doubts concerning Humboldt Bay. The board believed that two parallel jetties, built out from the sandy entrance heads and 500 yards apart, could result in a safer entrance to the bay. However, the Engineers were convinced that "such construction would be attended with immense difficulties and enormous expense."[40] One reason for the great expense was the absence of convenient quarries to provide the rock for jetty construction. The board also questioned whether jetties could be constructed on the sandy heads without collapsing because there was no supporting bedrock. Indeed, the members were divided on whether or not the "construction would be physically possible."[41] The three-member board had been unable to closely examine the bay entrance due to the rough condition of the bar, and so was unsure of the results that could be obtained by jetties. The board was aware of the dangers of the entrance and the need to improve the bay, however. When the coast steamer *Hassler*, on which they were traveling, arrived off the bay, the pilot had refused to guide the steamer over the bar even though the August weather was moderate. Furthermore, at the time the depth over the bar was 20 feet, and the *Hassler* drew only 12 feet. The pilot stated that he could not bring the ship into Humboldt Bay "without running the risk of the vessel striking bottom and her possible loss in the breakers."[42] The uncertain and often violent condition of the ocean near the entrance to Humboldt Bay influenced the board to deem it "highly improbable that a breakwater or jetties...be attempted here at the present time."[43]

Despite the two negative reports by the Corps of Engineers, William Ayres continued to lobby Congress for money and for further examination of Humboldt Bay by the Corps. His efforts finally met with success. The 14 June 1880 rivers and harbors act called for another study of the bay by the Corps of Engineers, with an emphasis on selecting some suitable way to improve the entrance. Congressman C.P. Berry of Eureka was instrumental in getting the authorization. Lieutenant Colonel George Mendell of the San Francisco District was tasked with finding ways to stabilize the entrance and make the bay a safer port. In the fall of 1880, Mendell traveled to Eureka to examine the bay and its dangerous entrance. He concluded that the bay should be dredged and that the Corps official overseeing the work also should seek ways to stabilize the shifting sands that created the hazardous entrance.[44]

The increasing trade on the bay and the growing prosperity of the region contributed to Mendell's favorable report. The *Annual Report of the Chiefs of Engineers, 1882* noted the dramatic increase in shipping on the bay:

> ...from July 1, 1853 to May 31, 1854... there arrived 143 vessels with a total tonnage of 22,060 tons; lumber shipped from the bay 18,932,000 feet. In the year 1878: number of vessels 306, with a total tonnage of 134,371 tons; lumber shipped from the bay: 48,000,000 feet.[45]

Large quantities of redwood lumber produced around the bay were being shipped directly to foreign markets, increasing the economic worth of the region. However, even after Humboldt Bay had been made a port of entry in 1882, its entrance still hampered the expansion of markets. The high waves and stormy conditions often prevented ships from leaving port for several days. And when they did they frequently were forced to leave half empty in order to cross the bar.

Following the lead of the 1877 engineering board, Mendell discussed constructing jetties to help solve the problem of crossing Humboldt Bar. He theorized that jetties would create a deeper tidal prism that would help scour out and maintain a single deep channel through the bar.[46] However, because he had reservations about the feasibility of constructing the jetties at the stormy exposed entrance to the bay, Mendell opted for the more traditional approach of dredging. Dredging, at least temporarily, would increase the tidal prism of the bay so that the tidal scour could deepen the entrance channel. An added benefit of dredging was that it would also deepen the bay channels (the bay was displaying a tendency to shoal because of the amount of tailings being dumped into it by the many mills around the bay). In 1881 Congress approved Mendell's recommendations and appropriated $80,000 for the dredging. William B. English, a local contractor, began work on the dredging project on 15 September 1881.[47] Assistant Engineer A. Boschke of the San Francisco District was assigned to oversee the project and to seek other ways to improve the entrance on a more permanent basis. The dredging was but a temporary measure. The bay was to shoal quickly, affecting the depth of the entrance channel.

NOTES

[1]U.S. Army, Corps of Engineers, *Annual Report of the Chief of Engineers, Fiscal Year 1917* (Washington, DC: Government Printing Office, 1917), part 2, p. 1634. Hereafter these reports are cited as *Annual Report*, with their appropriate year.

[2]Henry A. Finch, "The Humboldt Bay Jetties," *Dock and Harbor Authority* (June 1934): 215.

[3]William Wright Harts, "Harbor Improvement on the Pacific Coast of the United States," *Professional Memoirs* 3 (October-December 1911): 620.

[4]Finch, *op. cit.*

[5]*Ibid.*

[6]Clarence Pearsall, *et al.*, *Quest for Qual-a-wa-loo* (Oakland, CA: Holmes Book Co., 1966), p. 188.

[7]*Ibid.*, p. 180.

32 HUMBOLDT BAY

[8]Lynwood Carranco, *Redwood Lumber Industry* (San Marino, CA: Golden West Books, 1982), p. 85.

[9]*Ibid.*

[10]*Annual Report*, 1891, part 3, p. 3126.

[11]U.S. Coast and Geodetic Survey, Survey Map, 1851, Humboldt Bay, CA.

[12]Chad L. Hoopes, *Lure of the Humboldt Bay Region* (Dubuque, IA: Wm. C. Brown Book Co., 1966), p. 64.

[13]George Crook, *General George Crook, His Autobiography* (Norman, OK: Univ. of Okla. Press, 1946), p. 9.

[14]Work Projects Administration, *Survey of Federal Archives Project: Ship Registries and Enrollments, Port of Eureka, California, 1859-1920* (San Francisco: Nat. Arch., 1941), p. 8.

[15]*Humboldt Times*, Eureka, CA, 19 Feb. 1870, p. 3, col. 1. Hereafter cited as *Humboldt Times*.

[16]Ralph C. Shanks, Jr., *Lighthouses and Lifeboats on the Redwood Coast* (San Anselmo, CA: Costano Books, 1978), p. 155.

[17]*Ibid.*

[18]*Ibid.*, p. 158.

[19]U.S. Congress, *Removal of Lighthouse at Humboldt Harbor, California*, House Ex. Doc. 91, 49th Cong., 1st sess., 1886, p. 2.

[20]*Democratic Standard*, Eureka, CA, Nov. 10, 1877, p. 2, col. 1. Hereafter cited as *Democratic Standard*.

[21]Harry Taylor, "Civil Works of the Army Corps of Engineers," *Military Engineer*, 17 (March-April 1925): 98.

[22]See "Enter the Schooner," Susie Baker Fountain Papers, unpublished collection, newspaper clippings and personal notes on Humboldt County history, vol. 104, p. 228, Humboldt State Univ. Library, Arcata, CA. Collection hereafter cited as Fountain Papers.

[23]*Democratic Standard*, 27 April 1878, p. 2, col. 1.

[24]*Ibid.*

[25]*Ibid.*, 6 April 1878, p. 2, col. 1.

[26]*Ibid.*

[27]Albert E. Cowdrey, *Land's End* (New Orleans, LA: U.S. Army Engineer District, 1977) p. 22.

[28]*Ibid.*, p. 20.

[29]*Democratic Standard*, 22 Feb. 1879, p. 2, col. 2.

[30]*Ibid.*

[31]*Ibid.*, 15 March 1879, p. 2, col. 1.

[32]*Ibid.*

[33]*Annual Report, 1871*, part 2, p. 922.

[34]*Ibid.*

[35]*Ibid.*

[36]*Ibid.*

[37]*Ibid.*, part 2, p. 921.

[38]*Ibid.*

[39]*Ibid.*

[40]*Annual Report, 1877*, part 2, p. 1052.

[41]*Ibid.*

[42]*Ibid.*

[43]*Ibid.*

[44]*Annual Report, 1881*, part 3, p. 2480.

[45]*Annual Report, 1882*, part 3, p. 2540.

[46]*Annual Report, 1881*, part 3, p. 2480.

[47]*Ibid.*

CHAPTER II

Why Build Jetties?

The citizens of Humboldt County were excited at the prospect of the government work, and local newspapers closely followed the progress of the dredging. As the *Democratic Standard* phrased it, "to deepen our channels and wharfage ground, to interest the federal government in effecting some improvement of our bar... redound[s] to the benefit of every resident of Humboldt County to a greater or lesser extent."[1] Even more important than the dredging were the surveys being done on the bay entrance by Assistant Engineer Boschke from the San Francisco District office. The surveys were believed to be a preliminary step in finding some way to improve the hazardous entrance. Many felt that a safe entrance to the bay would result in a dramatic increase in shipping and achieve economic stability for Humboldt County. The eyes of the community turned to the dredging project and the surveys of Assistant Engineer Boschke, or "Captain" Boschke, as he was known in the local newspapers.

Boschke, in turn, reported on the area's prosperity and economic future to his superiors in San Francisco. When he arrived at Humboldt Bay in August 1881, he found a thriving metropolis developing alongside the harbor. Landing at one of the busy wharfs at Eureka, the largest city on the bay, Boschke saw the melding of maritime and lumber interests. The Eureka waterfront was lined with schooners waiting to be loaded with lumber bound for San Francisco or some other foreign or domestic port. Many of the schooners had been built at one of the shipyards around the bay. From his steamer Boschke also observed the many lumber mills, both large and small, as well as their landings for loading lumber. One of the largest was the Dolbeer and Carson Company mill at Eureka. Other large mills included John Vance's, across the bay from Eureka at Samoa. North of Eureka, at Arcata, a two-mile-long wharf stretched into the bay so that ships could load with lumber from the mills along the Mad River. In addition to the mills close to the bay, many inland mills were connected to the bay wharves by railroads. The Pacific Lumber Company at Scotia, formed shortly before Boschke arrived in the region, had its own railroad and wharf at Fields Landing. Boschke and the other travelers on the steamer witnessed the fact that the lumber industry of the north coast was growing rapidly, recovering quickly from the 1870s depression. As they walked through the wharf area into the business section of town, they passed stacks of lumber waiting to be loaded. Reflecting this boom, William Carson in 1885 built a mansion on the bluff overlooking his mill. The house included a cupola on the roof so that Carson could watch his ships loaded with lumber cross over the Humboldt Bar.

Lumber, however, was not the only product being shipped from the bay. Since the late 1860s farmers had been homesteading in the rich inland valleys of the county, and they had been shipping their produce to the markets in the San Francisco region. The oats and wheat grown in Humboldt County were considered some of the best in the state, but the major exports were fruit and dairy products. Homesteaders found that the inland valleys offered ideal conditions for growing apple trees, and many of the logged-over river flats were replanted with fruit trees. The bottomlands closer to the bay were well suited for raising dairy cows, and Humboldt County butter was soon in demand in San Francisco. Other items produced in the area and shipped south were canned salmon, caught in the annual runs in the Eel River, and rolls of tanbark to be used in tanning hides. While not as important or as valuable as lumber, these other products represented a substantial part of the local economy.

The Eureka business district reflected the needs of the region's homesteaders and farmers. The large mercantile establishments, such as Hans Buhne's, carried farming supplies as well as equipment for the lumber camps. The town's two daily newspapers, the *Humboldt Times* and the *Democratic Standard*, carried news of special interest to the farmers and reported which ships were in port and the length of their voyages. The two newspapers also described the general prosperity of the region in articles on the many new buildings under construction or those recently

The *Pomona* was one of the passenger steamers serving the Humboldt Bay region in the 19th century. She crossed the bar many times with the aid of one of H.H. Buhne's tugboats. *Courtesy D. Tuttle.*

completed. And William Carson was not the only Eurekan to display his success by building a large Victorian mansion. Hans Buhne owned a splendid mansion, as did most other wealthy and influential members of the community. In Arcata, John Vance's house was a showplace and gathering place for the community. Pride in the county was growing as well. In 1875 Eureka had celebrated its 25th anniversary along with the nation's centennial. Plans were underway to replace the old wooden courthouse in Eureka with a three story stone and cement structure. The courthouse, started in 1885, was resplendent with porticoes, Grecian columns, and statues. The rapid growth as well as the region's potential influenced Boschke's favorable findings about improving the bay.

Boschke's arrival was heralded in the local newspapers. The hope was that his arrival marked a permanent commitment by the government to improving Humboldt Bay. Boschke informed the *Humboldt Times* that the increase in commerce on the bay had attracted the attention of Congress, and that more money would be spent for the bay's improvement. Boschke also pointed out that the community's hopes for future improvement were well-founded because the national trend was that "when the government began to improve a harbor, it did not stop until the work of improvement was completed."[2] Boschke's words foreshadowed the considerable time, energy, and money the Corps of Engineers would invest to achieve a measure of safety at the entrance to Humboldt Bay.

The start of work to improve the bay did not halt, however, the continued agitation by local residents and politicians for increased funds for further improvement. If anything, the success in getting the congressional appropriation for the dredging project stimulated activity. The new editor of the *Standard*, Frank P. Thompson, continued William Ayres' work by calling for more financial support to end the isolation of Humboldt County. In fact Thompson declared on the front page of each issue of his paper that the *Humboldt Standard* was "devoted to the development of Humboldt County."[3] In an August 1883 editorial Thompson reminded county citizens that it was only by "dint of continued agitation and effort, in the face of much opposition that we have secured Government recognition."[4] That recognition had included making Eureka a port of entry, dredging the bay, and conducting new surveys of the bay mouth. Thompson and other local citizens believed that in order to implement the findings of the surveys, an organized and sustained effort was needed to ensure the necessary congressional appropriations. However, Thompson was convinced that the campaign would be successful because Corps officials supported the project.

The dredging contract with William B. English was the first of many let to local businessmen for work or supplies for improving the bay. The federal government's continuing efforts to assure a safe, reliable navigation channel through the bay entrance brought various forms of economic support to the region. The Corps hired many local residents to work on the improvement projects and used local shipyards to provide boats to transport Corps officials to the bay entrance. One instance was in 1881 when Captain Boschke hired a launch from the Bendixson shipyards with which to examine the bay, determine the channels to be dredged, and most important, survey the entrance. From the first Boschke was aware of the violent wave action at the mouth of the bay and of the obstacles to any form of improvement. He conducted monthly surveys to determine the relative positions of the north and south spits and how tidal currents affected them, charted how the spits influenced the channel and helped to focus the tidal currents that maintained the channels, and gathered information about the changing positions of the principal channel through the bar and how storms affected the channel depth and location.

While Boschke was at the bay he witnessed some of the unpredictable changes in the entrance channel and in one case he attempted to control its shifting. In September 1881 the entrance channel had moved to a radically new position that began to erode the south end of the north spit. Boschke was worried about this disintegration because he and Colonel Mendell had discovered a correlation between the position of the spits and the depth of the channel. Boschke undertook several experiments to stabilize the sands that composed the north spit, which he outlined in his annual report to Colonel Mendell. He constructed a system of brush jetties, the first on Humboldt Bay, in a series of squares that he believed would prevent further abrasion of the north spit. These jetties were made of "fine pliable willow brush, about four feet long, set upright between 2 two inch planks."[5] A brush fence was made by compressing the planks against the brush with screw bolts. The resulting panels were 20 feet long. They were bolted to three four-by-four posts seven feet long that had been driven by a pile driver into the remaining sand at the end of the north spit. The finished product was a series of brush jetties set in a square, with only three feet of the brush panels above the sand.[6]

At first the brush jetties worked well. They halted the erosion of the north spit, and even helped rebuild the eroded head of the spit. The waves breaking across the spit met with the squares of brush, which limited the breakers' range and thus prevented abrasion of the spit. An added benefit was that the brush jetties collected the loose sand particles carried in the waves. Boschke was pleased with the initial success of his experiment and confident that the brush jetties not only had preserved the north spit "from the inroads of the breakers, but [also] built out [the spit] to assume the desired form and position."[7] However, the conditions that had allowed for the success of the brush jetties did not continue for long.

The shape of the bar, marked by the shallow breaker flat, and its position began to change during the spring of 1882. The southern portion of the breaker flat started moving toward the bay, limiting the bay's tidal capacity and therefore the bay's ability to maintain the entrance channel by tidal scour. As the months passed the entrance channel shrank, becoming narrow and winding. The bay mouth became more and more dangerous to enter as the shape of the bar changed throughout the year. The end result of the shifting of the bar was that with the winter storms "both the counter current and breakers attacked the end of the north spit to such an extent that the brush jetties were undermined."[8] Instead of helping to prevent erosion, the jetties began to accelerate the process. Boschke was forced to abandon his project as the violent wave action destroyed the first jetties constructed at Humboldt Bay. However, he had learned important lessons about the tidal currents and their effect on the bar. These lessons would be applied to future improvement attempts on the bay.

Based on his surveys, observations, and study of the bar's history, Boschke concluded that in order to stabilize the bay entrance it would be necessary to protect the south breaker flat from the scour of the Humboldt Bay tidal currents. It also would be necessary to maintain the bar channel's northwest position, the direction in which the channel meets the least resistance from the sea. Boschke was unsure how these two conditions could be met. From his extended and close observations of the bay, however, Boschke identified certain features that he thought needed to be considered in building structures capable of withstanding "the occasional severe exposures from the southwest storm seas."[9] He thought that the south spit, with its clay base, was an ideal foundation. He also felt that anything built out from the south spit would prevent scour of the south breaker flat. Boschke thought that any protective structure should be built in a northwesterly direction to prevent undermining. In essence, he was proposing a single high water jetty built from the south spit. However, Boschke was still unsure about resolving the technological problem of building on the sandy spit. He questioned whether "a structure of great weight [can] be placed or imbedded upon the inner margin of the south breaker flat at a reasonable cost."[10]

Where jetties had been built on the East Coast and in Europe they had been built on bedrock, or at least anchored on the natural rock formations. Humboldt Bay lacked such anchoring rock and Boschke feared that any structure built on the sand would be undermined quickly by scour and would collapse, as had the brush jetties. Furthermore, Boschke was uncertain about how successful jetties would be and if they could be built strong enough on the sandy base to withstand the violent wave action that had destroyed the brush jetties. Finally, he believed that the cost of constructing rubble-mound jetties that would be strong and sturdy enough to withstand the strong force of the waves would far exceed any benefit to be gained from the jetties in stabilizing the entrance channel.

The improvement work at Humboldt Bay was not the only such work being proposed or in progress in the 1880s on the Pacific Coast. The experience of the Corps officials at the mouth of the Columbia River and Gray's Harbor in Washington, and at Yaquina Bay and Coos Bay in Oregon contributed to a positive response in considering the cost and feasibility of jetty construction to improve Humboldt Bay. The three bodies of water had characteristics similar to those of Humboldt Bay. Their respective entrances were blocked by a roughly crescent-shaped shifting sandbar that often obstructed shipping. Crossing these various bars was always difficult, and it was commonplace for ships to be "bar-bound" for several days due to either the roughness of the bar or the shallow depth of the channel across the bar. Beginning in the 1870s the Corps of engineers grappled with the problem of finding ways to improve these bays. Observations of the different bars had led the Corps Engineers to conclude the bars were formed and shaped by the large accumulations of sand that were easily moved by the ocean currents. Improvement, then, depended on obstructing the bar formation process. Employing methods used successfully by Captain Eads at the mouth of the Mississippi and by the Corps at the Charleston, South Carolina, harbor, jetties were constructed at all three ports. They were designed "to serve the primary purpose of concentrating and directing the ocean currents to develop scouring effects over shoal bars, and the secondary purpose of protecting such crossing[s] from storms."[11] The Corps used different forms of jetties and construction methods at each harbor, providing various alternatives for jetty construction at Humboldt Bay.

The first jetty system on the Pacific Coast was built out into the ocean at Yaquina Bay in Oregon, which lies 115 miles south of the Oregon-Washington border. Because the jetty was the first riprap jetty extending into the rough seas of the Pacific Coast, its design was copied at other jetty construction sites along the Pacific Coast. That jetty construction began in 1881 and was completed in 1884; Captain Boschke and Colonel Mendell probably watched with interest.

   With conditions similar to those at Humboldt Bay, Yaquina Bay
is a narrow estuary approximately 20 miles long. Unlike Humboldt,
however, it is fed by a river. Even with the Yaquina River, the tidal
area was five square miles, and the Corps of Engineers found that
the fresh water did not have a great effect on the channel formation.
The shallow bay entrance averaged only seven feet in depth. The
residents of the Willamette Valley advocated improving Yaquina
Bay because they wanted "an outlet to the sea and the markets of
the world separate from, and independent of, the outlet by way of
Portland and the Columbia River."[12] The citizens of the valley
had convinced Congress and the Corps of the region's potential
and the need to develop the harbor.

   Major George L. Gillespie of the Portland District chose James
Polhemus, a civil engineer who had worked in the Galveston,
Texas, area, to oversee the improvement project. In 1880 he drew
up plans for a single 2,500-foot jetty to be built out from the south
side of the bay entrance. (Captain Boschke and Colonel Mendell
recommended the same plan for Humboldt Bay.) Polhemus was
confident that the short crib-work and stone single jetty built to the
level of the sea at mid-tide would halt the shifting sands and
provide a safe entrance with a depth of 17 feet. Major Gillespie
believed that the increased depth of the harbor would "make the
bay a shipping port of great importance, not only for the products
which are raised in the immediate vicinity, but for a great part of
the Upper Willamette Valley with which it is said that there will
soon be a railroad connection."[13]

   Corps engineers had decided to build the single jetty because of
the belief that any other form of improvement would not be
permanent. Dredging the harbor entrance was not a viable
solution; one winter storm could lead to new navigation hazards.
Polhemus was forced to develop different building techniques
than those used on the East Coast because of the rough seas found
even in the summer months along the north Pacific Coast. On the
Atlantic seaboard, the basic procedure for building a rubble-mound
jetty was to place boulders on top of brush mattresses. The brush
mattresses not only prevented the rocks and boulders from
scattering, but also limited the erosion of sand under the boulders.
On the East Coast the Corps had used scows and lighters to both
transport jetty materials to the construction site and place the
brush mattresses and boulders. When this technique was attempted at Yaquina, the rough seas along the coast prevented the
scows and lighters from holding their positions. The method used

in the East of constructing large wooden boxes, or cribs, which were then filled with rock and lowered into the water also met with failure.

After experimenting with several methods of jetty construction, Polhemus found that the only solution to the problem of the wave-tossed boats was a stationary platform. He settled on a tramway built out from the shore about 20 feet above the water.[14] Built to withstand the violent wave action, the trestle was further reinforced so that it could support the double set of narrow-gauge tracks and railcars that carried the stone for the jetty as well as a steam pile driver that hung over the end of the trestle "far enough to drive the piles of the next bent."[15] Another advantage of using the trestle was that it substantially improved the ease of building and placing the brush mattresses. The mats were built underneath the trestle and then lowered into the water. Large boulders dumped from the track above prevented the mattresses from being washed away. The tramway proved so effective that it was used on most of the jetties constructed along the Pacific Coast in the 19th century, including those at Humboldt Bay.

The tramway construction was not without problems, however. At Yaquina, for example, the single sawmill on the bay could not provide the large timbers needed for the trestle, so they had to be shipped into the construction site. Another problem with the tramway was that it was exposed to the rough winter storms, which often washed away large sections of the completed trestle. In one storm the trestle lost more than 90 feet.[16] Attempts to make the trestle more secure failed, in part because the supporting bulwarks presented a larger surface for the force of the waves to beat against.

Another problem with the tramway system was associated with the size of the railcars used to haul the rocks and boulders used from the local quarry. The railcars supported the sandstone boulders, whose average size was four tons to the block. The railcars were specially designed to facilitate the placing of the boulders. Their platforms tipped to discharge their loads. These cars were designed and built at Yaquina Bay and were periodically modified to achieve better results.

Just as construction techniques were altered over time, so too was the original plan for a single jetty. In 1886 the project engineers determined that the single jetty was not controlling the bar or the entrance channel. Though the south jetty was able to halt some of the movement of the sand, it failed to maintain a single channel

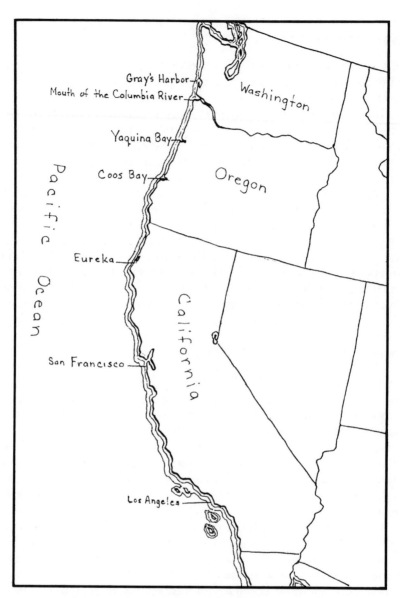

The West Coast of the United States. Drawing by M.B. Pritchard.

through the bar. The entrance remained treacherous. And while the jetty prevented the channel from forming to the south, the ocean currents still changed the channel's position. Therefore, in 1886 the Corps began building a north jetty as well as modifying the existing structure. The new jetty was to be built to the height of the water at mid-tide, and the south jetty raised to the same height and extended seaward 1,700 feet. These plans were changed in 1888, when the height of the south jetty was raised to above the high-tide mark. The north jetty height was similarly raised in 1892. The north jetty was built so that the heads of the two jetties converged slightly, instead of being exactly parallel. This new form of dual jetty system had proved very effective at Yaquina Bay and was recommended by the Portland District Engineers for the improvement of most of the harbor projects along the Pacific Coast.

The Corps completed work at Yaquina Bay in 1896. The entire project cost only $710,000.[17] The Army Engineers had increased the depth of the channel to 17 feet and stabilized its position. When completed, the south and north jetties were 3,700 and 2,300 feet long, respectively. An ironic note is that in 1899 a Board of Engineers concluded that Newport, the principal city on the bay, had not grown significantly since the Corps had begun to improve the bay's entrance; its population was still only 500. And though Major Gillespie had predicted in 1880 that improving the entrance would make the bay a "port of great importance," it had remained small, with few industries. The Board of Engineers in 1899 found only "two small salmon canneries, two sawmills, a creamery, a sandstone quarry, and a railroad repair shop."[18] Jetty construction and the outlay of federal funds for the region had not led to economic growth and development. Consequently, the Engineers believed that the commerce of the area would be adequately served by the existing jetties.

Another early jetty system influenced by the work at Yaquina Bay was built at Coos Bay, Oregon. A hundred miles south of Yaquina, Coos Bay was economically more important, deriving its commercial base from fir lumbering and lignite coal extraction. However, the bay was obstructed by a sandbar and had an average depth of only nine feet. Aware of the potential of this isolated port whose only means of commercial transportation was by seagoing vessels, the Corps as early as 1879 attempted to improve the bay entrance. Furthermore, the 1877 Board of Engineers had decided to develop the Oregon port as a much-needed harbor of refuge. Fearing that a jetty built out into the ocean would be destroyed rapidly in the rough waters, or would sink in the soft sands or be weakened by the scouring of the sand from underneath the structure, Major Gillespie, the officer in charge, determined that jetties would be built inside the bay entrance. Gillespie hoped that if built where "they were more or less protected,...this work would better the channel across the bars without extending the construction beyond the general line of the shore."[19]

The project was plagued from the start. The original proposal for two deflecting jetties to prevent the buildup of sand and the dangerous eddies was pared down to a single south jetty in 1879. Although the preliminary estimate for the cost of construction was $600,000 for the single 5,000-foot jetty, the final cost was almost triple that amount due to construction problems. An early problem surfaced when Major Gillespie found that it was impossible to use a pile driver at the rocky entrance to place the timbers that were necessary to hold the rocks of the jetty in place. When timber cribs filled with rocks were used, Gillespie saw that even in the shelter of the bay the currents would disrupt their placement. Because the cost was high in relation to the annual appropriations, work progressed slowly. In the first year, Congress allocated only $40,000 to the project. As a result, the Corps was able to place only 450 feet of cribbing by the fall of 1880. Work continued on the single jetty for nine years, with many different techniques being tried to place the stones.

Despite the continuing efforts, the deflecting jetty had little effect on conditions at the entrance. The Corps had been successful in building the riprap jetty out only 1,700 feet. In 1889 Corps surveys revealed that the jetty had caused the erosion of the north end of the north spit, "but had no useful effect on either the direction or depth of the bar channel."[20] Because the potential remained for Coos Bay to become a major shipping port for fir lumber and coal, another Board of Engineers in 1889 decided to attempt a new solution to the problem of the bar-bound bay. Encouraged by the success of the Yaquina Bay jetties, the board, on which Colonel Mendell served, proposed that two converging high-tide rubble-stone jetties be built at the entrance to Coos Bay. These jetties would serve "to control the sand movement at the entrance to the bay, to direct the tidal scour upon a special part of the bar, with the expectation of securing a minimum depth of 20 feet over the bar at mean lower tide, and afford an entrance along the most navigable lines."[21] In the following years, the jetties were even more effective in achieving these goals than the Corps had anticipated.

The Board of Engineers recommended that the 9,600-foot north jetty be built first and that the south jetty be built "when the needs of the harbor made it necessary.''[22] Extending the north jetty out to the original position of the sandbar would result in a 20-foot deep channel. The engineer at Coos Bay found that the project depth was reached even before the jetty was completed in 1894. Because the north jetty proved so successful, construction of the south jetty was delayed for almost 30 years. Work did not begin on the south jetty until 1922, and only after the stormy conditions of the Pacific Coast had washed away almost half of the north jetty. The Portland District authorized the building of the south jetty, partially as protection for the more exposed jetty, and the new system was completed in 1929. Meanwhile, the Coos Bay north jetty was forgotten. No allowance had been made for its maintenance, and the price of this neglect was its destruction, and with it, the deep-water channel it had maintained.

Corps engineers learned much from the construction of the Coos Bay jetties. In dealing with the stormy conditions at both Yaquina Bay and Coos Bay, the Corps found new ways to construct jetties and learned about the benefits and drawbacks of building the *pierres perdues* on the Pacific Coast. No one knew how long or how well the jetties would last, if the jetties would stop the littoral drift of the sands that formed the sandbars, or if the bar would simply form farther out to sea. Still, the Corps found that jetties were at least initially successful, and the Engineers continued to improve the construction techniques initiated at Yaquina Bay.

One of the places that benefited from the experiences of the Corps engineers at Yaquina Bay and Coos Bay was the mouth of the Columbia River. Its stormy climate and sandbar-blocked entrance resembled conditions at Humboldt. The channel changed often, and even the most experienced sea captains preferred to wait for a tug and a pilot to guide them into the river and its harbors. Corps officials tended to downplay its dangers, believing that they had been exaggerated. Astoria, Oregon, residents, disagreeing with the claim that the river entrance was no more dangerous than that of San Francisco Bay, in 1878 successfully petitioned Congress to allocate funds for improving the river mouth. The fact that the Columbia provided the Pacific Northwest interior with access to world markets helped generate support for the Astorians' petition. The improvement of the river's entrance would benefit more people in the long term than would improvements at any other port on the Pacific Coast north of San Francisco.

Despite the congressional mandate to improve the river entrance,

Major Gillespie was reluctant to begin. In a report to his superiors in 1879, he pointed out that "the building of [a] breakwater in open sea, to cover so wide a harbor entrance, and resting upon such an unstable foundation and exposed to such terrific seas, is an undertaking which any engineer may well hesitate to recommend and tremble to undertake."[23] Hesitant though he was, Gillespie recommended building a low-tide stone dike that would concentrate the current of the river and the tidal flow, thus creating and maintaining a single deep-water channel through the river mouth and across the bar. This proposal, made in 1880, was rejected by the Army Engineer Review Board of the Pacific Coast, which believed that the natural conditions would be adequate to maintain the channel.

Continued pressure from citizens living along the Columbia moved Congress to call again for some form of improvement of the river mouth. In 1882, therefore, the Review Board adopted a plan to build a single south jetty at the river mouth. The objective of this low-tide 4.5-mile-long jetty was to narrow the entrance of the river mouth, thus confining the water to a single 30-foot-deep channel through the bar. The project's estimated cost was $3.5 million. Congress finally authorized the project in 1884, and construction began immediately. As had happened with other improvement projects, low annual appropriations by Congress delayed completion.

With the initial allocation, Corps officer Captain Charles F. Powell established a wharf and dock, and began constructing the trestle for the tramway on the beach. The south jetty at the mouth of the Columbia was built much the same way as the north jetty at Yaquina, but on a much larger scale. The south side of the river mouth was exposed to the full fury of the ocean swells, causing severe damage to the trestle and to the completed jetty itself. The Engineer in charge of the project, Assistant Engineer Gustave Hegaardt, was acutely aware of the dangerous forces of wind and wave. At times the "rough ocean waters caused the outer portions of the tramway to sway so violently that he could not run trains on it."[24] In 1890 the weather was so stormy that 144 feet of tramway were washed away. Despite these harsh conditions, the south jetty was completed in 1895 at a cost of just under $2 million. It had taken ten years to build the structure, which was 30 feet high at its crest and from 80 to 90 feet wide at its base.

The south jetty produced a channel with an average depth of 30 feet. In fact a positive effect was seen as early as 1889. However, the jetty was unable to maintain the desired depth over time. The channel shoaled rapidly and within five years problems had developed. The public clamored louder than ever for more improvements, particularly since commerce on the Columbia had become dependent on the larger, more economical ocean vessels that had been using the newly improved entrance channel. In 1902 a Board of Engineers decided that in order to eliminate the shoaling and to reestablish a single, deep stable channel it would be necessary to repair the existing 4 mile jetty and add 2.5 miles to its length. Even this $8 million improvement plan proved inadequate to secure the Board of Engineers' proposed depth of 40 feet. The longer jetty deepened the channel to only 36 feet, so in the spring of 1914 the Portland District determined to build a north jetty on the Columbia River. Finished in 1917, the north jetty helped to focus the tidal and river currents so that a project depth of 40 feet was found even in what had previously been the shallowest portions of the entrance. With the two jetties in place, the entrance to the Columbia River became a safe port. As Colonel George A. Zinn of the Portland District reported in 1917, the two jetties "made it possible for the largest of vessels operating on the Pacific Coast to enter and leave at all normal stages of tide and in any weather except during [the] most severe storms."[25] The twin jetty system proved to be the most effective form of harbor protection on the Pacific Coast.

Jetty construction on the Pacific Coast can be best described as experimental and evolutionary. Though jetties had produced good results on the East Coast and in Europe, when work began on the Yaquina Bay jetties, the benefit to be gained from their construction was uncertain. Engineers believed that the single south jetty would create a deep and stable channel, but it was not known when it would first form or how long the channel would last. Nor could anyone predict the amount of maintenance the jetties would require. Moreover, though it was assumed that the improved harbor would benefit the community, forecasting the full economic effect of the project was impossible.

In applying technological lessons learned from one Pacific Coast project to another, inevitably mistakes were made. Some techniques worked well at one location only to fail at another. For example, the tramway method employed at Yaquina Bay was used effectively in modified fashion at both Coos Bay and on the

Columbia River. However, the successful crib technique used at Coos Bay was a dismal failure at Yaquina Bay. Engineers discovered the need to learn as much as possible about local meteorological and hydrological conditions. At Coos Bay the single interior deflecting jetty failed to improve the bay entrance. Likewise, at all three of the harbors, it was soon obvious that a single jetty could not prevent the littoral drifting that caused the dangerous sandbars. Experience proved that two slightly converging jetties created the best results along the stormy coast.

At the same time, the experience in building the jetties at Yaquina Bay, Coos Bay, and the mouth of the Columbia River enlightened the Corps as to the optimum size and height for the structure. Though each bay or river entrance was different, the Corps found that certain factors needed to be considered in order for jetties to function properly. One consideration was height. The Board of Engineers for the Pacific Coast in the 1870s originally proposed to build low-tide jetties on the coast; that is, jetties built only to the average height of the low tide at the site. Prevailing thought was that the low jetties could control the movement of sand and would be cheaper to construct than taller structures. However, Corps observers found that the low jetties allowed "large quantities of sand... [to] wash over them into the protected areas of the bay and that they [did] not maintain full control of the currents."[26] As jetties were built up to mid-tide, high tide, or even higher, they became increasingly better at maintaining open channels. They also became more susceptible to deterioration; the heads of the higher jetties were subjected to the most destructive forces of the waves. Hence, the ends often were eroded to low-tide levels, limiting their overall effectiveness.

Naturally, selecting the location of a jetty was important. While minor refinements of the jetty slope did not significantly affect the currents, the jetty base had to be placed so that it would not be subject to scour or to undermining from the tidal currents. Furthermore, to ease the passage of ships entering the harbor in foul weather, the jetty was placed where it would force the entrance channel to run in the same direction as the prevailing wind. The jetty also was built to extend far enough out into the ocean to offer substantial protection. In all, jetty construction is a delicate balance of cost and efficiency. Even after construction began it was often necessary to adjust the initial design. The Humboldt jetty system typifies the evolution of the construction and maintenance of jetty systems on the Pacific Coast.

The successes of the various jetty systems along the Oregon coast answered Assistant Engineer Boschke's question as to whether or not it was possible to place "a structure of great weight... upon the inner margin of the south breaker flat at a reasonable cost."[27] In January 1883 Colonel Mendell proposed to the Chief of Engineers that a single low-water revetment be built on the south spit at the entrance to Humboldt Bay. Mendell hoped that the low-tide jetty would hold the south sands in place, preventing the filling in and movement of the main entrance channel. The project was approved by a Board of Engineers at an estimated cost of $600,000. The structure was to resemble in cross section the one that had been approved at the mouth of the Columbia River that same year. The jetty was to be built from "a point near the end of the south spit, and extend in a northwesterly direction for about 5,000 feet."[28] This early design was to be modified many times before the jetties were completed.

NOTES

[1]*Democratic Standard*, 2 Oct. 1880, p. 2, col. 3.

[2]*Humboldt Times*, 15 Aug. 1881, p. 3, col. 3.

[3]*Humboldt Daily Standard*, Eureka, CA, 3 Jan. 1884, p. 1.

[4]*Democratic Standard*, 25 Aug. 1883, p. 3, col. 1.

[5]*Annual Report, 1882*, part 3, p. 2540.

[6]*Ibid.*

[7]*Ibid.*

[8]*Ibid.*, p. 2542.

[9]*Ibid.*

[10]*Ibid.*

[11]H.M. Chittenden, "Ports of the Pacific," *Transactions, Amer. Soc. of Civil Eng.*, 76 (Dec. 1913): 190.

[12]Thomas W. Symons, "Jetty Harbors of the Pacific Coast," *Transactions, Amer. Soc. of Civil Eng.*, 27 (March 1893): 160.

[13]William F. Willingham, *Army Engineers and the Development of Oregon. A History of the Portland District U.S. Army Corps of Engineers* (Portland, OR: U.S. Army Engineer District, 1983), p. 39.

[14]William W. Harts, "Description of Coos Bay, Oregon, and the Improvement of its Entrance by the Government, with discussion" *Transactions, Amer. Soc. of Civil Eng.*, 46 (Dec., 1901): 489.

[15]*Ibid.*

[16]Symons, *op. cit.*, p. 163.
[17]Willingham, *op. cit.*, p. 83.
[18]*Ibid.*
[19]Harts, *op. cit.*, p. 484.
[20]*Ibid.*, p. 496.
[21]*Ibid.*
[22]*Ibid.*
[23]Willingham, *op. cit.*, p. 41.
[24]*Ibid.*, p. 29.
[25]*Ibid.*, p. 64.
[26]Harts, *op. cit.*, p. 630.
[27]*Annual Report, 1882*, part 3, p. 2543.
[28]*Annual Report, 1883*, part 3, p. 1991.

CHAPTER III

Building the Jetties

Although construction of the south jetty at Humboldt Bay was approved in January 1883, actual work did not begin until May 1889. Three factors caused the delay. First, Corps officers at Humboldt Bay waited for the bar channel to reform in its northwest alignment, the most desirable position for construction. Second, low annual appropriations prevented starting work; six years passed before enough money was allocated to finance the project. And third, six landowners on the south spit were unwilling to settle on fair prices for their land, which was needed for support buildings and for placing equipment. Though frustrating to the local community, the long delay enabled the Engineers to apply the experience gained at the jetty works at Yaquina Bay and Coos Bay to the project at Humboldt.

One lesson learned at the two Oregon bays was the necessity of aligning the entrance channel to allow the easiest navigation in a storm. Because the Humboldt Bay channel lay in a northwest direction, both Assistant Engineer Boschke and Colonel Mendell recommended placing the channel in that position. Such an alignment would provide the most stable and the deepest channel. Accordingly, the Corps' 1883 proposal provided that the single south jetty be built in a northwesterly direction.[1]

Unfortunately for William Ayres and others who desired that the jetty construction proceed rapidly, the 1880s was a period when the direction and shape of the bar and channel changed rapidly. In 1882, for example, the channel's change of direction caused the north spit to erode and eventually destroy the brush jetties erected by Captain Boschke. In fact, the channel would change positions several times a year. In June 1884, for instance, the channel lay in a northerly direction, parallel to the north spit, but was very narrow.

By July the channel had closed. Simultaneously, a channel formed to the south of the bay entrance. The north channel continued to shoal, while the new channel drifted toward the west. In November the Coast and Geodetic Survey found the entrance channel to lay "nearly straight out west, and with excellent water."[2] However, that westerly channel began to shoal rapidly into a large sand flat in December. By January 1885, no new channel had formed. So little water covered the bar that shipping from the bay halted.

Problems continued throughout 1885. A new south channel formed in March and April, but it was very shallow and crooked. The unreliable condition of the bar wreaked havoc on the redwood industry of Humboldt Bay that year. Foreign trade almost ceased, because large transoceanic ships could not enter the port. Many of the "vessels in port and loaded were obligated to discharge parts of their cargoes and proceed elsewhere to finish loading."[3] Any attempts by the Corps to extend the jetty would be sabotaged by the vagaries of the channel. For example, while the channel lay in a southerly direction, its depth was too great to consider constructing a breakwater, because the current would wash away all of the jetty materials.

The channel continued to move and change direction throughout the decade. During much of 1886, it returned to the advantageous north-northwest position. Then in October, it began to shoal from its greatest depth of 16 feet, working its way south. The new channel was very narrow, and passable only at high tide by vessels with a draft of between 14 and 15 feet. By spring of 1887 a new channel had appeared, this time running almost due west. Because of rapid fluctuations of the channel and its depth, pilots were needed to guide every vessel over the bar, even if the ship's captain was accustomed to sailing into the port. Hans Buhne, one of the bay's bar pilots, remained convinced that little could be done by the Corps of Engineers or any private engineer to improve the stability of the bar channel.

The Corps of Engineers itself was unsure whether the breakwater it had proposed could control the channel. Army Engineers were confident of two factors: (1) that when aligned to the north the channel was fairly stable and (2) that the sands of the south spit acted as a natural breakwater that partially focused the tidal action, thereby helping to maintain a deep channel to the north. Colonel Mendell anticipated that $600,000 would be sufficient to build a low-tide structure from the south spit. However, the annual congressional appropriations were far below that amount. Furthermore, Captain A.H. Payson, the Corps officer assigned to the bay, feared no more would be forthcoming. In the original proposal in 1883, Mendell and Boschke had asked that the sum be appropriated in two consecutive years, thus assuring a "successful operation."[4] They believed that without the large biannual appropriation the stormy north coast of California would destroy any works that had been extended seaward.

The need for a large aggregate sum before construction could begin was a common theme in the annual reports of Captain Payson and other Corps officials responsible for the improvement of Humboldt Bay. In 1884 Payson pointed out that "the cost of the work is likely to be much increased if only small annual amounts of money are given."[5] In fact, Payson feared that without sufficient funding, the project would not be completed at all. He asserted, "there is no safe middle ground of compromise as to what money it shall have in this kind of work."[6] Despite Payson's pleas, by July 1886, three years after approval of the project, only $62,363.64 was available for construction. This amount was far short of the estimated cost of the jetty construction.

Throughout the six-year period before construction began, Corps officials continued to worry about the lack of available funds. The 1885 appropriation was "hardly more than sufficient for the establishment of the necessary wharf, buildings, track, and miscellaneous plant on the south spit."[7] Because undertaking this preliminary construction would have depleted the jetty fund, it was thought best to wait until the project was under way. The theme was continued in the annual report for 1886, which noted that the best results could be obtained only if enough money were available to both provide for constructing the necessary support works and to push "actual construction to the utmost during an entire working season."[8] Another concern of the engineers was that the wharf and tramway, if constructed prematurely, would be subject to damage from teredos, boring worms that would destroy wooden structures submerged in the salt water for more than two years. Mendell and Payson believed that the project could be completed in two years. Therefore, if the support works were built immediately before actual construction began, they would not need to be replaced.

Another complication related to the high prices demanded by the landowners on the south spit whose land was needed for the wharf and other support buildings. In 1885 the joint owners of the 17-acre parcel informed Payson that their land could not be had for less than $9,000 to $12,000. An infuriated Captain Payson called the land "quite worthless, save from the presumed necessities of the government."[9] Because the price demanded would have depleted the project's coffers, Payson asked for permission from his superiors at the San Francisco District to begin a condemnation suit. However, he was turned down because the existing appropriation for the project was too meager to cover legal expenses. Payson feared that when sufficient funds were finally available for construction the cost of the property could further delay work. He pointed out that the Corps would find itself either "yielding to the exorbitant demands of the land owners or the loss of another season through the legal delays of condemnation."[10]

This gloomy forecast was overtaken by events. The Rivers and Harbors Act of 5 August 1886 required "that none of the money thereby appropriated for the improvement of the bar should be expended until the United States had obtained a title free of expense to the land desired on the south spit."[11] On hearing the conditions of the act, local citizens interested in the bay's improvement took action. In 1887 a committee, led by lumber magnate John Vance, was formed to seek a compromise between the six landowners and the federal government. Vance, also president of the Eureka Chamber of Commerce, was vitally interested in the harbor improvement. He and the committee decided that they would contribute "money to purchase the said tract from the original entrymen... to the end that the Government might get the land free of cost."[12] After buying the south spit tract they would give it to the government and construction could begin.

The committee members were acting in their own best interests; they depended on coastal shipping to get their products to market. The men hoped that improving the entrance would increase profits and expand the foreign markets for redwood as predicted by William Ayres. Vance and his supporters paid the six property owners $300 each, an amount significantly lower than the $9,000 figure quoted to Payson. All of Vance's powers of persuasion had been required to convince owners such as Stephen Whipple to lower their asking price for the small strip of land. Vance was also able to convince some of the landowners, such as the Pacific Lumber Company, to donate their share of the property to the government project. The process was not without legal stumbling blocks. When Assistant Engineer Boschke began a title search he found yet another snag in obtaining the land. A young child named Gertrude Smith had inherited a one-sixth interest in the land, but had no control over the transfer. Proceedings in probate court in San Francisco had to be initiated to empower the child's guardian, Caroline Taber, to convey the property to Vance. In all, it took nearly a year to obtain a clear title to all of the land needed.

The next step was obtaining a written opinion from the U.S. District Attorney on the legality of the deed. After securing a "proper deed for the property referred to" the final stumbling block was overcome.[13] On 11 June 1888 Vance deeded the property to the United States to be used "for the purpose of erecting wharves and works thereon to improve the said entrance to Humboldt Bay."[14] Assistant Engineer Boschke was appointed as a deputy U.S. surveyor to survey and chart the lands.

With ownership of the land and clear right-of-way the federal government finally could begin constructing the single jetty as soon as the bar channel was aligned in the optimal northwest position. Questions had arisen about the wisdom of building a single jetty at the bay entrance, but no action had been taken to authorize a second jetty. As early as 1886 Captain Payson had formally stated his apprehensions about the erosion of the north spit. He feared that work begun on the south jetty without any "measures being taken for the protection of the north [spit] will be followed very quickly by large changes in the latter."[15] Problems with the single jetty system at Yaquina Bay contributed to Payson's apprehension. The jetty had proved insufficient to maintain the channel and, moreover, had caused additional erosion on the spit opposite the jetty. Payson's personal experience with both the Yaquina Bay and the Coos Bay jetties had made him well aware of the dangers of erosion and scour.

Notwithstanding Payson's concerns, in the fall of 1888 the Corps prepared to build a single low-water south jetty. Enough money was available to make the work feasible, the channel was finally in the northwest position, and the title to the lands at the end of the south spit had been cleared. After advertising throughout the nation, the San Francisco District accepted six bids for building the single jetty. One was from as far away as New Orleans, submitted by the Louisiana Jetty and Lighting Company. The proposals were opened on 30 November 1888. The contract was let to the low bidder, American Bridge and Building Company of San

Francisco. The winning bid of $250,000 included placing 88,000 tons of rock, constructing and placing the brush mattress, building the pier and tramway, and laying the track connecting the pier to the tramway.

The San Francisco company spent the next few months preparing for the work. Company employees surveyed the region and selected a quarry east of Eureka. They built a rail line to the quarry and quarters for their workers at both the quarry and the south spit. The company also began shipping equipment to the remote construction site. Though visible from Eureka, the spit could be reached only by crossing the bay or by a long, circuitous overland route. By water and land the contractor brought the railcars and engines to haul the rock on the tramway, the scows to transport the rock across the bay, and the steam pile driver — one of the most important pieces of equipment. The government built an office on the south spit to oversee the operation, and a large pair of scales to weigh the railcars' loads of rock, while the firm constructed a wharf and landing there.

The residents of Humboldt Bay were elated to witness the construction of the Corps plant for it symbolized the federal government's commitment to improve the entrance to Humboldt Bay. The editor of the *Humboldt Daily Standard*, J.F. Thompson, was particularly interested in the work, discussing the project in detail with Colonel Mendell when the latter came to Humboldt to inspect the site in March 1889. Mendell was confident that the work would be successful in deepening the channel over the bar, referring Thompson to the work done at Wilmington Bay in Los Angeles County. There the depth of the entrance channel had been increased from 3 feet to 12 feet. Mendell omitted mentioning that the conditions there were far different than those at Humboldt Bay. For example, the work at Wilmington had been more or less protected while the proposed jetty at Humboldt would be exposed to what some ship captains considered the roughest section of ocean along the Pacific Coast. Mendell was aware of the violent seas, but expected that the jetty would be completed without disaster. If problems did occur, such as the washing away of a portion of the jetty, that still would not "be any certain indication that the ultimate object will not be obtained."[16] Mendell's confidence inspired Thompson, who published a portion of Mendell's annual report for 1888 that outlined the work to be done on the south spit.

A month later, in April 1889, Thompson had an opportunity to travel to the south spit and inspect the construction site. He was accompanied by W.P. Smith, the engineer overseeing the project for the government, and Smith's assistant, Frank Bert. On the boat ride across the bay Smith explained to Thompson that south spit construction activities included building crew quarters for the American Bridge and Building Company employees and a protective wall around the spit to shield the buildings from the high tides which had washed away eighty feet of the south spit. Thompson was impressed with all the buildings at the site: the superintendent's quarters, the boardinghouse for the fifty-man crew, the blacksmith shop, the tool shop, and the office for the Corps officials. He predicted that soon "vessels drawing twenty feet will be able to enter [the bay] at low tide."[17]

The plant was completed, and in May 1889 construction began on the jetty. No immediate effect on the channel was seen during the first year of construction, but none was expected. The jetty could be effective only when it was built out at least one mile from shore, and in 1889 only 728 feet of the training wall had been built. This wall was only four to five feet high. In order to reduce scour and erosion its 20- to 30-foot-wide base rested on brush mattresses. The basic construction technique resembled that used at Yaquina Bay. The mattresses were placed below a tramway that was built out from the shore and 20 feet above the water. The rocks anchoring the mattresses and forming the rubble-mound jetty were dropped from the trestle. Running on the sturdy redwood tramway were the pile driver and standard-gauge railcars pushed by a steam locomotive. Powered by a donkey steam engine, the pile driver, used to drive the large redwood timbers of the trestle into the sand, was an integral part of jetty construction.

In this first year of work, the crew encountered no major problems. The work was done fairly close to shore and was not subject to the fierce, destructive action of the breakers on the Humboldt Bar. Although the project proceeded at a fairly regular rate, inadequate funds prevented as much construction as had been anticipated by Major William H. Heuer, the Engineer in charge of the project. The money had been spent on building the plant and little was left over for the next work season. Heuer estimated that only $337,500 was needed to finish the project and he asked that the appropriation be made in a lump sum so that the project could be finished in one year. He was afraid that the longer the work was carried on, the higher the cost would be. He cited the rapid deterioration of the tramway piers due to the teredo worms as one single example of how cost would increase if the project was not carried through immediately. If the contract took longer than two years to complete, the pier and portions of the tramway would have to be rebuilt at a cost of $50,000 before any new work could be done. Heuer's cost estimate was based on building a single low-water jetty. He pointed out that the cost would increase if it were found necessary to build the jetty to high water, a plan he thought should be considered by a Board of Engineers. Reports from the other jetty construction sites on the Pacific Coast indicated that the higher jetties were more efficient than the low-water jetty being built at Humboldt. Before such a board could meet to consider his proposal, construction based on the original project plans had stopped.

The shore protection work at the south spit as well as the work on the trestle and the construction of the brush mattresses had proceeded according to schedule. The American Bridge and Building Company had almost completed these projects by December 1889. However, all of the contract conditions had not been met. The company had delivered little more than half of the rock specified by the Corps, which severely slowed construction. The mattresses, for example, could not be sunk without sufficient rock, lest they be washed away. Each mattress required approximately "six tons of rock per running foot to properly sink and hold the brush mats; the balance of the rock was used in raising the shore end to high water."[18] Though dissatisfied with the contractor, the Corps of Engineers extended its contract until October 1890. The company did little, however, during the first months of 1890, because that spring was unusually stormy.

Once work resumed in May it proceeded rapidly. The first loads of rock from the Mad River Quarry began arriving and by the end of June 3,448 tons of rock had been delivered to the construction site. But even at that rate, the contractor was unable to transport the stipulated amount of rock needed to complete the contract. Although the contract was extended to 31 October 1890, the company was able to supply only about 46,000 tons of rock, over 41,000 tons short of the contracted amount. Consequently, the Corps of Engineers annulled the contract and stopped work on the south jetty for 1890. At the end of the working season, the jetty was 3,039.7 feet long and an average of 45 feet wide.

Meanwhile, Corps officials had other problems with the improvement project. Although the nascent jetty was one-third completed, the channel showed no signs of stabilizing. In fact, in the first six months of 1890 the channel changed position so often and so rapidly that Major Heuer feared that the newly extended south jetty must be the cause. Engineering surveys revealed that most of the change was confined to the entrance channel and was related to the erosion of the tip of the north spit. As in 1881, the north spit's rapid deterioration had greatly expanded the bay entrance. In fact, in a single year the bay entrance had widened by 1,300 feet. Corps surveys showed that the small south jetty was actually accelerating bar formation. These conditions threatened all of the work done at the entrance by the Corps of Engineers.

Major Heuer called for a Board of Engineers to analyze the problem. In addition to providing solutions for halting the erosion of the north spit, the board was asked to review the advisability of raising the project height of the south jetty to above the high-water mark. The recent work done at Yaquina Bay had indicated that the higher the jetty the better it controlled the littoral drift of the shifting sands. The board, consisting of Colonel Mendell, Lieutenant Colonel W.H.H. Benyaurd, and Major Heuer, met in Eureka on 11 December 1890. After analyzing the data compiled by W.P. Smith, the Assistant Engineer in charge of the jetty construction, the board decided that the only solution was to build a north jetty.

In the 1871 and 1877 recommendations for the improvement of the bay entrance the two Boards of Engineers had stated that two jetties would be needed to sufficiently control the tidal currents. (Later surveys by Colonel Mendell and Captain Boschke had proposed only one jetty to produce the desired results. The north spit had proved to be less stable, however, than anticipated by these officers.) The newly proposed north jetty would be built to the high-tide mark, parallel to the south jetty. As revised by the 1890 Board of Engineers, the project called for the north jetty to be 6,750 feet long, built in the same way as the south jetty. In addition, the south jetty would be extended to a length of 7,800 feet and raised to the high-tide level. When finished, the two jetties would be 2,100 feet apart at their seaward end. The estimated cost of the new work plus the additions to the south jetty came to $1,715,115. The board submitted its final recommendations to the Chief of Engineers, Brigadier General Thomas Casey, on 13 March 1891. He quickly approved.

Prior to this approval, bids for a new contractor to continue the project had been advertised. A modified construction plan had been drawn up by the Board of Engineers at their Eureka meeting to provide for the immediate construction of the new jetty if approved by the Chief of Engineers. Because of the board's foresight the contract for the project was awarded before final approval was received. Only three bids were submitted by the 12 January 1891 deadline, two from Eureka contractors and one from a San Francisco firm. The bid of James Simpson and Thomas Brown of Eureka was the lowest, and on 7 February 1891 they became the second construction company to enter into a contract to build the Humboldt Bay jetties. Their contract specified that they would provide 57,000 tons of rock, 13,000 cubic yards of brush, and build 2,000 feet of pier and an apron wharf and approaches as well as 1,000 feet of track along the shore. This work was to be completed by December 1891. Simpson and Brown believed that they could do the job for only $157,950.

In February 1891 Simpson and Brown opened a new quarry and laid track to it. By 1 May they were ready to begin work on the jetties, delivering their first load of rock to the south jetty on 5 May. In two months the contractor brought more than 8,000 tons of rock to the south jetty in order to build up the already constructed jetty to the high-tide level. By the end of June over half of the completed jetty was raised to the newly specified level. Simpson and Brown did no extension work on the south jetty and it remained at less than half of its final projected length.

In May 1891 the north spit began eroding even more rapidly, requiring that work begin on it immediately in order to protect the rest of the spit. The erosion of the north spit widened the entrance to 5,100 feet; the previous year it had been only 3,000 feet wide.[19] But before the north jetty could be built, Simpson and Brown had to build a breakwater inside the bay mouth to protect against further erosion. The breakwater extended to the original uneroded end of the north spit. From there, not from the newly eroded land end, the north jetty would be built. Because the jetty required a solid base to prevent its destruction, the majority of the work on the north jetty that year consisted of preparing and building the breakwater.

The breakwater was built in the same way as was the south jetty, complete with its own tramway. The object of the protection work,

A sketch of the trestle on the south jetty. Drawing by M.B. Pritchard.

in addition to preventing further erosion of the north spit, was to "narrow the entrance somewhat and to remove the shoal which [had] formed just to the eastward of the entrance."[20] The work on the breakwater was finished by the end of July, and Simpson and Brown turned to the business of building the north jetty. As work began, Assistant Engineer Smith discovered that the north spit sands had begun to reform behind the breakwater and on the north side of the jetty. By late September Simpson and Brown had built the north jetty out to 1,480 foot. By then their experience had helped them to find ways to decrease the expense of construction. For example, instead of using one brush mattress to form the base of the jetty they used two. One mattress was sunk on top of the other, thus reducing the amount of expensive rock needed in construction. They also were able to increase their profits by using only half the amount of timbers in the north jetty trestle work that

had been used on the south jetty. The north jetty was more
protected than the south jetty, which bore the brunt of the rough
waters of the south breaker flat.

On 31 October 1891 Simpson and Brown completed the terms of
their contract with the Corps of Engineers. They had delivered
more than 15,900 tons of rock to the north jetty and twice that
amount to the south jetty and had built the required trestle and
other support works. They had done all this in less than six
months, a shorter time than called for in their contract. This
successful conclusion, however, signaled the end of work on the
jetties for that year and the next. Work on harbor improvement
ceased because the jetty construction had exhausted the money
previously allocated by Congress. No new appropriations had been
made in 1891 nor were any made in the spring of 1892. In his 1892
report Major Heuer asked for a $700,000 appropriation, stating
that anything less would be insufficient and would cause increased
cost in the long run. He again cited the ravages of teredos in
increasing the final cost of the project, pointing out that the
various contractors counted on being reimbursed for constructing
the plant. It was common practice, according to Heuer, for the
contractor bidding on a project to calculate his proposal "so as to
reimburse himself for the outlay in his plant, costing $40,000 to
$50,000 in every contract."[21] On 13 July 1892 Congress did
appropriate $150,000 for the Humboldt Bay jetty project but the
amount fell far short of Heuer's recommendation. As a result no
new contracts were let in 1892. Not until 1893 did work resume on
the jetties.

In the meantime, the local community continued to call on
Congress for money for the harbor improvement. To attest to the
vitality of the Humboldt Bay economy and its dependence on
coastal shipping, the Humboldt County Chamber of Commerce
included a statement on the economy of the region in the Chief of
Engineers 1891 *Annual Report* to Congress. In addition to stating
the amount of exports and the quantities of redwood shipped to
foreign ports, the chamber stressed Humboldt Bay's unique status
as one of the few natural harbors on the Pacific Coast. Because the
bay sat almost halfway between San Francisco and the mouth of
the Columbia River, it was, according to the Chamber of
Commerce, the ideal location to develop a harbor of refuge. The
chamber also cited the growing U.S. Navy and the need for coast

defenses: "the strength and safety of the Pacific Coast and of the Government's naval power call for the improvement of Humboldt Bay."[22]

The Chamber of Commerce's final reason for soliciting government aid in developing the bay concerned the delivery of mail. Eratic mail service to Humboldt Bay had plagued the region since its settlement in 1850. Local residents depended on coastal steamers to carry the mail, and often the steamers could not cross the Humboldt Bar. The mail steamer *Columbia* for weeks would be prevented from entering the port, and often the local editor's only comment was "passed by again." By the 1890s, the residents found the situation intolerable. The Chamber of Commerce believed that the federal government was obligated to provide fast and reliable mail service. In its opinion, "the convenience and prosperity of 25,000 people, so far as they can be affected by communication, are at the mercy of a bar that the Government has neglected to improve."[23]

In 1892, a year after the Chamber of Commerce's report, Congress appropriated additional funds for the project. The lawmakers also authorized in that year's rivers and harbors act the letting of a continuous contract to complete work on both the north and south jetties. The continuous contract meant that Congress was committing the government to spend the estimated $1 million needed to finish the project. For a third time the San Francisco District office advertised for bids. The eight-bid response was greater than for any of the previously advertised Corps contracts for work on the Humboldt jetties. Four bids came from San Francisco; one came from the firm of Hughes Brothers and Bangs of Syracuse, New York; and another came from N.J. Blagen of Portland, Oregon. Two Humboldt County contractors also bid for the contract. The Pacific Coast Contracting Company of Eureka submitted one of the lower bids, but was underbid by John C. Bull, Jr., of Arcata. Bull's $750,660 bid was the lowest, and he signed a contract with the government on 16 December 1892.

In 1893, the Humboldt County Chamber of Commerce published a pamphlet extolling the northern California county. It was titled *In the Redwoods Realm, By-ways of Wild Nature and the Highways of Industry, as Found Under Forest Shades and Amidst Clover Blossoms in Humboldt County, California*. The pamphlet represented the feelings of county residents, who were proud that the area had risen to sufficient prominence to warrant a congressional appropriation of more than $1 million for improving Humboldt Bay. Once work was resumed, more than 200 men were employed on the jetties, and the chamber was confident that the structures soon would be completed. Most of the materials used on the jetties were obtained locally, again illustrating the county's value as a commercial center. The chamber pamphlet pointed out that the effects of the improvement already could be seen, and soon the one impediment to the commerce on the bay, the shifting sandbar, would be removed. The Chamber of Commerce also applauded the fact that a county resident, the Arcatan John Bull, had been awarded the contract.

John Bull was not a typical contractor, however. He had done no construction work prior to receiving the Humboldt Bay contract. Bull's varied career included apprenticeships as a plumber and coppersmith after his family came to California from Massachusetts in 1851. He settled in Humboldt County in 1856, after his parents had established a hotel in Arcata. Bull later ran a ranch and a butcher shop in Arcata and served as county sheriff from 1875 to 1876. According to his biography, although Bull carried out his affairs in a modest manner, he "was on the lookout for opportunities... thus it was that he came to take the government contract for the jetty... a work of great magnitude and one requiring executive qualities and intimate knowledge of local conditions possessed by few."[24] Bull's awareness of the hazards of the bay entrance led to his success in building the two jetties, although the project took seven years to complete. Ironically, Major Heuer felt that Bull's bid was "about 12 per cent too low and would lead to failure."[25]

When Bull began constructing the jetties in April 1893, he found that the existing structures had been damaged badly by storms the year before. Both the north and south jetties had to be repaired before they could be extended. Much of the damage had occurred when large redwood logs washed into the ocean from the nearby mouth of the Eel River. The logs became wedged against the trestle work of the jetties and caused more than 100 feet of the tramway to collapse. In addition the storms had washed away a large portion of the sandy beach on the ocean side of the north spit, narrowing the unstable ground that the jetty was being built on. The ocean also washed away 1,000 feet of the shore railroad track that carried the rocks and other building materials and supplies to the north jetty construction site. The south jetty, which did not have as much vulnerable trestle work, sustained very little damage during this time.

Bull spent two months of valuable construction time repairing the protection work and building the existing north jetty to a level above that of the highest storm tides. Only after this work was completed could he begin extending the north jetty seaward. In order to control the erosion of the north spit, the Corps of Engineers had decided to concentrate on the north jetty and its protection work. Hence, the north jetty's position had been modified slightly to incorporate the protection dike. Once the north jetty was as long as the south jetty, the two would be extended simultaneously. The Board of Engineers had decided on this construction plan because they believed that the south jetty had caused the erosion of the north spit and would, if extended faster and made longer than the north jetty, ultimately destroy the north jetty by directing the tidal scour toward the rubble-mound structure. By June 1893 the north jetty had reached a length of 2,293 feet, and Bull turned his attention to extending both jetties concurrently.

When Bull began shipping rock from the Jacoby Creek quarry to the two construction sites, he experienced the same problems as had his predecessors. The rock was metamorphic sandstone and required special handling. Some of it disintegrated before it could be used. Hence Bull and his employees had to use extreme caution to select rock that the Corps believed to be durable. Compounding this problem was the fact that the Corps claimed that the rate at which the rocks were delivered fell far short of contract specifications and the size and quality of the rock also was unsatisfactory. Lieutenant Herbert Deakyne, the Corps of Engineers officer in local charge of the project, stated in his annual report for 1893 that though "promises were freely made,... they were not kept."[26] Deakyne believed that quarry workers broke the rock into unusably small pieces through careless blasting. Often the rock delivered was too small to be used even in mattress sinking, yet it had to be removed from the quarry before more suitable rock could be transported to the jetties.

The jetties continued to be built by the trestle and brush mattress method. The mills around the bay could easily supply the large redwood timbers used in the trestle. The brush used was mostly alder and willow, although the alder was slightly brittle and tended to break easily. Then, in May of 1894, Bull and Deakyne discovered that the brush mattresses were not preventing the scour of the sands beneath the jetty trestle. The powerful tidal currents had begun eroding away the sand around the tip of the north jetty. Before anything could be done to prevent jetty damage, the heavy spring seas washed away the end of the completed trestle that had been undermined by the scour. Bull lost several uncompleted brush mattresses in addition to the new trestle work. The loss brought about modifications to the pile driver that made it more stable and reduced expenses. At that time, however, the brush mattresses were not modified and they continued to be used in the jetty construction.

It was fortunate that Bull developed a better pile driver, because stormy weather continued to plague the construction work. In November, for example, the first great storm of the winter destroyed several bents of the recently completed trestle work and washed away a completed brush mattress that had not yet been sunk. At the height of the storm the pile driver, which had been withdrawn from the end of the trestle to a more protected position, broke loose from its moorings. It pitched forward and was washed away by the ocean waves, but was not carried far before it grounded. Although Bull was able to retrieve the machine, he estimated damages in excess of $1,000.[27]

The November storm heralded a particularly violent winter season, bringing an early close to the year's work season. Deakyne recorded the progress of the jetty construction, as well as its destruction by the winter storms, by numbering each 16-foot bent on the trestle. In one storm in 1893 six bents were destroyed and twice as many damaged. Drifting logs also caused damage to the trestle work each year, requiring extensive repairs.

By 1893 the jetty construction was showing some results. The bar channel had stabilized in one position at an average depth of 19 feet. Deakyne found that since the resumption of construction "no vessels were prevented from leaving the harbor on account of lack of depth on the bar, although on a few occasions they were prevented from doing so by rough sea."[28] One unanticipated aspect of the improved channel was the deepening of the bay mouth beside the south jetty. Surveys by Deakyne in the summer of 1893 revealed that the entrance channel was encroaching on the jetty, threatening to undermine the structure. To prevent its collapse, Deakyne decided to build spurs or projections out from the main jetty into the channel to support the structure, much like the flying buttresses used in cathedral construction in the Middle Ages. Four spurs were built, each approximately 36 feet long by 25 feet wide. Built perpendicular to the jetty, they were constructed in the same manner as the rest of the jetty but to a height of only 3.3 feet. However, the brush mattresses were dropped from a scow instead of from a trestle, and rock was added from the jetty to add stability. A special steam crane was used to lift the larger rock onto the spurs from the railcars on the jetty. Because the spurs cost approximately $900 each, they were an unexpected cost that added greatly to the overall expense for the year.

With the exception of the spur construction, no work was done on the south jetty in 1893 or 1894 even though it was only half completed. The bar channel had moved to a southerly position and passed immediately past the end of the south jetty. The channel at this point had scoured to depths of 35 to 50 feet. Deakyne knew that in these depths the pile driver could not properly drive the piles to support the trestle. Furthermore, even if the trestle could be built, the scouring current would wash away the mattresses before the rocks could be placed to secure them. Deakyne therefore stated that no work should be done to extend the jetties. He was not alarmed by the repositioning of the channel, for he was confident that the "recurring changes would again move the channel northward and cause shoaling, thereafter rendering extension work feasible."[29] A consequence of the greatly deepened channel and the halting of work on the south jetty for two years was the destruction of the existing trestle work. Before any new work could be done on the south jetty, it would be necessary to rebuild the entire structure.

In March 1895, Deakyne took soundings at the head of the south jetty and learned that the channel there was beginning to shoal. The channel finally had moved to a more northerly direction and "for a distance of a 1,000 feet ahead of the trestle there was depth of only 18 to 22 feet where formerly it had been 35 to 50 feet."[30] Deakyne considered the new depths favorable for construction, and the work of extending the south jetty resumed in July. June was spent repairing the trestle and replacing large segments that had washed away. By the end of June the trestle had been rebuilt to within 17 feet of its length in 1893 when extension work was abandoned. Yet, even as the trestle was extended seaward, the sand in front of the line of the proposed jetty began to erode again. Since March, when Deakyne's soundings revealed the

shallower conditions satisfactory for construction, the water depth
had increased by ten feet. On 12 July, when the trestle had been
extended only another 336 feet, Deakyne was forced to admit that
"the depths ahead were so great as to render jetty construction
both hazardous and expensive; it was therefore stopped for the
season."[31]

While work on the south jetty consisted mostly of repairs and
shoring up, the north jetty was extended seaward at a rate that
exceeded the expectations of Major Heuer, the Engineer in charge
of the project. The weather and sea conditions were favorable for
construction, "and excellent progress was made."[32] By February
1896, the trestle on the north jetty was built out 8,059.6 feet, and
the completed rubble-stone jetty built to above the high-water
mark was 6,570 feet long. But, like the south jetty, the north jetty
was subject to the destructive forces of the pounding waves along
the coast and the equally damaging threat of scour. During the
winter, when work was stopped, a watchman was posted at the bay
entrance to look for scour or other potentially hazardous conditions
around the jetties.

In March 1895 Lieutenant Deakyne received a telegram from
the watchman at Humboldt Bay advising him that the north jetty
was being undermined by scour along the entrance side of the
jetty. When Deakyne reached the bay on 17 March he found that at
one point there was a depth of 42 feet at low tide, only 65 feet from
the center of the jetty. Concerned that the rocks of the jetty might
topple into the entrance channel, Deakyne immediately contacted
John Bull. By March 24, rock began to arrive for building a
protective work. The work consisted of a revetment or support
work built for 162 feet along the side of the jetty where the scour
was the most severe. In a few days, Deakyne and Bull had secured
the jetty against immediate danger. They continued the revetment
work until mid-April to ensure no further damage. Deakyne
found a significant amount of scour also was occurring along the
north side of the head of the jetty. He had revetment work done
there as well.

Hoping to prevent future erosion and to forestall the destruction
of the rock used on the jetty, Deakyne instituted a rigid inspection
plan. From observations of rock that had been placed previously on
the jetties, he learned what kinds of rock disintegrated fastest.
After his analysis, Deakyne refused rock having any of the

following characteristics: "(1) a fine-grained blue rock full of seams and so soft it crumbled in the hand; (2) a surface rock of yellow-grey color; (3) a conglomerate, crumbling on slight pressure; and (4) a rock containing seams of slate."[33] Even with these new requirements, rock shipments increased greatly in 1895, exceeding all previous annual deliveries. More than 197,000 tons of rock were directed to the north jetty alone. Deakyne credited the increase to John Bull's new superintendent of jetty construction, W.E. Dennison. Dennison increased the scale of the operations by adding to the fleet of scows and railcars that delivered the rock to the construction sites. He also introduced electric lights at both the quarry and the jetties so that work could continue late into the night. In the two months following these improvements, more than 10,000 tons of rock were delivered to the two jetties.

Dennison recorded the dramatic aspects of the jetty construction in the September 1896 issue of the *Overland Monthly*. His article brings to life the large-scale operation and portrays the experiences of the workers who were pushing back the forces of nature. He began by describing how the rocks were brought from the quarry to the construction site in 1896. The center for the elaborate operation was in Eureka, where a dispatcher was connected by telephone lines to both of the jetties; to the Jacoby Creek quarry; to the quarry pier at Bayside, a small community on the bay near Arcata; and to the railroad from the quarry. The dispatcher coordinated rock delivery, controlling the operation by means of a board on which he pegged the various positions of the two sternwheel steamers and one tug that towed the seven barges throughout the day and night. The steamers notified the dispatcher of their positions through a system of whistles. Three blasts indicated that the barge was loaded and headed for the jetties while two meant that it was empty and en route to Bayside for another load.[34] The barges had three sets of rails built on them, and were long enough for seven cars to fit on each railtrack. The barges simply carried the loaded or empty cars, thus saving on loading and unloading. In a matter of ten minutes a steam locomotive waiting for the barge at either the Bayside or jetty wharves could unload the 21 cars, and the steamer with barge in tow would be on its way to the quarry or jetties.

The sight of the quarry along Jacoby Creek often startled visitors just emerging from a large stand of redwoods. The bluff above the creek was exposed to its full height of 420 feet, with the quarry extending some 3,000 feet up the creek. Two hundred men were employed there to remove the rock for the jetties. By 1896 more than 600,000 tons of rock had been shipped to the construction sites, even though the quarry had not yet been fully opened. Dennison wryly commented that "enough waste rock lies on the dumps to macadamize every road in the country."[35] Once removed from the bluff, the rock was loaded onto railcars by ten steam derricks. Jacoby Creek provided the water to run both the steam machines and the force for the small hydraulic monitor, similar to those used in hydraulic mining, to blast away unusable rock. The quarry site itself was a complete work camp, similar to those used by the lumber companies for their woods crews. As in the wood camps, housing and food were provided for all 200 men.

With the aid of the slight downhill grade, the fully loaded railcars made the return trip to the quarry wharf in only 20 minutes. The train was loaded by gravity onto the waiting barge and then towed to the jetty construction sites. According to Dennison, the quarry was capable of yielding six train loads of rock a day and, on a good day, as many as seven. The trip across the bay to the jetties was the longest portion of the journey, the steamers taking two hours to pull the laden barges down to the bay entrance. Once at the jetty wharf destination, on the bay side of either spit, a hoisting engine pulled the loaded railcars onto the wharf, where they were weighed three at a time. From there a steam locomotive pushed them out onto the jetty trestle, where the rock finally was dumped onto the jetty. The railcars had a hog back center so that they could be easily unloaded with a crowbar. A special hydraulic car was used to dump the larger boulders in place. More than 300 men worked on the jetties, making the brush mattresses and unloading the railcars. These men, like those at the quarry, were housed and fed at a work camp right at the jetties. Married couples also lived at the construction site. A child, David Thompson, was born to one of those couples at the south spit camp in 1895.

Dennison was confident that with the large workforce the jetties soon would be completed. By the end of the 1896 work season, the north jetty was nearly finished, having been pushed out nearly 1.5 miles seaward and reaching the crest of the sandbar. The south jetty work was proceeding more slowly, but Dennison believed that it would be finished in short order also, possibly within the next work season. Deakyne and Heuer had found that winter work resulted in more damage than successful construction. Hence they had mandated a work season lasting from 15 April to 15 October. Dennison also believed that with extension of the jetties all speculation about their inability to improve the entrance had been dispelled. Since 1894, the *Pomona*, the largest steam vessel entering the bay, had been able to do so both day and night without the aid of a tug. The 1896 survey of the Coast and Geodetic Survey team marked a channel that was 1,500 feet wide across the bar and 24 deep, even at low tide. Dennison thought that in less than two years the channel would "be declared permanent and the work completed."[36]

Despite Dennison's confidence, Corps officials faced several problems before the jetties could be completed. One was the continual threat of scour. Major Heuer decided that the best defense would be a revetment alongside the jetty. A revetment was cheaper to place and easier to maintain than the elaborate spurs built along the south jetty, which often required the construction of their own trestles. Furthermore, the revetment did not obstruct the flow of the tidal channel as did the spurs. (The spurs were often the sites of eddies and whirls of water, causing further scouring. In some cases these eddies had destroyed the spur, weakening the jetty in the process.) Nevertheless, not even rock revetment would completely prevent the erosion of the sand around the base of the jetty.

Another problem Major Heuer and Deakyne encountered was the criticism of their management of the construction by the *Daily Humboldt Times*, which carried the letters of local resident David Evans. Evans claimed the officers' negligence had led to the erosion of the north spit. Evans and his supporters sent letters condemning the Corps' construction techniques to members of Congress from California. One of Evans' complaints concerned the quality of rock used. In 1894 he accused Deakyne and Heuer of using limestone rock that slaked away, eroding easily. He also claimed that the rock was too small and was being washed into the channel, making it unnavigable. Based on his own inspections and observations, Evans believed that the Corps officers had been delinquent in their duties and that therefore the jetties soon would disintegrate.[37] The other daily newspaper, *The Humboldt Daily Standard*, defended the Corps officers, claiming that they knew more about engineering than did Mr. Evans.

Heuer and Deakyne were far more concerned, however, over the battering of the trestle work by the destructive waves. Both the north and south jetty trestles were destroyed regularly by high waves during the winter storms. The damage required extensive repair work during the first month of every working season. Though many attempts were made to strengthen the trestles, none proved particularly successful. If the trestle was supported with extra braces, the brace work interfered with the construction and placement of the brush mattresses. Moreover, the bracings exposed a greater surface area to the waves, and actually contributed to the destruction of the trestle. By 1896 Major Heuer had resigned himself to the annual winter damage. He decided that it was cheaper to replace the damaged trestle work caused by winter storms than to try to modify the existing method. Heuer found that the damages, though "extensive, [were] not costly to repair."[38] The necessary timbers were easy to obtain and reasonably priced in a port whose principal economy was the production of redwood lumber.

In May 1895, Deakyne discovered that teredo worms had honeycombed the wharf on the north spit where the railcars of quarried rock were unloaded. Two of the support pilings had given way and the wharf had collapsed. The pilings, which had been placed in April 1894, were destroyed in only thirteen months. Bull immediately replaced the collapsed support work and in June added eight more pilings for increased support. Late in June, another piling gave way after being in the water only five months. The teredos had attacked it twenty-two feet below the water level. During the final years of construction, many more pieces of the wharf and trestle had to be replaced because of teredo damage.

Delays in the construction of the Humboldt Bay jetties were not limited to the caprices of nature, however. In June 1894, for example, work ground to a halt because of a series of strikes. The pile-driving crew struck on 30 June 1894, demanding a pay increase of $.50 a day. Bull and his Jetty Construction Company refused to bargain with the men, firing them and importing "a crew from San Francisco to take their places."[39] The new crew started pile-driving on 7 July. Bull's strike problems were not resolved, however. Undeterred by the company's reaction to the pile-driver strike, the workers walked off of the quarry on 2 July 1894 in an attempt to get free board. The men were paid between $1.25 and $2.00 a day, and were charged $.50 a day for board whether they worked or not.

Enraged by these conditions, approximately ninety of the workers left the quarry and went to the contractor's main office in Eureka. The Jetty Construction Company responded by paying off the men. Jetty construction halted when the rest of the crew followed the lead of the original ninety. Conditions remained stalemated for a week, then on 9 July the strikers and the company reached a compromise. The entire crew met in Eureka with W.E. Dennison, Bull's representative. The company, faced with the prospect of having to hire a new crew, offered the men a raise of $.25 a day and exemption from paying board on Sundays unless they worked that day. In addition, married men would not have to pay the hospital fee, nor would single men who had certificates from other hospitals. At the end of the meeting Dennison told the men "that the steamer *Silva* with a barge would wait until 9 o'clock...for their decision."[40] The men at first refused Dennison's offer, but later decided to return to work. The following day, 10 July 1894, the strike officially ended and the men traveled to the quarry wharf aboard the *Silva*. Yet another strike was threatened when the jetty construction crew complained about the food. Bull averted this third strike by hiring a new cook.

Although the men at the quarry and on the jetties did not complain of the hazards of their jobs, they worked in very dangerous conditions, especially the men on the jetties. A grim reminder of the dangers of the jetty construction occurred on 22 July 1896. That afternoon Angus McDonald, Ed "Shorty" Inman, and Kenneth Ferguson were unloading several railcar loads of rock. Taking advantage of the calm weather, they were working overtime near the end of the south jetty trestle and had dumped all but the last two carloads of rock for the day. They were using the hydraulic railcars that were lifted with locomotive steam in order to deposit their loads of rock. The two cars were set up to empty their load onto the channel side of the jetty. As one of the cars was readied, Inman stood between the two cars while McDonald stood on the truck at the side of the car. Where the other men were was never determined. According to an eyewitness account, the car the crew had prepared to dump into the channel was tilted slightly in the direction of the channel when it unaccountably reversed its position. The force of the momentum threw both of the cars, their loads of rock, and the workers into the water. Inman and McDonald were swept out to sea, their bodies lost forever. The other men were thrown across the trestle to the other set of tracks. Ferguson was injured badly and later died of complications from a fractured thighbone. Considering the hazardous conditions of the Humboldt Bar and the damage done to the jetties during construction, that only these three men were killed during the project's construction is amazing.

Despite the loss of trestle and the tragic deaths of the men, work progressed steadily on the jetties. Because construction on the north jetty had not been halted since 1893, Bull was able to complete that jetty in four years. Captain Cassius E. Gillette, the Corps of Engineers officer responsible for the Humboldt project in 1897, declared the work complete on 17 April 1897 when the north jetty received its last load of rock. The jetty was not built up to its full projected height above the high-water mark, because the rock near the head of the jetty was liable to be washed away. Captain Gillette believed, however, that "the jetty [would] retain sufficient height to fully accomplish the purpose for which it was constructed."[41] The north jetty was designed to help confine the tidal currents and to prevent the erosion of the north spit. When completed, the north jetty jutted westward into the ocean for a mile and a half, to the Humboldt Bar.

Work continued for another two years on the south jetty. One of the greatest obstacles to completing this jetty was the tendency of the tidal currents to scour out twenty to thirty-foot depths directly in front of the construction. (This occurred before the brush mattress was placed.) Because it was difficult and expensive to drive the piles of the jetty trestle in such depths, in 1898 Major Heuer tried an experiment that revolutionized the way jetties were built on the Pacific Coast. He substituted "a layer of small rock, one pound and upward," for the brush mattress.[42] The advantage of the small rock was that it could be placed faster than brush mattresses, thereby avoiding much of the scouring around the piles.[43] In 1901 Major William Harts, who had been responsible for the construction of the Coos Bay jetties, discussed the advantages of rock mattresses in a paper he presented to the

The apron wharf on the south spit was a scene of great activity as it received the loads of quarried rock delivered to the jetties. *Courtesy D. Tuttle.*

American Society of Civil Engineers. Harts believed that the layer of rock was more effective on the Pacific Coast than were the brush mattresses, and recommended its use for all jetty works in the region.

The new technique worked well at Humboldt Bay, especially on the south jetty, and prevented the scour that had been slowing the completion of the project. Another modification to the original construction proposal was the decision to use extra-strong fastenings on the south jetty trestle, because of the violent wave action against the jetty as it was extended to the Humboldt Bar. The waves' force kept beating down all of the rocks and boulders placed far below the line of the low-tide mark, so the end of the jetty was always under water. Bull found it difficult to keep the rubble mound jetty at the height thought necessary to achieve the best results; despite the several thousand tons of rock that were delivered to the jetty since 1897 the jetty still sloped down at its head. The north jetty had this same problem, so even when completed in 1899 both jetty heads were below water.

On 30 August 1899, after more than 1,148,144 tons of rock had been delivered to both jetties, the Humboldt Bay jetties were declared completed and the project accepted. The south jetty extended seaward for 7,408 feet and was separated from the north jetty by 2,100 feet. The north jetty was 8,068 feet long. The final cost of the ten-year project was $2,040,203.35, which was approximately $17,000 less than the Board of Engineers' 1891 estimate.[44] Both the San Francisco District and the local residents viewed the jetties as a success. The jetties maintained a stable entrance channel with an average depth at low water of twenty-five feet and with ample width. For the first time since the settlement of the region in 1850, large vessels could enter the bay, even at low tide, and without the aid of a tugboat and pilot. Commerce to the bay increased rapidly. A year after the jetties' completion, in 1900, exports had grown to more than $1 million annually and by 1910 they had tripled.[45] The jetties were not the only cause for the rapid growth of the region's commerce, but they played a significant part in establishing the economic security of the region and in fulfilling the dream of William Ayres.

NOTES

[1]*Annual Report, 1883*, part 3, p. 1991.
[2]*Annual Report, 1885*, part 3, p. 2352.
[3]*Ibid.*
[4]*Ibid.*, p. 1991.
[5]*Annual Report, 1884*, part 3, p. 2199.
[6]*Ibid.*
[7]*Annual Report, 1885*, part 3, p. 2352.
[8]*Annual Report, 1886*, part 3, p. 1920.
[9]*Annual Report, 1885*, part 3, p. 2352.
[10]*Ibid.*
[11]*Annual Report, 1887*, part 3, p. 2447.
[12]Humboldt County Recorder's Office, Humboldt County Courthouse, Grantors Book 26, Eureka, CA, p. 661. Hereafter cited as Humboldt County Recorder's Office, Grantors Book.
[13]*Annual Report, 1888*, part 3, p. 2135.
[14]Humboldt County Recorder's Office, Grantors Book 26, p. 661.
[15]*Annual Report, 1886*, part 3, p. 1920.
[16]*Humboldt Daily Standard*, 6 March 1889, p. 2, col. 1.
[17]*Ibid.*, 3 April 1889, p. 2, col. 3.
[18]*Annual Report, 1890*, part 4, p. 2919.
[19]*Ibid.*, p. 2920.
[20]*Annual Report, 1891*, part 4, p. 3122.
[21]*Annual Report, 1892*, part 4, p. 2658.

[22]*Annual Report, 1891*, part 4, p. 3127.
[23]*Ibid.*
[24]Leigh H. Irvine, *History of Humboldt County, California, with Biographical Sketches* (Los Angeles: Historic Record Co., 1915), p. 1221.
[25]W.E. Dennison, "Humboldt Bay and its Jetty System," *Overland Monthly* (September 1896): 385.
[26]*Annual Report, 1894*, part 4, p. 2545.
[27]*Ibid.*, p. 2547.
[28]*Ibid.*, p. 2549.
[29]*Annual Report, 1895*, part 4, p. 3313.
[30]*Ibid.*
[31]*Annual Report, 1896*, part 4, p. 3210.
[32]*Annual Report, 1895*, part 4, p. 3314.
[33]*Ibid.*
[34]Dennison, *op. cit.*, p. 386.
[35]*Ibid.*, p. 387.
[36]*Ibid.*, p. 390.
[37]*Daily Humboldt Times*, 26 June 1894, p. 4, col. 3.
[38]*Annual Report, 1896*, part 4, p. 2211.
[39]*Daily Humboldt Times*, 3 July 1894, p. 4, col. 3.
[40]*Ibid.*, 10 July 1894, p. 4, col. 3.
[41]*Annual Report, 1897*, part 4, p. 3366.
[42]*Annual Report, 1898*, part 4, p. 2949.
[43]Harts, *op. cit.*, p. 505.
[44]*Annual Report, 1900*, part 4, p. 4243.
[45]Fountain Papers, Vol. 104, p. 174.

CHAPTER IV

The Disappearing Jetties

When the Humboldt Bay jetties were declared complete in 1899, no provision was made by the Corps of Engineers, Congress, or the local community for their maintenance. By 1910 the Corps of Engineers realized the jetties were indeed vulnerable. In the ten years since their completion the jetties had been battered down to below the level of low water, and thus required extensive work to rebuild. The history of the jetties in the 20th century is marked by the Corps' continued attempts to ensure that the Humboldt Bay jetties remain as permanent structures that can withstand the erosive forces of the ocean. Through all the expensive reconstruction the residents around the bay have stood firm regarding the need for the jetties and their importance in the development of the region.

Even after the completion of the Northern Pacific Railroad in 1914, the jetties were still considered the key to the economy of the Humboldt Bay region. While the railroad offered an alternative transportation route for the lumber companies in Humboldt County, new industries on the bay were dependent on the deep-water channel. In the 1920s a fishing fleet was established on the bay, and it has grown to be one of the county's leading industries. The crab and salmon fishermen must rely on the safe entrance to Humboldt Bay. The wood pulp mills built in the early 1960s on the north spit are equally dependent on the deep-water channel. Large tankers bring chemicals for the plant while others transport bales of paper from the two mills. These large tankers require a 40-foot channel through the entrance as well as in the bay. The deeper channel has been used by deep-water vessels since shortly after World War II. At that time the international lumber trade, especially that with

Japan, became dependent on the deeper channel and open entrance. With these new, modern demands on the bay and its mouth, the Corps of Engineers has had to work continuously to ensure the deep-water entrance by rebuilding the jetties and occasionally dredging the bay.

Another justification for the large government expenditures on the jetties is the need for a port of refuge on the stormy Pacific Coast. Humboldt Bay is one of the few deep-water ports between San Francisco Bay and the mouth of the Columbia River offering a safe port for vessels in distress. In January 1986, for example, the Polish ship *Plock* began to have engine problems, and could make no headway in the strong southerly winds. Invoking an international law that allows vessels to enter territorial waters when in danger, the *Plock* with its cargo of fish meal took refuge in Humboldt Bay.[1] While the vessel stayed only a day for necessary repairs, the incident illustrated Humboldt Bay's importance as a port of refuge.

When the jetties were first completed, the citizens of Humboldt County were convinced that the bay would become a prominent harbor, rivaling San Francisco in exports. In 1905, however, Eureka residents realized that not only was the deep channel originally created by the jetties slowly filling in, but the jetties themselves were disintegrating. With the collapse of the jetty system, businessmen saw the collapse of the booming economy that the jetties had helped generate. Even more alarming was the shifting of the channel and the reforming of the hazardous sandbar across the bay's entrance. Some felt that Hans Henry Buhne had been right. There was no way to improve the hazardous entrance permanently.

U.S. Coast and Geodetic Survey maps trace the deterioration of the Humboldt jetties and, in consequence, the deep entrance channel. The 1903 map, for example, shows the channel, though still deep, beginning to narrow. Three years later, the channel had changed direction, to almost due west. The entrance was starting to show signs of shoaling, as seen by the buildup of sand along the north side of the south spit. Stimulating the accumulation of sand was the breaking apart of the jetties. A survey map by the San Francisco District in 1905 shows large gaps in the jetties. Only seven years after completion, the south jetty could not prevent the

Even with the jetties completed, the bar remained dangerous. In 1907 the steamer *Corona* wrecked while crossing the bar. *Courtesy D. Tuttle.*

littoral currents from passing into the entrance, carrying large amounts of sand into the channel and reforming the Humboldt Bar.

Because no maintenance work had been done, waves washed away the smaller stones that had helped to secure the large boulders. Once the stones were gone, the large rocks soon followed. In addition to the large gaps in the jetty structure above the water level, the ends of the jetties, which were already at sea level, were worn down further. Soon they were covered with 15 to 18 feet of sand and were completely useless. Conditions at the bay's entrance became reminiscent of the 1870s and 1880s. After 1907, ship captains found a "crooked channel, difficult in all weathers and unusable in times of fog and storm... [and] during these unfavorable years even coast-wise vessels, on regular runs to Humboldt Bay, had to secure the services of local pilots."[2] In 1909, stimulated by the Eureka Chamber of Commerce, the Corps of Engineers recommended to Congress that new appropriations be authorized to improve the entrance of Humboldt Bay. At the time, having already spent over $2 million, "the United States could only show two dilapidated enrockments [for its money], at which the waves ceaselessly pounded."[3]

In 1910 Congress responded to the Corps recommendation by authorizing "the restoration of [the] jetties to [their] original condition, [at a] cost [of] $1,037,400."[4] The 1911 Rivers and Harbors Act granted another continuous contract for what was "considered the most urgent work in... [the San Francisco] District."[5] Of the two jetties, the south jetty was in the worse shape, with large gaps that allowed sand to wash into the entrance channel. Lieutenant Colonel Thomas H. Rees of the San Francisco District, recognizing the importance of the south jetty in controlling the littoral drift, authorized the restoration of that jetty first. In 1911 a contract was let to begin the work. The Morton L. Tower Engineering Company began rebuilding the south jetty the following year.

Before work could begin a major engineering problem had to be solved. An innovative technique was required for placing the new jetty materials onto the existing structure. In 1912 the compact rubble remains of the south jetty prohibited the construction of a new trestle (the one used in the original project had long since washed away). According to civil engineer Morton L. Tower, the

In 1911 Morton Tower developed a new technique for jetty construction that utilized the battered remaining structure of the original jetty. The redwood rail ties used can still be seen today. *Courtesy D. Tuttle.*

old south jetty had been beaten into "a compact mass, such that it would have been necessary to place a portion of the piles of each bent in the sand to give any lateral stability."[6] The trestle also would have had to be reinforced to support the standard-gauge railroad and railcars used in construction. The construction company used standard instead of narrow gauge because the larger cars had a higher resale value and could handle the twenty-ton boulders the Corps deemed necessary to rebuild the south jetty. Tower estimated a cost of approximately $45,000 to build a tramway on the remains of the old jetty. Given the increased costs of the rock and other construction materials, both Tower and the Corps of Engineers considered this cost excessive. However, there were few alternatives.

The problem of rough water preventing the dumping of rock from barges still remained. In fact, no work was possible from September 1912 through January 1913 because the "jetties were subjected to an almost continuous pounding from extraordinarily heavy waves."[7] Tower came up with an economical solution to the problem when he proposed that the compacted jetty remains be used as a base. Starting from the shore, the old jetty would be built up with rock and concrete to about 14 feet above the high tide level. Instead of random dumping from railcars, the jetty rock would be placed by a large crane that ran on tracks imbedded in concrete on top of the jetty. The concrete cap which had been placed on the old structure greatly reduced the cost. According to Tower's estimates the cap cost only $18.10 per linear foot to construct. It also greatly diminished the wave damage and "when finally broken up by the settlement and washing away of the rock slopes it [would] still be of value as jetty material."[8] The technique proved effective and was used at other jetty maintenance projects on the Pacific Coast, including those at Coos Bay and the mouth of the Columbia River.

The jetty was extended in a leapfrog fashion, the most recently completed section providing the base for the work on the next segment. The existing structure was built up with medium-sized rock (from one-half to ten tons) to within two feet of the new fourteen-foot height of the jetty. Workmen put smaller pieces between the rock to fill in gaps and to obtain a somewhat even surface. They then placed a metal form on the top of the jetty and poured a very dry concrete mixture onto it. The concrete was

mixed with as little water as possible so that it would dry quickly in
the damp conditions of the wave-washed jetties. Forty-foot-long
redwood ties, whose length matched the width of the jetty, were
placed and spiked on top of the still damp concrete. Finally, an
aggregate cement mixture was poured around the ties to secure
them to the concrete. The tracks for the steam crane and railcars
were placed on the ties, and the process repeated on the next
section of the jetty. The work crew soon became very proficient;
eight laborers were able to "build a section of track 18 to 20 feet in
length in two hours and fifteen minutes, including the construction
of forms and placing ties and rails."9 In all, a force of fifty men
worked on rebuilding the south jetty. Yet, despite the large work
force and new construction technique, the south jetty took three
years to complete.

Construction was slow for several reasons. Although the Corps
was concerned about the fierce winter storms that limited construction to certain months of the year, the Engineers were even more
disheartened about the inadequate funding. Just as the Corps had
suspended work in 1892 because of low annual congressional
appropriations, the Army Engineers were forced to discontinue
work again in August 1914. However, this time little damage was
done to the jetty structure during the hiatus because of the
protective concrete cap. After additional funds were appropriated
for the project, work was resumed in February 1915 and the Corps
completed the construction in June. The south jetty was rebuilt at
a cost of $1,537,000. The highest appropriation was $467,000 in
June 1913; the lowest was $150,000 in June 1910.

One engineering decision had increased both the time and cost
of jetty construction. The San Francisco District and the Morton
L. Tower Construction Company had decided to select large
boulders at the quarry and then to use the steam crane to place the
boulders on the jetty, rather than placing them haphazardly as had
been done formerly. A separate contract was let to obtain the
necessary rock from the same Jacoby Creek quarry that was used
in the original construction. The contractor, Hammon Construction Company, was responsible only for removing the rock and
transporting it to the south jetty landing. The company employed
more than 100 men to remove and transport the 519,000 tons of
rock required over the three year period of the contract. Renamed
the Pacific Engineering and Construction Company in 1913, the

contractor used the same methods to move the rock as had been used in the 1890s. A steam derrick was used to load the rock onto flatcars, which were hauled by a steam locomotive the seven miles to the loading wharf, about nine miles north of the south jetty. Once at the construction site the rocks were weighed and graded, and then turned over to the Tower Construction Company.

Unlike its predecessor, John C. Bull, however, the Pacific Engineering and Construction Company needed to supply four different grades and sizes of rock, as specified by the Corps. Class one rock was the most important of the four grades. Weighing between ten and twenty tons, it was used to build up the height of the jetty and formed the base of the rebuilt jetty. During the work season, the contractor had to deliver 500 tons of this size rock daily to the south jetty. The next class of rock was smaller and was used to fill in around the boulders, bringing the jetty structure up to its required height. Class two stone weighed between one-half ton and ten tons; 1,000 tons were required daily to complete the south jetty on schedule. The third class of rock was used to level out the top of the jetty, making a uniform base for the concrete cap. This smaller rock was used mainly in the early stages of the jetty construction. By the time the end of the jetty was reached, only ten tons a day were used. The fourth class of stone was used to make the concrete and was either river gravel or the crushed remains of the larger rock. The contractor provided approximately seventy tons a day of this class stone.

Although the concrete cap and carefully placed rock prevented the rapid erosion of the top and sides of the jetty, a major problem still confronted the Engineers. Experience with other jetties on the Pacific Coast had shown that the most important portion of the jetty was its head. The higher the head of the jetty, the more effective it was at controlling the littoral drift, preventing sandbar formation, and focusing the tidal scour to keep open a deep-water channel. However, the head had suffered the most damage of all portions of the jetty, for waves had rapidly eroded the rock at the jetty head to below the level of even low tide. By 1915, when work on the south jetty had reached the head, the end of the south jetty was buried in sand. In fact, in the original construction John C. Bull had been able to complete neither the south nor the north jetty heads to the high-tide mark because of the rapid erosion. The rock itself was not sufficient to withstand the exposure to the

Hauling rocks to end of south jetty, c. 1914. *Courtesy L. Carranco.*

violent waves. Furthermore, the concrete cap alone was not able to hold the jetty head together. Given these conditions, a new solution was required. The Corps of Engineers representative at the site, George F. Whittemore, decided to "build a monolithic reinforced concrete block for a jetty head of about 1,000 tons weight, in order to afford a good protection to the weakest, as well as the most vital part of this. . . structure."[10] Whittemore, Junior Engineer at the project, oversaw the construction of the monolith and described the challenging engineering feat in an article for the Corps of Engineers journal, *Professional Memoirs.*

The monolith formed the remaining 50 feet of the jetty, surrounded and protected by the largest boulders. The steam crane was run out to the end of the completed jetty to place these 20-ton rocks, whose positioning was critical. A good true slope of the south jetty rocks was needed, according to Whittemore, "as scouring and undermining were feared at the end of the jetty, where the currents are very strong."[11] With the boulders creating a buffer between the work crews and the ocean, the men began excavating the pit to hold the concrete block. Once the pit was five feet deep, workers attempted to make the bottoms and sides of the excavation water-tight with a foot-thick concrete lining.

Whittemore believed that reinforcing the concrete made it better able to withstand the exposure to the rough seas. Therefore, the next step in building the concrete blocks was the placing of reinforcing steel bars. A total of 796 linear feet of steel rails and steel cables was used to strengthen the huge monolith. The reinforcement consisted of first placing 60-pound steel rails horizontally and transversely. These rails were intersected by 50-pound rails set vertically, then further strengthened by clamping ⅝-inch cables horizontally to the vertical rails. The reinforcement was designed so as not to interfere with the pouring of the concrete by bucket.[12] The reinforcement also protected the workers during the construction. Most of the cable and rails used were recycled from earlier projects on the jetty, reducing the monolith's cost. For example, the cable required no cash outlay, and the 446 feet of rail cost only $60.[13] The steel reinforcement contributed significantly to the longevity of the monolith in maintaining the desired height of the jetty head.

With the steel reinforcement in place, the site was ready for the pouring of the concrete. The weather conditions of a calm sea were

A cement plant was built on the south spit to supply all of the material needed for the 1911 jetty reconstruction. In 1915 it was moved to the north spit. *Courtesy D. Tuttle.*

met at 2:30 A.M. on 25 June 1915 with the falling tide. Two crews of 27 men each worked steadily until 9:30 A.M. on 27 June. The block was built from the sea end toward the shore, allowing the far section to dry and prevent damage to the inner portions. The concrete was mixed at the end of the jetty and poured by the steam crane a bucketload at a time. Whittemore estimated that twenty buckets were placed in an hour, each bucket yielding about six-tenths of a yard of concrete. The 473 cubic yards of concrete, therefore, was deposited irregularly as to strata depths and lengths.[14]

In addition to the steam crane, two locomotives, several railcars, and a cement mixer were used in the construction. One of the train engines brought work materials such as rock and sand as well as supplies, while the other was used to supply water to the mixer tank.[15] Because the supply yard was 1.625 miles from the construction site, these two engines were in constant use.

When completed the monolith weighed 950 tons, was 30.5 feet wide and was built to a height of 19 feet above the low-water mark. The total building cost was $3,517.40.

Only twenty-two hours after the monolith was completed, the concluding reconstruction work on the south jetty began. The steam crane was used to place more of the class one rocks around the concrete block to further protect the jetty head. Steel cable and concrete were also added. When the work was finished, the jetty head was 50 feet wide and more than 100 feet long. The San Francisco District office then ordered the south jetty plant moved to the north jetty for the impending work there. Less than a month after the end of the construction, Whittemore found that the "southwestern slope [had] washed down to high water capped with large stones fastened with cable and concrete."[16]

Whittemore's superiors expected that the million-dollar investment in the reconstruction of the south jetty would make it able to withstand the violent wave action and maintain a steady, deep-water channel through the bay entrance. But the Corps of Engineers did anticipate that future work would be required to maintain the jetties. In the 1915 annual report District Engineer Colonel Thomas H. Rees concluded that "only very substantially built jetties can be expected to be reasonably permanent in this locality and that regular maintenance work is more economical in the long run than the abandonment of all work upon first completion of the

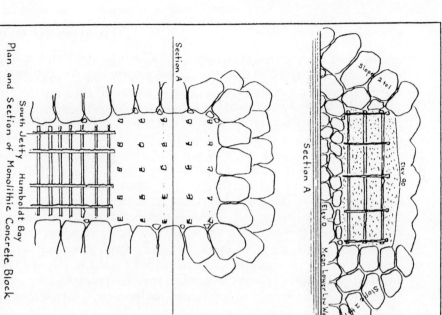

Plan and Section of Monolithic Concrete Block

South Jetty   Humboldt Bay

Section A

Section A

Slope 2 to 1

Elev. 20

Elev. 0

Mean Lower Low Water

Slope 2 to 1

South Jetty - Humboldt Bay Jetties
Plan and Elevation of
Jetty Head

Mean Lower Low Water Line

Top of Slope

Edge of Concrete

Block

Mean Lower Low Water

Concrete Cap

Concrete Block

From *Professional Memoirs* #8, pp. 35 and 37. Drawing by M.B. Pritchard.

jetties."[17] This decision committed the Corps to maintaining the jetties, and ensuring that they would never again become a broken, wave-battered rubble mound.

Shortly thereafter, repairs were begun on the north jetty. Stimulating the decision for immediate action was Whittemore's discovery that the north jetty played a critical part in controlling the littoral drift and in maintaining the entrance channel. Furthermore, Whittemore's surveys had revealed that the erosion and destruction of the north jetty had been accelerated by the reconstruction of the south jetty, just as the original construction of the south jetty in the early 1890s had caused the rapid erosion of the north spit. Repair work began on the north jetty late in July 1915, using the same techniques that had proven so successful on the south jetty. A concrete cap was placed on the surface of the built-up jetty, and a concrete monolith was constructed at the jetty head. Because no money was allocated to the project during World War I, work on the north jetty stopped in 1917.

However, between 1915 and 1917 significant steps were taken to strengthen and rehabilitate the jetty. One of these, moving the construction plant from the south spit to the north spit, illustrates the conflict caused by the low annual appropriations and the need for future repair work. Whittemore had opposed the move; he felt that in light of the need for future maintenance work, "a large part of this plant might be left there [on the south spit] to advantage for use in jetty repairs from year to year — such as tracks, scales, [and] buildings."[18] Offsetting Whittemore's concern about the wisdom of the $10,000 move was the uncertainty of the yearly congressional appropriations, which were never guaranteed for the project.[19] Whittemore proved to be right. In 1917 new buildings had to be constructed on the south jetty to support some minor maintenance work.

In August 1915 a wharf was constructed on the north spit so that the newly moved plant would be in place when the shipment of rocks resumed. The project was not simple, for large gaping holes torn in the structure by the corrosive force of waves on the Humboldt Bar needed to be closed. Progress was slow, but by 1917 the north jetty had been completed to within 500 feet of its original length. As usual, the work was insufficiently funded and often stopped by the treacherous weather conditions. Furthermore, many companies were reluctant to contract with the government due to the uncertainty of the appropriations and the difficulty of the work involved.

In light of the low appropriations prior to World War I, Whittemore continued to seek more economical ways to fulfill his duties. One of his solutions focused on finding a safer and cheaper method for taking cross sections of the north jetty. The cross sections were needed to determine the location of the north jetty where it had eroded to below the level of low water. Whittemore had to know where the center line of the old jetty was as it formed the base of the new one and prevented erosion, much as had the brush mattresses in the original construction. The widespread practice of taking cross sections by using three rowboats and a tag line was impractical and dangerous at Humboldt Bay. In fact, one of the jetty engineers, Morton L. Tower, was killed on 17 April 1915 when he was washed overboard while attempting to take a cross section. The system was not only dangerous, it was expensive and often inaccurate. Surveys done by the Corps after the project was completed revealed that portions of the rebuilt jetty were not built in the best alignment with the original.

Whittemore's solution was to suspend a 120-foot outrigger platform from the revolving steam crane and from this platform take fast and accurate soundings. Experience proved that "for locating the submerged old jetty enrockment ahead of construction, and for taking borings through the sand blanket over the old stone, this outfit [was] especially suited."[20] In addition, the new system did not cost much to build or to maintain, because it was made from scrap materials at the construction site. The outrigger could be operated by as few as five men so wage expenses also decreased. Whittemore used the outrigger successfully from 1915 to 1917 without any complications. When work resumed in the 1920s, the jetties were built up sufficiently to require no further cross-section work.

Although the work produced a deeper channel, the bay entrance remained dangerous. In December 1916 one of the U.S. Navy's new submarines, the H-3, was shipwrecked, as was the *Milwaukee*, a recently commissioned cruiser, in January 1917. The H-3 along with three other vessels was on a cruise "to gather information about facilities at [Pacific] coast ports for the care of submarine vessels."[21] Having already stopped at Gray's Harbor, the mouth of the Columbia River, and at Coos Bay, the convoy was en route to

Humboldt Bay when the H-3 developed engine troubles. The diver lacked adequate navigation equipment and had little visibility. Hence, the sub's commander, Lieutenant Harry Bogusch, headed for the relative calm of Humboldt Bay to have the damaged diesel engine repaired. Bogusch was unfamiliar with the bay entrance, and proceeded cautiously along the foggy coast. Mistaking the lights of the Hammond Lumber Company mill on the north spit for the north jetty warning lights, Bogusch headed his sub inland, only to find that he had grounded the little sub in the breakers 300 yards off shore. The crippled engines could not move the diver back out to sea and the 27-man crew was stranded in the wave-tossed sub for nearly ten hours before they were rescued from shore.

The other vessels in the convoy soon heard of the wreck of the H-3, but were unable to help. The breakers prevented them from rendering immediate assistance, and the bay entrance channel was too treacherous for the other two submarines to cross. The submarines H-1 and H-2 proceeded to San Francisco, while the monitor *Cheyenne* stayed at the bay to see if she could salvage the diver. As the local residents had predicted, all attempts by the *Cheyenne* to pull the H-3 off of the breakers failed. The Navy, after considering several civilian offers to salvage the H-3, decided that the 24,000-horsepower engines of the cruiser *Milwaukee* would be more than sufficient to pull the sub off the sandy north spit.

Instead, the ever-present fog, the high surf, the unpredictable currents, and the sudden breaking of a tow line conspired so that at about "4:10 a.m., January 13, 1917, the *Milwaukee* was in twelve feet of water, broadside to the beach, and tilting at a twenty degree list."[22] George Whittemore tersely recorded in his work journal that the "U.S. Cruiser *Milwaukee* went ashore on Samoa beach."[23] Though the crew was rescued, the *Milwaukee* was a total loss. Although the local community correctly concluded that nothing could be done to rescue the sub, the Navy as well as state and national newspapers sought to find out who was responsible. The *Oakland Tribune*, ignoring the almost thirty years and several million dollars spent by the Corps of Engineers on the bay entrance, partly blamed the federal government. The newspaper claimed that "the coast near Eureka [was] the most dangerous and treacherous along the entire Pacific coast line but the federal government had done little toward making navigation in this section less perilous."[24] In reality, the government had done a great deal to improve the safety of the bay entrance, but little could be done to control the rough conditions that continued to plague the region.

Contrary to the criticism in the *Tribune*, local bay residents applauded the work that had been done to improve the bay entrance. But they were increasingly concerned about the condition of the jetties in the 1920s. No new work had been done and maintenance had been minimal during World War I. Consequently, the recently rebuilt jetties were deteriorating rapidly. A 1925 letter from the Eureka Chamber of Commerce to First Lieutenant Aubrey H. Bond, of the San Francisco District Corps of Engineers, described the decrepit conditions of the jetties. The letter expressed the concern that unless soon repaired the badly damaged south jetty would revert to its 1911 condition when it could no longer control the shifting sands or maintain a single deep-water channel at the bay entrance. R.J. Wade, the secretary for the chamber, pointed out that "the construction of these jetties is of inestimable value to the constantly increasing commerce moving in Humboldt Bay, and we urge continuance of this work."[25] Even though the railroad linking the Humboldt Bay region to the San Francisco Bay area had been operating for ten years, ocean shipping was still critically important to the region's economy.

World War I had given the shipping industry on Humboldt Bay a big boost. In 1917 San Francisco Mayor James Rolph opened a new shipbuilding plant on the bay near the north jetty. The shipyard turned out wooden supply ships for use in the war effort. Yet Rolph's shipyard was only one example of the increase of exports and industry along the bay. The lumber mills of John Vance and William Carson continued to operate on a large scale and other lumber companies began to compete with them. The Pacific Lumber Company of Scotia, for example, owned a fleet of steamers and maintained its own wharf and landing, as did the Falk Lumber Mill and the Hammond Lumber Company. In 1925 forty wharves lined the bay, mostly catering to the redwood lumber industry. Railroads linked these wharves to more mills in the mountains behind the bay. This period of regional prosperity depended on the deep-water channel through the entrance maintained by the jetties.

Despite the complaints of the Chamber of Commerce, some

The most common maintenance needed on the jetties is the repair of gaps caused by the wind and wave erosion. Here timbers from the 1915 reconstruction span holes where rock and concrete have been washed away from the jetty surface. *Author photo.*

work had been done on the jetties. In 1920 the San Francisco District began action to re-extend the north jetty and to repair it where it had eroded. The north jetty construction had been abandoned in 1917 by the San Francisco District, and during World War I the end of the north jetty had receded rapidly. In 1917 the jetty had been 3,937 feet long; three years later the jetty extended only 3,730 feet. The base of the north jetty was beaten down by the waves to a level nearly even with the bay at low water.

The waves swept over the battered structure and began washing away the beach behind the jetty. Accelerating the destruction of the north jetty was the comparatively undamaged south jetty, which focused the waves toward the north spit. Because the erosion of the north spit was rapid, soon several government buildings, including the old lighthouse tower built in the 1860s, were threatened. The placing of more rock prevented further erosion, and in 1922 the Corps of Engineers began work on the north jetty proper.

In worse shape than it had been in 1915, the end of the jetty was still 550 feet shy of its original length and required a massive infusion of rock. George Whittemore and the new District Engineer, Colonel Herbert Deakyne, decided in 1921 to extend a railroad four miles south from the community of Samoa to the north jetty, thus connecting the construction site with a branch of the Northwestern Pacific Railroad. They hoped the government railroad would cut the "high rates charged by contractors for barge deliveries to the north jetty."[26] However, the railroad was less successful in this regard than anticipated. The line was expensive to maintain because it was exposed to the corrosive salt air and the rails were subject to burial by the blowing sands of the north spit. To retard the movement of sand, the Corps of Engineers planted yellow bush lupine, as had the Coast Guard in 1904. Today, this introduced shrub covers the north spit, although the railroad has long since been removed.

With the line's completion early in 1922, rock delivery began in earnest. As expected, the violent waves and rough seas slowed progress. In fact, San Francisco District Engineer Lieutenant Colonel Henry A. Finch described the work as a "battle." Even with the use of the concrete cap method, the project was plagued with setbacks. In one year alone, 1924-1925, more than "462 feet of concrete cap and 42,000 tons of stone were washed out of the north jetty."[27] The effort to extend the north jetty a mere 500 feet took five years. In 1925 a concrete monolith, identical to the one placed on the south jetty ten years earlier, was built on the north jetty head, marking the end of the first authorized project to rebuild the jetties at Humboldt Bay. Colonel Finch declared that "a hard fight had to be waged to carry the north jetty out its final 500 feet, but this battle was won,... and a monument, in the form of a monolithic jetty-head...was erected on the battlefield."[28]

The end of the first reconstruction project, however, did not signal the end of the rebuilding of the Humboldt jetties. When work was finished on the north jetty in 1925, the south jetty was in dire need of repairs. The concrete monolith required the most work. Furthermore, portions of the concrete cap had washed away, and the sides of the jetty had begun to erode. The jetty head had settled and was beginning to wash away. Rebuilding the head was necessary because it no longer prevented the shifting sands from filling in the entrance channel. The channel was shoaling rapidly, jeopardizing the 25-foot-deep channel. By 1927, more than $5 million had been spent for jetty reconstruction. The jetties were proving to be more difficult to keep in place than the Corps officers had anticipated.

Faced with spiraling maintenance costs, in the 1920s the Corps of Engineers began experimenting with structures that would resist the constant erosive forces and help maintain the bay's deep entrance channel. Local community support remained vital to obtaining congressional funds, but equally important was the Corps' commitment to providing the engineering solution toward maintaining the jetties. As San Francisco District Engineer Finch saw it, "the engineers [had become] so deeply involved there could be no drawing back."[29] For the next fifty years numerous experiments on the jetties sought the best method for withstanding the violent waves at Humboldt Bay. These experiments finally met with success in 1972 with the placement of more than 4,000 dolosse, the 42-ton jack-shaped concrete armor units developed in South Africa.

Earlier experiments had met with varying degrees of success. The concrete monoliths built at the ends of each of the jetties were one early solution to the problem. Unfortunately, the monoliths proved vulnerable, showing an alarming tendency to settle and erode. In 1926 Lieutenant Colonel Finch and Senior Engineer Whittemore attempted to make the monoliths more stable by adding concrete tetrahedrons to the sides. They hoped that these "wings" would deflect the waves and "act as highly efficient protection for the rubble foundation of the crown block."[30] However, the wings were only partially successful. Those that remained close to the jetty did protect the monoliths. However, most of the wings settled away from the jetty and failed to prevent the washing away of the base of the monoliths.

The jetties are constantly battered by waves, especially the exposed jetty heads. They required constant work, as evidenced by this 1934 aerial photograph showing damage to the south jetty head. *Courtesy D. Tuttle.*

Another experiment that was tried in the late 1920s consisted of thickening the concrete cap from one foot to seven feet where it joined the monolith. This part of the cap was an historically weak and vulnerable point of the jetty, most exposed to wave action and unprotected by the concrete armor blocks. Senior Engineer Whittemore, who developed the concept, hoped that as the greatly thickened cap was undermined and broken apart the material would fill in the gap, thus creating new jetty materials and slowing the disintegration of the jetty core.[31] The thickened cap also acted to hold the jetty materials together, retarding the erosive action of the waves.

Even with concrete monoliths and concrete caps, the jetties still required large boulders, each weighing up to 20 tons, to fill in eroded gaps along the jetty sides. By the early 1930s these boulders cost $3.62 per ton. Some were imported from Oregon because the local quarries were nearly depleted and often supplied unsatisfactory rock such as sandstone which disintegrated rapidly. Alarmed by both the expense and poor quality of these boulders, Corps officials began to experiment with using concrete blocks instead.

Finch and Whittemore tried using several different weights and sizes of concrete blocks around the jetty heads to protect against wind and wave action. Their experiments with fifty-ton blocks proved to be disastrous. These large blocks were made in two stages. First, a twenty-ton precast concrete container, divided into two sections, was placed near the jetty head where the block was to be situated. The sections then were filled with more concrete and, after curing, the block was tipped into the ocean. Four of these fifty-ton concrete cellular blocks were made, and all "soon broke up into separate sections or settled below low-water level — at any rate nothing was seen of them after the first winter of their service."[32] Part of the reason for the rapid deterioration of the blocks was that they were not reinforced with steel. Finch and Whittemore eventually settled on the use of 21-ton blocks. They found the 21-ton blocks to be cheaper and more efficient than boulders as protective rip-rap material around the jetty head. These armor tetrahedron concrete blocks became the most common form used to repair and maintain the jetties from the early 1930s to the late 1960s.

During this same period, the only changes in the approach to jetty work related to the weight and size of the tetrahedrons. The largest tried was a 100-ton block that shattered just as the fifty-ton block had; the equipment used was inadequate to accurately place these larger blocks. The smallest block used, twelve tons, was placed in the 1930s and 1940s. Recent research has shown that "these units were considerably smaller than [coastal engineers] would now consider stable."[33] This fact was borne out on the Humboldt jetties, where the smaller blocks disintegrated rapidly.

Not all of the innovations in jetty maintenance were limited to experiments with the size and shape of concrete blocks to be used as jetty armor stone. One of the Corps officers who worked on the Humboldt Bay jetties in the late 1920s, Captain Aubrey H. Bond, became concerned with the damage done to the jetties by the high waves, especially those driven suddenly by distant summer storms. He began to correlate information about distant storms and sought ways to increase public awareness of the factors influencing the wave action at Humboldt Bay. Bond found that "the wind diagrams appearing on the annual project maps [were] practically worthless as reliable indications of the forces of destruction brought to bear upon exposed jetties by heavy seas."[34] During the 1924 work season a sudden and destructive sea washed up over the jetty. As the crew withdrew to safety on shore, they watched while the ocean swept away the vulnerable small stones and displaced several of the large boulders.

Bond believed that if a correlation did indeed exist between distant storms at sea and the destructive waves, both time and money could be saved. The San Francisco office of the U.S. Weather Bureau acceded to Bond's request to inform the Corps officials at Humboldt Bay "whenever a disturbance at sea was noted."[35] At first difficulties in communication and the remoteness of the region hampered the system. Often reports of storms would arrive several days after the storm had already struck. As methods of communication improved, however, the system did aid in jetty construction and repairs. By knowing when storm-tossed waves could be expected the Corps was able to save on materials that would no longer be washed away before they could be placed. Time and effort were also not expended needlessly. Perhaps most important, the improved prediction system helped make the jetties a safer work environment.

Although the jetties had been regularly maintained from the 1930s to the late 1950s, they began to erode. Following the unusually heavy winter storms in 1957-1958, and because of damage done to the jetties in the 1955 earthquake, they required full-scale reconstruction. The concrete monoliths needed to be replaced, as did their protective armor units. In January 1959 a local newspaper editor vividly described the condition of the jetties as a result of the recent storms: "even the rails that once were set so firmly in concrete [had] been torn loose and twisted about like bale wire in many places. Huge rocks [had] been battered loose like children's playthings."[36] The San Francisco District mounted a large-scale operation to repair and re-extend the concrete monolith. Yet, the District Engineers tried no new construction techniques but instead depended on the time proven 1920s method of building a steel reinforced concrete monolith and protecting it with concrete armor. Repairs began on the north jetty in 1960 and were completed in November 1961. Similar work began on the south jetty the following year and was completed in 1963.

The newly repaired jetties did not remain in a sound condition for long. The severe winter storms in subsequent years wreaked havoc on the recently rebuilt jetties. The severe flooding in the Eel River drainage area caused by the December 1964 storms sent large logs to the coast, where they floated north and battered the jetties. High seas caused further damage. Most of the 116 recently placed 100-ton concrete blocks were washed away during the winter of 1964-1965. Without their protection, both the north and the south jetties began to deteriorate rapidly. Only six years after the winter storms of 1964-1965 "the heads of the jetties were totally destroyed and another major rehabilitation work was required."[37]

Instead of simply replacing washed-out portions with more concrete, Corps officials determined to find a new approach, one that would withstand the erosive force of the waves at the bay mouth better than had the simple concrete blocks. Between 1931 and 1964 more than $4.5 million was spent on repair work at the Humboldt jetties.[38] In the late 1960s studies were authorized at the Waterways Experiment Station (WES) at Vicksburg, Mississippi, to find the best way of protecting the fragile jetties on the stormy northern California coast.

WES engineers in 1968 constructed a scale model the size of a football field and tested various design shapes, including concrete blocks, tetrapods, and stones. The form that was best able to withstand conditions simulating those at Humboldt Bay was an hydraulically interlocking armor unit developed in South Africa. Roughly jack-shaped, it is named dolos, because it resembles the ankle bone of a South African goat of the same name. The plural of the term is dolosse.[39] WES recommended the dolosse for Humboldt Bay because of their ability to interlock, forming a solid chain of protection against the force of the waves. The engineers at WES were further impressed with the record of the dolos at the Port of East London in South Africa where they had been in place since 1964. The dolos had been developed by Eric Merrifield, the Harbor Engineer at East London. He had observed over a period of four years that the twenty-ton concrete unreinforced dolosse used at the port had "interlocked so well that they formed a stable protection against the waves for the bank to [be] built behind them."[40]

To the WES engineers an even more important characteristic of the dolosse was the reaction to scour, one of the leading factors in the deterioration of the Humboldt jetties. At East London Merrifield had found that scouring actually served to make the dolosse "move forward and interlock more effectively."[41] Another advantage to using the dolosse was that no single surface of the dolos is large enough to be struck with the full force of the wave. Instead, the wave's force is absorbed and dissipated in the maze of shapes created by the interlocking dolosse. The WES engineers believed that by deflecting the full fury of the waves the dolosse would protect the fragile and exposed jetty heads, preventing their gradual erosion to below sea level.

WES engineers decided that for the best protection the dolosse would be placed around the sea ends of both jetties, and also landward 700 feet along the sides of each jetty. Thereby the dolosse protected the weakest portion of the jetty structure, which is "especially susceptible to sometimes unpredictable stability problems."[42] The dolosse offered other advantages. For example, when on a tour of the north jetty construction site in 1972, Johan Zwamborn, head of the Hydraulic Research Unit of the South African Council for Scientific and Industrial Research, explained to the local newspaper, the *Times-Standard*, that because the dolosse had been developed by a government agency and was therefore unpatented, the Corps of Engineers was not subject to paying royalties. On the same tour, Orville Magoon of the Coastal Engineering Research Center pointed out that the dolosse not only protected the jetty, but also "provided ecological enhancement by providing a home for fish. An artificial reef is created with the placement...of dolosse around each jetty."[43]

Even as the WES recommended dolosse for use at the Humboldt Bay jetties, it modified the final form to be used there. Fearing that the twenty-ton dolosse originally designed and used at East London harbor would be too small, WES authorized the use of larger dolosse. Forty-three-ton dolosse would protect the seaward tip of the jetty head; forty-two-ton dolosse would be placed along the sides. The dolosse would be cast from a very dense concrete mixture, each dolos requiring twenty-two cubic yards of concrete.

During the bidding phase of the project, the dolosse were modified again. The original design called for no reinforcing of the large jacks, as with the dolosse used at East London. However, the San Francisco District began to consider the issue of the large dolosse's stability and fragility. Aware of the unreinforced concrete forms having broken at Humboldt Bay after only a few years' use, the District engineers required that each dolos be reinforced with steel. Hence, all of the dolosse made in 1971 included 1,400 pounds of steel. When these large dolosse were placed on the jetties in 1972 and 1973 they marked the first time that this artificial armor stone was used in the United States. They were also "the largest dolosse ever to be cast, to that time, in the world."[44]

With the decision made to use the dolosse, it was necessary to call for bids and to draw up precise specifications for the repair work to be done at Humboldt Bay. Because of the short work season, 1 May to 15 October, the project would last three years. During that time the contractors restored the concrete monolith heads, cast the dolosse, and then placed the dolosse randomly around the head to protect it. The contract stated that "dolosse weighing 42 tons each will be placed pellmell [*sic*] in two layers along the periphery of the heads and extending out a maximum of 163 feet from the edge of the monolith."[45]

Due to the project's complexity and innovative nature, the San Francisco District engineers met with the prospective bidders several times to ensure that all aspects of the project were understood. One of the questions raised was the definition of "pellmell," which the San Francisco District interpreted to mean that the dolosse were to be set so that they interlocked, but in no particular pattern. A year later the contract to place the dolosse and repair the north and south jetties was given to the Umpqua River and Navigation Company of Oregon, the lowest bidder. In fact, their $9,185,000 bid was lower than the Corps' estimate for the project.

The Corps had kept the local community well informed about the planned rehabilitation of the jetties. The Board of Harbor Commissioners had even flown to Vicksburg in 1969 to examine the scale model testing of the dolosse. They brought back pictures that were published in the *Times-Standard* showing the jetty model being subjected to a tidal wave, and the resulting effects on the miniature jetty. The model graphically illustrated the destructive forces of nature against the jetties by using simulated 100-ton concrete blocks, which were easily moved and destroyed by the test waves because the blocks presented a solid wall for the waves to work against, unlike the dolosse which present no single side. The dolosse's designer, Eric Merrifield, cited another advantage of the dolosse. He pointed out that the dolos could "be manufactured and handled by standard contractor's equipment."[46] Colonel Charles Roberts of the San Francisco District pointed out that the "dolosse have been scientifically designed specifically for the...[Humboldt jetties and were] the most deliberate design on the West Coast."[47]

Nevertheless, when the time came for the dolosse to be placed on the jetties, the local community voiced some doubts. Humboldt Bay residents were well aware that the placing of the dolosse marked the third major repair work done to the jetties, and "in both previous times the jetty was expected to last."[48] The *Times-Standard* typified the community's wait-and-see attitude in writing: "Designers say dolosse will last, but remember the Titanic, Zeppelin?"[49] The newspaper also ran photographs including one of the cracked and broken monoliths of the south jetty.

Work on the south jetty began in the fall of 1970; actual placing of the dolosse was scheduled for June 1971. A large manitowic crane, which handled payloads of 400 to 500 tons, attracted much attention. The largest crane ever to be brought to Humboldt Bay, the manitowic could be seen from across the bay at Eureka. The Umpqua River and Navigation Company found it necessary to place large boulders up to 200 feet from the end of the jetty to help support the dolosse. While the rock was being placed, the dolosse themselves were being built. At a plant on the south spit, the

In 1971 and 1972 a large manitowic crane carefully placed the dolosse so that they would interlock, providing protection for the fragile jetty head. View of south jetty. *Author photo.*

contractor experimented to find the right mix of concrete to achieve the density required by the Engineers. The contractor had "felt the concrete mix stipulated by the Corps was unworkable."[50] However, Corps officials deemed an aggregate stone and sand mixture satisfactory and full scale production began.

The dolosse constructed in the 1970s at Humboldt were made by weaving steel reinforcing bars into elongated egg-shaped cages in a mandrel shed. During the height of construction the crew shaped 1,382 pounds of steel rebar every thirty minutes. The long cages then were placed on a jig where they were tied into the jack shape of the dolos. Workers then encased the rebar cage in a prefabricated metal form and poured the concrete. The dolosse remained in the metal molds for several days and later were moved to a fenced-in twenty-acre site where they were allowed to cure further. During the casting stage each dolos was given a serial number to be used in monitoring its performance and to record its final location on the jetty. During this phase of the construction the contractor averaged eighteen to twenty-four cast dolosse for every ten-hour working day.

In 1972, when making the dolosse for the north jetty, a new technique for making the concrete armor unit was tried. This was a result of problems the contractor had experienced with the rebar reinforcement during the south jetty work. Not only was the rebar expensive, but when it was exposed to salt water it rusted, causing the dolosse to collapse. In line with the experimental nature of the project, a new form of reinforcement was developed at the north jetty construction plant: metal shavings were mixed into the concrete itself. The mixture proved to be both "more economical than conventional concrete and yet. . . a stronger product."[51] These new dolosse were placed on the north jetty after being tested in several ways by the Corps of Engineers. The forms were tested for durability and stability and test directors kept records on their actual performance. One test involved raising the dolos up on one leg and then dropping it to see if it would break. Another consisted of placing pressure against the dolos at its weakest point, its joints, with hydraulic jacks. The reinforced dolos worked better than the plain concrete, while the mixture of concrete and steel shavings was more durable than the other forms. As for the rest of the dolosse, whether reinforced with rebar or steel shavings, they "are being tested by the sea."[52]

Once the dolosse were made, the next task was to place them on the ends of the jetties. A Euclid truck with a special cradle carried one dolos at a time from the curing yard to the end of the jetty. The manitowic crane lifted the dolos off the truck, placing it so that it interlocked with those around it. The contractor and District Corps officials prepared a diagram showing the best location for each dolos in a random pattern along the slopes of the jetty. The forty-three-ton dolosse were placed farthest out from the jetty head, forming the base of the interlocking structure. Eleven dolosse were placed in each 1,000-square-foot area. The careful placement was to achieve "the interlocking necessary to insure the stability of the dolos structure during a storm."[53] The dolosse placed closer to the actual jetty were positioned on the jetty slope so that their legs protruded higher than the top of the jetty, thus protecting more of the structure. In order to meet the contract terms requiring that the job be finished within three years, the contractor placed between fifty and one-hundred of the dolosse every working day. Ultimately, nearly 5,000 dolosse were placed on the heads of the jetties. One more was set beside the Eureka Chamber of Commerce building. The single dolos represents the millions of dollars spent by the federal government through the Corps of Engineers to improve Humboldt Bay's entrance and the continuing work by the residents of the region to have the bay improved, an effort that dates to the late 1870s.

However, the placing of the last dolosse in 1973 did not mark an end to the Corps' work at the entrance to Humboldt Bay. A survey of the jetties in the early 1980s by the San Francisco District showed that after nearly twelve years most of the dolosse remained intact, "demonstrating their ability to withstand the impacts of the waves."[54] One of the reasons for the durability of the dolosse at Humboldt was their steel reinforcement. Dolosse used at other locales had not been as successful. For example, in 1978 all of the dolosse used in Portugal were found to be defective. The dolosse had not been reinforced in any way and proved to be structurally weak. At Humboldt, though, few signs of breakage were found. However the survey did indicate that the forty-three-ton dolosse at the tips of the jetty had begun to settle into the sandy ocean floor. The settling threatened the stability of the entire interlocking structure. In 1983 a $3.5 million contract was awarded to the Claude C. Wood Company of Lodi, California, to build 1,000 more dolosse.

Unlike the previous contract, the Wood Company was responsible only for constructing the dolosse. Another contract was let for placing the structures. The new dolosse differed slightly from those built in the early 1970s. Instead of being made with rebar or metal shavings, they were reinforced with a wire mesh. More durable than the metal shavings, the mesh did not destroy the entire dolos if exposed to rust, as was the case with the rebar-reinforced ones. The metal in the mesh simply rusted to a point where it was no longer exposed to salt water. The mesh was not easy to work with though, and the contractor spent several weeks developing a suitable concrete mixture. The problem was in determining when to add the metal reinforcement. If mixed in too soon the fine metal wires binded together, instead of blending through the concrete. Another problem involved the chemicals used in formulating the mix; the ratios needed to be in precise quantities to achieve the level of hardness required by the San Francisco District.[55]

Once the formula was perfected, the Wood Company began casting ten dolosse a day in 1984. All of the dolosse placed on the north and south jetties in 1985 were built at the same plant on the

In 1984 a thousand new dolosse replaced those that had broken or
settled around the jetties. Reinforced with a steel mesh, the new
dolosse were allowed to cure for a year before being placed, creating
"Humboldt's Stonehenge." *Author photo.*

south spit. The rock used in the concrete was hauled by truck from
the same Jacoby Creek quarry that had supplied rock for both the
original construction and the first rebuilding of the jetties. The
concrete and wire mesh mixture was poured into steel prefabricated
forms and allowed to dry. Then the newly formed dolosse were left
to dry for more than a year, creating what the *Times-Standard*
dubbed "Humboldt's Stonehenge."[56]

The next task was to transport and place the dolosse around the
jetties. In 1985 a $4 million contract was awarded to Reidel
International, Inc., of Portland, Oregon, to put the new dolosse
around the heads of the jetties. Reidel also was responsible for
dumping 150,000 tons of rock around the "base of the dolosse for
additional support."[57] Again the dolosse were placed with a
manitowic crane. The decision remained on how to get the 450
dolosse to the north jetty from the seasoning plant on the south
spit. The San Francisco District suggested that the dolosse be
barged to the site or trucked overland. Reidel, given responsibility

for the final choice, researched both alternatives. The company rejected the bay route, finding it too "expensive to move...[the dolosse] over water with barges, cranes and tugboats."[58]

After some deliberation, Reidel accepted the proposal by the Dutra Trucking firm of Arcata to move the dolosse one by one over the circuitous 35-mile land route. Dutra estimated a cost of $2,500 to move each dolos to the north jetty. The Humboldt County Board of Supervisors issued a special permit so that the dolosse could be hauled over the small county roads connecting the south spit with Highway 101. The permit required "inspection of the roads for possible damage, posting of signs [warning motorists about the large loads] and purchase of a $10 million insurance policy in case of an accident."[59] In July 1985 Dutra Trucking began hauling the dolosse using new Kenworth V-12 trucks with specially built lowboy trailers to cradle the dolos. The route to the north jetty required driving through downtown Eureka. Many of the businesses along Highway 101 in Eureka vibrated when the oversized trucks rolled by. At the end of the project, the truck drivers hoped "to never haul a dolos again."[60] By September Reidel had placed the 450 dolosse on the north jetty and another 550 on the south jetty.

In all, more than $20 million has been spent so far in maintaining the simple rubble-mound structures at the entrance to Humboldt Bay. This most recent expensive repair of the Humboldt jetties will most probably not be the last, as the heavy ocean waves still pound the structures.

NOTES

[1] *Times-Standard*, 1 Feb. 1986, p. 1, col. 1.
[2] Finch, "The Humboldt Bay Jetties," June 1934, p. 250.
[3] *Ibid.*
[4] Index, Humboldt Bay and Harbor California, Corps action, 1880-1938. *South Pacific Division*, Main Office, General Administration files, 1913-1944, Record Group 77, National Archives, San Bruno, CA.
[5] *Annual Report, 1910*, part 3, p. 2364.
[6] Morton L. Tower, "Rebuilding Jetties at Humboldt Bay, California," *Professional Memoirs* 5 (Sept.-Oct. 1913), p. 504.
[7] Finch, *op. cit.*, p. 250.
[8] Tower, *op. cit.*, p. 506.
[9] *Ibid.*, p. 510.

[10]George F. Whittemore, "Construction of Concrete Block at end of South Jetty, Humboldt Bay, California," *Professional Memoirs*, 8 (Jan.-Feb. 1916) p. 32.

[11]*Ibid.*, p. 36.

[12]*Ibid.*, p. 34.

[13]*Ibid.*, p. 38.

[14]*Ibid.*

[15]*Ibid.*, p. 36.

[16]*Ibid.*, p. 40.

[17]*Annual Report, 1915*, part 2, p. 1984.

[18]George F. Whittemore, "Moving Plant from South Jetty to North Jetty, Humboldt Bay, California," *Military Engineer* 8 (March-April 1916), p. 196.

[19]*Ibid.*, p. 201.

[20]George F. Whittemore, "Taking Cross-Sections, Humboldt Jetties, California," *Professional Memoirs* 9 (Sept.-Oct. 1917), p. 540.

[21]Lynwood Carranco, "Maritime Fiasco on the Northern California Coast," *California History* 60 (Fall 1981), p. 212.

[22]Lynwood Carranco, *Redwood Country* (Belmont, CA: Star Publishing Company, 1986), p. 205.

[23]Humboldt Room Collection, Humboldt State Univ. Library, Work Journal, 1917, Humboldt Bay Jetties, 13 Jan. 1917, Arcata, CA.

[24]Carranco, *Redwood Country*, p. 211.

[25]Eureka Chamber of Commerce to Lt. Aubrey Bond, 14 May 1925, San Francisco District, Main Office, General Administration files, Record Group 77, National Archives, San Bruno, CA.

[26]Henry A. Finch, "The Humboldt Bay Jetties," *The Dock and Harbor Authority*, July 1934, p. 267.

[27]*Ibid.*

[28]*Ibid.*

[29]*Ibid.*, p. 270.

[30]*Ibid.*

[31]See *Ibid.*, p. 268.

[32]George F. Whittemore and Henry A. Finch, "Concrete Blocks Replace Stone in Jetties Battered by Sea," *Engineering News-Record*, 115 (8 Aug. 1935), p. 193.

[33]Orville T. Magoon, Robert L. Sloan, and Nobuyuki Shimuzu, "Design and Construction of Humboldt Bay Jetties, 1880-1975," Proceedings of the Fifteenth Coastal Conference, Honolulu, 11-17 July 1976, p. 2480.

[34]Aubrey H. Bond, "Meteorological Studies at Humboldt Bay," *The Military Engineer* 19 (Nov.-Dec. 1927), p. 507.

[35]*Ibid.*, p. 508.

[36]Fountain Papers, Vol. 104.

[37]Magoon, *et al.*, *op cit.*, p. 2481.

[38]U.S. Army, Corps of Engineers, *Brief Design Memorandum, Repairs to Humboldt Harbor and Bay Jetties* (San Francisco, U.S. Army Engineer District, 1970), p. 8.

[39]Greer E. Coursey, "New Shape in Shore Protection," *Civil Engineering*, 43 (Dec. 1973), p. 69.

[40]Eric M. Merrifield, "Dolos Concrete Armour Protection," *Transactions, Amer. Soc. of Civil Eng.*, 134 (Dec. 1969), p. 842.

[41]*Ibid.*

[42]Robert W. Whalin, "Maritime Works," *Centenary of the Permanent International Assoc. of Navigation Congresses*, 1985, p. 698.

[43]*Times-Standard*, 8 July 1972.

[44]Joseph Jeremiah Hagwood, *Engineers at the Golden Gate* (San Francisco: U.S. Army Engineer District, 1980), p. 345.

[45]U.S. Army, Corps of Engineers, *Brief Design Memorandum, Repairs to Humboldt Harbor and Bay Jetties*, p. 10.

[46]*Times-Standard*, 7 Nov. 1970, p. 9.

[47]*Ibid.*

[48]*Ibid.*

[49]*Ibid.*

[50]Hagwood, *op cit.*, p. 349.

[51]*Times-Standard*, 8 July 1972, p. 3.

[52]U.S. Army, Corps of Engineers, *Humboldt Harbor and Bay, Repair of Jetties, Humbodlt County, California* (San Francisco: U.S. Army Engineer District, 1978), p. 4.

[53]Coursey, *op cit.*, p. 69.

[54]*Times-Standard*, 3 March 1985, p. 3.

[55]Oral interview with J.M. O'Hara, employee of Claude E. Wood Company, by Susan J. Pritchard, Weott, CA, 17 April 1986.

[56]*Times-Standard*, 23 Aug. 1985, p. 1.

[57]*Ibid.*, 7 July 1985, p. 3.

[58]*Ibid.*

[59]*Ibid.*, 10 July 1985, p. 3.

[60]Oral interview with Ken Nichols, truck driver for Dutra Trucking, by Susan J. Pritchard, Fortuna, CA, 17 July 1986.

CHAPTER V

Changes Wrought by the Jetties

The Humboldt Bay jetties have done much more than create a safer entrance to Humboldt Bay by preventing the reformation of the Humboldt Bar. The jetties' success in maintaining a deep-water channel also has helped increase the shipping of lumber products and made new economic ventures possible. At the same time, the attempts to get federal money to improve the jetties have influenced the political development of the county. The jetties have also become a favorite recreation area for local residents, who enjoy fishing from the sides of the breakwater. But the environmental changes stimulated by the jetty construction have provided the most visible and dramatic effect.

Boosterism, the promotion of a region's attributes to attract new businesses and residents, has been a part of Humboldt County development since its settlement in 1850. The push to build and maintain the Humboldt jetties has been a central theme in that boosterism. The jetties have been a symbol of both commercial expansion and regional pride. In the 1870s the economic future of Humboldt County was perceived by the newspaper editors to be tied to transportation, specifically to the ability of ships to cross the Humboldt Bar. The community, recovering from a national depression, was convinced that individual success in business was linked to the overall prosperity of the region.

Social historian Don H. Doyle in his book *The Social Order of a Frontier Community* describes how western communities defined themselves and established a social order through boosterism. By generating editorials about the potential of the county, William Ayres was in effect creating the necessary "enterprising public spirit [which] would inevitably boost the community toward a

self-determined future of prominence."[1] Once Ayres determined
that the jetties were the key to solving the remote region's problem
of transportation, he began to seek support for the project. To gain
the community's backing for the jetty construction, Ayres linked
the future and "goals of individual opportunity to the collective
destiny of the town."[2] Through the voice of the *Democratic
Standard*, Ayres convinced the community that its continued
prosperity and growth would be guaranteed only with the
construction of the jetties. This thinking has been characterized
in all articles and arguments for the presence and maintenance of
the jetties. Though the jetties' effect on the economy of the region is
often overstated, they continue to be viewed as one of the economic
keystones of the region.

Attitudes regarding the importance of the jetties have been
well-publicized throughout Humboldt County history. For example, in the 1920s D.L. Thornbury, a Eureka teacher, published
a travelogue called *California's Redwood Wonderland: Humboldt
County* that emphasized the jetties' economic importance to the
region. In 1923 Thornbury described Eureka as "the principal
commercial city in northern California and...the gateway through
which pass the products of a territory larger than Pennsylvania,
and not limited by the boundaries of Humboldt County."[3] He
asserted that the jetties would ensure that Eureka retained this
status.

Throughout the 20th century the federally built jetties and the
deep entrance channel they provide have attracted new businesses
and industries to the region. Many area residents believe that the
deep entrance channel is vitally important to Humboldt County's
economic future despite continued economic instability in the
region. The Chamber of Commerce and the Board of Trade have
long pointed to the presence of the jetties and the development of
the bay by the Corps of Engineers as reasons to invest in the
region's economy. Eureka City Councilman Jim Worthen also
believes that the presence of the jetties and the improved bay
entrance will draw more businesses to the area.[4] While not creating
a port to "rival San Francisco's," the jetties continue to represent
the region's potential for future development even though they
have been completed for nearly eighty years.

William Ayres' editorials promoted the idea of using jetties to
improve the bay entrance, and Ayres was also the first area resident

The jetties, when complete, protect the deep-water channel and prevent the drifting sands from forming a bar across the bay's entrance. *Courtesy D. Tuttle.*

to call for community involvement in obtaining federal funds. The ad hoc committees formed in response to Ayres' editorials established the future roles of the Humboldt and Eureka Chambers of Commerce in the development of Humboldt Bay. John Vance, the lumber baron, for example, was one of the first chairmen of the Humboldt Chamber of Commerce when it was formed in the late 1880s.

In an effort to promote the economic needs of the area, the Humboldt Chamber of Commerce itself petitioned Congress for financial aid and worked directly with the Corps of Engineers when seeking improvements to the harbor and its entrance. In the 1890s the San Francisco District included statements in the *Annual Reports of the Chief of Engineers* by the chamber emphasizing the importance of the region's commerce. Besides compiling economic documents for the Corps, the chamber continued to stress the need for the jetties in its publications. For example, in the 1893 booklet outlining the importance of Humboldt County, *In the Redwoods Realm*, the chamber pointed out that the partially completed jetties already had helped improve the entrance. The chamber continually publicized the economic benefit to be derived from having a "channel through the bar that will have sufficient depth of water to admit vessels of any draft, even at low tide."[5]

In the 1920s the chamber pointed out to the Corps that because the businesses around the bay had become dependent on the deep-water port, the Corps of Engineers was responsible for maintaining the deep entrance channels. In a 1925 letter to Engineer Lieutenant Aubrey H. Bond, the chamber argued not only for repair of the decrepit jetties but also for dredging of the bay. One reason the chamber cited was that the redwood lumber industry, which depended on ocean trade, had "shown a substantial increase during the last five years."[6]

In the 1930s the Chamber of Commerce became even more active in attracting the Corps' attention to the need for improving Humboldt Bay. Modern ships, carrying larger loads of lumber, could not call at the Eureka port because the entrance channel and the bay channels were not deep enough to accommodate them. In addition, the chamber desired the "removal of [the] bar shoals outside [the] end of the jetties, either by maintenance work or by extension of jetties, [and] raising of entrance jetties to sufficient height to prevent seas throwing sand into [the] entrance channel."[7]

To substantiate the claims, the secretary of the Chamber of Commerce, Lantz D. Smith, solicited letters of support from the major shippers on the bay. All of the diverse firms that responded acknowledged the economic potential of the bay, but also pointed out that their ships could not leave the harbor if fully laden.

In response to the chamber's lobbying, the Corps held several public hearings at the Chamber of Commerce's offices in the Eureka Inn in 1933 and 1936. While no immediate action resulted, local leaders did express their concerns about the bay's poor position in competing with other ports for commerce. One of the principal issues raised was that the cargoes from the bay often had to be reshipped, instead of being sent directly to a foreign market, thus increasing costs and reducing profits. The chamber invited to the hearings representatives from the area's largest lumber companies, such as the Hammond Lumber Company and the Pacific Lumber Company, and members of both foreign and domestic shipping firms. The political community was represented by the mayor of Eureka, members of the Board of Supervisors, and State Senator H.C. Nelson.

The development of the redwood lumber industry had led to the rapid settlement of the county, and the interests of the community were closely tied to the lumber economy. Although shipping catastrophes at the bay entrance had limited the expansion of the lumber industry, the situation was rapidly reversed following the completion of the jetties. By 1906 lumber exports were almost double those for 1898. Correspondingly, when the jetties were destroyed and the deep-water channel began filling in 1908 and 1909, the amount of shipping from the bay decreased. In 1907 the amount of freight crossing the Humboldt Bar was 834,635 tons, while the following year only 601,787 tons of freight were shipped.[8] The state of the jetties continued to affect the amount of commerce on the bay throughout the early twentieth century. The deep entrance became even more crucial to the development of the lucrative foreign market after the completion of the Northwestern Pacific Railroad in 1914.

The railroad accommodated most domestic trade, but it could not compete in the foreign market. Consequently, the local shipping industry began to rival San Francisco ports for foreign trade. Following World War II, the majority of foreign trade from the bay was with Japan. However, significant amounts of lumber products, including plywood and wood pulp, were also shipped directly to northern Europe, the Mediterranean, South Africa, South America, Australia, and the Far East. In the 1960s the local lumber industry expanded into the rendering of wood waste products to make paper pulp. Two large pulp mills were built on the north spit peninsula across from Eureka. With over 200 employees, the pulp mills are responsible for some of the largest current shipments over the Humboldt Bar. For example, to create the paper pulp, large tanker loads of chemicals are required. The resulting bulk paper products are shipped from the bay in large cargo vessels. In 1974 local pulp products comprised forty percent of the exports from Humboldt Bay.[9]

One of the oldest industries on the bay is the business of guiding the large ocean vessels across the Humboldt Bar. Hans Buhne was the first bar pilot, having guided the *Laura Virginia* into the bay in 1850. He continued to guide ships over the bar for the rest of his life. When the jetties were first finished in the early 20th century, it seemed as if the services of the bar pilots would no longer be necessary. A deep channel was open and the steamers could easily enter and exit the bay. But this situation was short lived. With the larger ships of the twentieth century, the services of the bar pilots became increasingly important. Today's ships are even larger than those used in the early part of the century, and are therefore "much slower and harder to handle while entering the treacherous 'jaws' of the jetties."[10]

Shipbuilding was another area closely tied to both the lumber industry and the need for the Humboldt jetties. In the mid-1860s shipbuilders began to cater to the redwood lumber industry, building ships specifically designed to cross the Humboldt Bar. The leaders of the industry, Hans Bendixson and Euphronius Cousins, actively promoted improving the bay entrance because their vessels, with flat bottoms and smaller cargo holds, could not compete with those of other firms along the coast that did not have the same limitations. Once the bar channel stabilized, their boats became competitive with others along the Pacific Coast.

Although shipbuilding began to decline in the 1920s because of the replacement of the wooden steamers by metal ships, World War I saw a final burst of construction. San Francisco Mayor James Rolph, using the resources of the Hammond Lumber Company, took over Bendixson's operations to supply wooden ships for the war effort. This short-lived effort marked the end of large-scale shipbuilding around the bay. In the 1980s a proposal by a Washington State firm, Wright Schuchart, brought a resurgence of interest in the industry. The Seattle firm proposed to refit World War II tankers at Humboldt Bay to be used as deep-water fish-packing plants. The idea, while still in the planning stages, represents the potential for further development of the shipbuilding industry and more expanded use of the Humboldt harbor. The project depends on the ability of the large vessels to cross the bar and is another link in the economic chain of development predicated on the performance of the jetties.

The deep-water entrance was also important to the development of new industries in the region. In the 1930s, for example, the Humboldt Brewing and Malt Company of Eureka began large-scale production. In 1933, after having spent more than $336,000 on improvements to the old brewery, the company contracted with the Safeway Corporation to supply $25 million worth of their product for the grocery chain's Pacific Coast district over a ten year period.[11] Accessibility to a deep-water port had been critical in, first, deciding to implement large-scale production and, second, obtaining the Safeway contract.

Another industry that began to grow in the 1920s and the 1930s because of the jetties was the fishing industry. Prior to the completion of the jetties, local commercial fishing was limited to what could be caught on Humboldt Bay or in the local rivers. The majority of fish sent to San Francisco from the Humboldt wharves was salmon caught along the banks of nearby Eel River. Ocean fishing was rare because the rough entrance was as dangerous for small fishing boats as for the larger lumber steamers. In 1892 the excitement over the discovery of halibut banks was mitigated by the conditions of the entrance. One of the local newspapers commented that "there is no doubt but what our markets will be continually supplied with this excellent fish when our bar will admit of the passage of small boats."[12] With the completion of the jetties, the entrance became safer for the fishing boats.

In the twentieth century the fledgling fishing industry grew to be a principal contributor to the local economy. The twelve-vessel fishing fleet of the 1890s grew to more than 100 vessels in the 1930s, and more than 300 men worked on the boats. Two canneries began permanent operations in the 1920s; Tom Lazio and

Theodore Weissich were among the first to be involved in the packing industry on the bay. They found San Francisco to be a ready market for the salmon, halibut and bottom fish caught in the area. The industry continued to grow in the twentieth century. In the early 1970s more than 200 boats were berthed permanently at Eureka, and 500 more used the harbor facilities. A Humboldt County Planning Department Survey in 1974 revealed that "more than half the fish consumed in California is landed at the port of Eureka."[13] The Planning Department estimated that the fishing industry's contribution to the local economy was in excess of $15 million.

Of the fish caught in the waters offshore from Humboldt Bay, the most important and valuable are king salmon. Not only do commercial fishermen depend on the annual salmon season, local party boat operators also base their income on the summer catch. The growing use of the bay has fostered an increased awareness of the dangers of the bay's entrance. The California State Department of Navigation and Ocean Development recently published a brochure on "Safe Boating Tips for Humboldt Bay" which stresses the dangers of the bar and advises how to safely cross. The treacherous currents are one of the department's main concerns. Despite repeated warnings, accidents still occur, and often end in tragedy. In January 1986, for example, a small pleasure boat capsized while crossing the bar. Both of its occupants drowned.

The Humboldt fishing industry has also included whaling and shark fishing. In 1947 Maritime Industries, Inc., established a whale-rendering plant at Fields Landing, a small community across from the bay entrance. That same year they harvested thirty-eight whales. The company employed thirty men to hunt sperm, humpback, and finback whales. The whale oil, for use in perfumes, was marketed in San Francisco. Between 1938 and 1947 shark fishing was a flourishing local industry. The shark was rendered for cod liver oil at the canneries on the bay.

In the early 1980s the Exxon Corporation considered building deep-water drilling platforms on a site on the north peninsula of Humboldt Bay. The firm chose the bay as a possible location to build the platforms when Exxon's existing sites in San Francisco Bay would not accommodate taller platforms because of the bridges spanning the bay. Also, because Humboldt was a deep-water port the large edifices could be moved for use in new deep-water drilling areas off the Santa Barbara coast. Exxon ultimately decided to contract with a firm in Korea, but the excitement stirred by the company's interest in Humboldt Bay focused new attention on the jetties and their role in developing the area's economy.

Beyond enhancing the potential for regional development, the jetties have become important recreation areas for county residents. Tourists and residents alike traveled to the bay entrance to view the construction of the rubble structures extending out into the ocean. After completion, the jetties became one of the wonders of Humboldt County, and excursions to view the manmade enrockments continued. On 13 July 1913, anthropologist Llewellyn L. Loud wrote to Alfred Kroeber stating that he "took advantage of a launch excursion to 'The Jetty' on south spitt [sic]."[14] Loud was on the bay examining the remains of the Wiyot tribes, but was glad to also have the opportunity to travel to the south spit to see the famous construction site. Ten years later, D.L. Thornbury described a similar trip to observe the jetties and their reconstruction. Impressed by the scale of the operation, Thornbury and his companions lingered at the south jetty, walking out "the jetty as far as...[they] were allowed and watched the work of bringing rock and dumping it into the sea to build up the jetties." Thornbury goes on to comment, "the two stark masts of the old *Corona* wreck at the entrance remind one of the danger of this coast."[15]

Several years later another visitor to the jetties experienced the same feelings of wonder at the jetty construction and the terrific forces of the waves. Clyde Dillworth wrote an article for a local newspaper about the recent completion of a new gravel road along the north spit to the north jetty. He described walking along the jetty, where he was joined by many other weekend visitors who "were treated to a splendid spectacle as the huge waves caused by an 8-foot tide swept over the end of the jetty."[16] Later in the day, Dillworth walked out onto the jetty, feeling "as secure as on dry land" until his guide, Alvin Lee, the government caretaker for the property, reminded him that "there were times when these huge rocks were tossed about as easily as a toy boat in a...still pond."[17] Dillworth also described the jetties as an excellent location for fishing: "A day spent on the jetty is well spent, and if you like to fish, it is doubly pleasurable."[18]

Fishermen can be found on calm days along the inner sides of either jetty trying for a "variety of perch, greenling, rockfish and an occasional salmon."[19] An additional incentive to fishing from the jetties is that a California Department of Fish and Game Fishing license is not required. Diving and spearfishing also are permitted from the jetties. However, the "Recreation Map and Guide to Humboldt Bay," a Kiwanis brochure, warns that "certain precautions should be exercised,... diving should be done only on an incoming or slack tide."[20] Diving is allowed only on the inner sides of the jetty; around the rocks of the jetty the skindivers can spearfish for the same fish caught from the surface, or hunt for crabs and clams.

Because of the hazards caused by the sudden and powerful waves sweeping across the jetties, the Corps of Engineers has attempted to block them from public access. But quite often fishermen and sightseers ignore the warning signs posted along the length of the jetties. Occasionally, tragedy results. One such case occurred in November 1986 when two high school students drove their pickup truck onto the south jetty. While they drove along the jetty, "a large wave swept over the jetty and swept the truck into the sea." One boy managed to swim back to the safety of the jetty, but the other occupant of the truck, 15-year-old Arrion Dean Reid, drowned. As a result of the tragedy, the County Sheriff's Department "issued a warning against driving vehicles onto the jetty at any time and even walking on them in stormy weather."[21]

Another unexpected side effect of the jetty construction and maintenance has been the erosion of the shorelines of Humboldt Bay, particularly the disintegration of Buhne Bluff. The tidal currents are focused by the jetties onto the bluff site which is directly across from the entrance. When the jetties were completed in 1899 the bluff was 500 feet high; it is now only slightly above sea level. According to Donald C. Tuttle, the Humboldt County Environmental Services Manager, "approximately 188 acres of Buhne point were lost in 102 years."[22] The erosion of the bluff was accelerated whenever the jetties were repaired, and was slowed when the jetties were damaged by the frequent storms.

The erosion of Buhne Point and the surrounding land caused severe problems for the residents of the King Salmon land development. The wave action has washed away portions of a county access road to the small community, and has damaged sections of the railroad that parallel the bay. To combat the erosion the San Francisco District in the early 1980s constructed a new beach and two protective rubble-mound groins to protect King

Salmon. The erosion of Buhne Point had been arrested in 1952 by the Pacific Gas and Electric Company when they built a 3,000-foot-long seawall in front of the bluff. (The Northwestern Pacific Railroad also had constructed a seawall there in the 1930s.) Other points of land within the bay have been eroded by waves reflected from Buhne Point. One of these sites is adjacent to the north spit, where from 1939 to 1984 "a 60 to 80 foot wide sandy beach...has been eroded."[23]

The jetties have caused other shoreline changes around the bay, particularly to the shape of the north and south spits. One early example was in 1890 when the north spit receded 1,500 feet in a few months. During construction of the two jetties in the 1890s, the District officers had to change their original plans for building the low riprap jetties because of the power of the tidal scour. Surveys by the Corps officer at the site, Lieutenant Deakyne, showed that "on the channel sides the currents scoured the sand out, so as to seriously endanger the foundation of the jetties."[24] To combat the eroding scour, which also threatened the trestle works, low-water revetments were built along the sides of the jetties.

The purpose of the jetties was to control the littoral drift of sand and to prevent the reformation of the shallow bar with its treacherous breaker flats blocking the bay entrance. The suspended particles of sand are carried by the ocean currents from the north to the south, providing the building materials for the north and south spits and the sandbar. The normal flow, interrupted by the jetty construction, was forced seaward where the sandbar reformed. With the north jetty blocking the littoral drift, the north spit also has advanced seaward along the side of the jetty. The south spit has not receded correspondingly because "the periods were short in which the jetties acted as completed littoral barriers. These periods were ended when littoral transport continued in normal volume either through or around the jetties."[25]

The natural course of beaches, as currently understood by geologists, is that they shift in size and shape, and indeed they "must be unstable to survive."[26] In some locations where jetties have been built on the East Coast, the result has been that the sand movement forming the beaches has been controlled, and the beaches are eroding because the sand is not being replaced. This has not happened at Humboldt Bay because the sand often could penetrate the structures. Ronald Noble, who has extensively studied the shoreline changes at Humboldt, believes that the prevalence of southwesterly storms affects the north-south transport of sand. Hence, the south spit is supplied with particles to replace those blocked by the jetties. The south spit is also replenished by the dredged material from the entrance channel. (The forty-foot entrance channel is beyond the equilibrium depth maintained by scour, so it needs to be dredged annually.) The north spit does not need to be replenished, having changed little since the jetties were completed.

The jetties are indeed, as Colonel Finch called them, the site of one of the longest battles on the Pacific Coast between man and nature. The struggle has resulted in an improved harbor entrance at Humboldt Bay, but only at great cost and risk. Moreover, the battle must be fought continually or the jetties would soon deteriorate to their condition of 1910. The construction and maintenance of the Humboldt jetties has spurred the development of new techniques for building and protecting the seawalls from the violent waves found in the area. These advances include installing the concrete monoliths at the heads of the jetties, and keeping them above the level of water at high tide. The most widely copied protection technique was the construction and use of the forty-two-ton steel-reinforced dolosse.

The Humboldt Bay jetties have had a profound effect on the economic development of the county, remaining central to all future plans for commerce around the bay. As a consequence they continue to be repaired and maintained.

In recognition of the difficulties involved in constructing and maintaining the jetties, and of their role in the development of the region, they have been declared a California Historic Civil Engineering Landmark by the San Francisco branch of the American Society of Civil Engineers. In 1981 the jetties were named a National Historic Civil Engineering Landmark by the same organization. The designation commemorates not only the construction, but the jetties' evolution in "adaption to extreme local conditions."[27] Long before they were recognized as state and national historic landmarks, however, the jetties were local landmarks. The community has valued the structures both as a recreation area and as an opportunity for economic development. The Humboldt Bay jetties signify the battle between man and nature in a region that has been struggling against the elements since it was first settled.

NOTES

[1]Don H. Doyle, *The Social Order of a Frontier Community* (Chicago: University of Illinois Press, 1983), p. 63.

[2]*Ibid.*, p. 62.

[3]D.L. Thornbury, *California's Redwood Wonderland* (San Francisco: Sunset Press, 1923), p. 11.

[4]Oral interview with Jim Worthen by Susan J. Pritchard, Eureka, CA, 3 Oct. 1986.

[5]J.M. Eddy, compiler, *In the Redwoods Realm, Humboldt County California* (Eureka: Humboldt County Chamber of Commerce, 1893), p. 13.

[6]Humboldt Chamber of Commerce to Lt. Aubrey H. Bond, 14 May 1925, San Francisco District, Main Office, General Administration files, Record Group 77, National Archives, San Bruno, CA.

[7]Letter to Eureka Chamber of Commerce from William Groundwater, Director of Transportation, Union Oil Company. Transmitted to Lt. Col. H.A. Finch, Corps of Engineers, 11 Aug. 1933, San Francisco District, Main Office, General Administration files, Record Group 77, National Archives, San Bruno, CA.

[8]*Annual Report* 1910, p. 925.

[9]Humboldt County Board of Supervisors, *Humboldt County Atlas* (Eureka: Humboldt County Board of Supervisors, 1974), p. 70.

[10]*Times-Standard*, 29 July 1985, p. 1.

[11]Eureka Chamber of Commerce to Col. Finch, 11 Aug. 1933, San Francisco District, Main Office, General Administration files, Record Group 77, National Archives, San Bruno, CA.

[12]Fountain Papers, vol. 35, p. 232.

[13]Humboldt County Board of Supervisors, *Humboldt County Atlas*, p. 54.

[14]Robert Heizer, ed., *An Anthropological Expedition in 1913* (Berkeley: University of California Press, 1970), p. 8.

[15]Thornbury, *California's Redwood Wonderland*, p. 61.

[16]Fountain Papers, vol. 35, p. 185.

[17]*Ibid.*

[18]*Ibid.*

[19]Eureka Kiwanis Club, *Recreation Map & Guide to Humboldt Bay* (Eureka, CA: Marine Advisory Extension Services, Humboldt State Univ., circa 1975).

[20]See *Recreation Map & Guide to Humboldt Bay.*

[21]*Times-Standard*, 22 Nov. 1986, p. 1.

[22]Don Tuttle, "Problems of the Sea at Buhne Point," *The Humboldt Historian* 30 (Aug. 1982), p. 11.

[23]Don Tuttle to B.N. Tilghman, 16 May 1984, Files, Public Works Department, Natural Resource Division, Humboldt County, Eureka, CA.

[24]Ronald M. Noble, *Shoreline Changes, Humboldt Bay, California.* (Berkeley: Univ. of California Hydraulic Engineering Laboratory, 1971), p. 7.

[25]*Ibid.*

[26]F. Housley Carr, "Return of the Jetties," *Sierra*, 70 (March-April 1985), p. 23.

[27]Carroll W. Pursell, "Historical and Technological Significance of the Humboldt Bay Jetties, Humboldt, California," report dated 22 Sept. 1981, p. 20.

Oceanside Harbor

by
GREGORY GRAVES

Preface

When officials of the Department of the Navy built a military harbor adjacent to the City of Oceanside, California, in 1942, their decision left a dramatic imprint upon the recent history of northern San Diego County. The Navy built the facility for the use of the U.S. Marine Corps at recently-established Camp Joseph Pendleton during the height of preparations for the Second World War. Not only was there tremendous socio-economic impact on the small community of Oceanside with the coming of the huge military base; the harbor, built directly north of the city, heightened erosion on the public beach to the south. However, the harbor also provided the city with sufficient cause to build a civilian small-craft marina sharing the same entrance channel as the military facility. While the harbor complex has proven to be an economically sound one for Oceanside and the Marine Corps, chronic entrance channel shoaling has occurred consistently, resulting in frequent and costly maintenance dredging operations. Severe erosion has continued to afflict the beach south of the harbor.

Personnel of the U.S. Army Corps of Engineers, public officials of Oceanside, and a host of federal, state, county, and local individuals have attempted to ameliorate these chronic problems for several decades. This is a history of their efforts to establish and maintain an operational harbor, while meeting the demands of a number of diverse public interests. The coastal resources of the earth are limited, and yet there is intense demand for their development and use. The building of structures has proven that coastal land is sensitive environmentally, and that actions at one point often have an impact elsewhere along the coast.

Demand for shoreline use near Oceanside exemplifies the magnitude of problems that coastal development can cause. It also reveals the severe challenges coastal engineers have faced in attempting to maintain an operable harbor and a sandy beach to the south. Chronic harbor shoaling and beach erosion have plagued Oceanside for decades, and both problems are the result primarily of the harsh wave environment at that location. Placement of jetties north of the city both exacerbated beach erosion and clogged the harbor entrance channel with the rapidly moving sand. In battling these problems, coastal engineers have dredged tens of millions of cubic yards of sand from the harbor and placed all of it on the beach to the south. Moreover, they have placed tons of additional material from inland locations on that beach — all to be washed out to sea or back into the harbor.

In the 1980s, the Corps of Engineers constructed an elaborate and expensive sand bypassing system at Oceanside. All those who have been involved in maintaining the harbor and beach hope that this experimental system will at least ease the severe shoaling and erosion problems in this difficult setting. While there are other systems in operation which pump sand from harbors through fixed pipelines and distribute the material elsewhere, none functions in a harsh wave environment like Oceanside. The success of the first construction phase of this system depends on Corps officials' ability to solve a variety of technical and economic problems which will determine if the next phases will be built. If sand bypassing proves economically feasible in reducing the costs of maintenance dredging at Oceanside, engineers may use similar systems elsewhere to solve the same problems.

The events leading to the sand bypassing experiment at Oceanside provide a case study of the Corps of Engineers and its interactions with the aggressive city government of Oceanside. They also highlight the Corps' dealings with the Marine Corps (which shares the harbor with the city), a number of federal and state environmental and resource agencies, and interested private citizens during the last fifty years. That the experiment is taking place at Oceanside instead of another harbor experiencing shoaling is attributable to the public and private individuals influencing policy there. Oceanside demonstrates the difficulty in balancing human needs and desires to develop and use coastal land with environmental and aesthetic considerations. Moreover, it under-scores the extreme challenges coastal engineers face when they attempt to build and maintain structures which modify the forces of nature.

CHAPTER I

Oceanside: Beach City
on the Open Pacific

Oceanside, California, incorporated in 1881 and located in northern San Diego County, has long been a community dependent on its coastal resources. Tourists, swimmers, and sun bathers from all parts of North America have taken advantage of the city's majestic, yet uncrowded shoreline since the late nineteenth century. The economy of Oceanside has relied since the city's foundation on a proximity to the Pacific Ocean. Some of the largest waves in all of southern California thunder on Oceanside's beach, making it very popular for all wave recreation activities. A mild climate with minimal temperature extremes has helped to make Oceanside a very popular recreational spot on the California coast.

Providing moderate weather patterns, as well as meeting the commercial and recreational needs of the region, the Pacific has for the most part lived up to its serene name since European settlers first came to California in the eighteenth century. Yet the ocean has at times in the past century lashed out at human development along the shoreline. Powerful waves have undermined structures, sweeping them out to sea, and then rearranging them up or down the coast according to the ocean's own design. While much of the southern California coast is guarded from the awesome power of the Pacific by a series of large islands, Oceanside has one of the least protected beach areas. In summer, it is vulnerable to waves from the southern hemisphere. During winter months, waves emanating from far in the North Pacific and only partially diminished by the Santa Barbara Channel Islands churn the Oceanside beach sands. Storm waves from either direction often break more heavily at Oceanside than anywhere else in southern California, assuring that

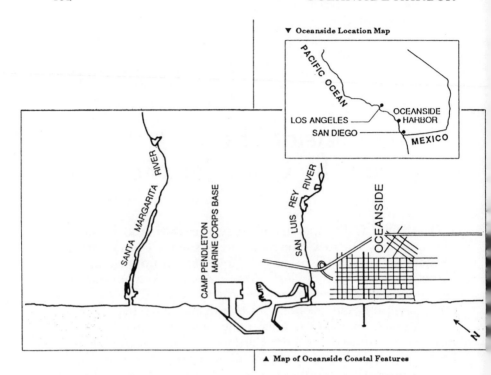

▼ Oceanside Location Map

▲ Map of Oceanside Coastal Features

in any given year hundreds of thousands of cubic yards of sand will
be in motion within the Oceanside littoral cell. The problems that
this phenomena of extreme littoral fluctuation have presented to
recreational and commercial development are basic to a history of
coastal engineering in the vicinity of Oceanside.

Upcoast and downcoast movement of littoral material, known as
longshore transport, is a principal factor in beach sand supply. In
addition to longshore transport, rivers provide another major
source of sand. Bordering Oceanside on the north is the San Luis
Rey River, and about two miles further north is the Santa
Margarita River. Between them lies a sandy estuary, rich in marine
life. Historically, during periods of heavy precipitation inland,
these rivers delivered great quantities of sediment to the shoreline.
In the present century, however, significant sediment delivery has
occurred only twice. The largest occurred in 1916, when heavy
winter rains caused a major flood on the San Luis Rey, burying
thousands of coastal acres of cultivated land with inland silt,

washing out all major roads, and isolating Oceanside for nearly two weeks. The raging river carried silt hundreds of feet into the ocean, forming a large sandbar at the mouth of the stream. This was the flood that prompted the construction of a dam in 1922 creating Lake Henshaw on the San Luis Rey, thereby reducing its uncontrolled drainage by more than one-third. Ironically, it was also this flood which blessed Oceanside with much of the sand which contributed to "its wide flat beach and very gradual inshore and foreshore slopes."[1]

The Oceanside business community enjoyed the benefits of the city's beach resource for the next two decades, as tourists flocked to the city. In response to the increasing tourism, the city council in 1927 authorized construction of a recreational beachfront known as "The Strand," centerpieced by the longest pier in southern California. These attractions helped Oceanside residents weather the economic crises of the 1930s, as the city's close proximity to Los Angeles and San Diego made it a popular vacation spot. While minor floods nourished the beaches during the 1926-27 and 1936-37 storm seasons, neither matched the 1916 event, and drought conditions were common. Meanwhile, the ocean continued inexorably to move millions of tons of sand in and out of the Oceanside littoral cell. Natural sediment delivery, often below

Oceanside Beach, 1939.

normal from drought and after 1922 interrupted by Henshaw Dam, failed to replenish the eroding beach at the same rate as the sand was disappearing.[2]

Most people were unaware that inland water impoundment was having a gradual, but significant impact on beach nourishment. After damaging coastal flooding occurred during winter storms between 1936 and 1938, San Diego County and several local officials appealed to the United States Congress for additional flood control measures on both the San Luis Rey and Santa Margarita rivers.[3] Soon Congress authorized the U.S. Army Corps of Engineers, through its Los Angeles District Office, to examine the possibilities of creating flood control structures on these rivers. The District Office was interested not only in reducing the risk of flooding for the Oceanside area; it also was considering the need for water conservation and hydroelectric generation. In conducting separate studies for each river, the engineers found that while water supplies were sufficient for that time, they would soon become deficient under even the most conservative estimates of population growth. Their preliminary studies argued that additional flood control and water conservation measures were probably justified economically (the requirement for construction of any federal development project) on both river basins, and that they should begin to conduct surveys to determine the best plans.[4]

By 1940, the Los Angeles District engineers had studies underway for both rivers, and had issued a plan of improvement for the San Luis Rey. Three alternatives called for dams varying from 242 to 279 feet in crest elevation which would be built on the lower drainage of the river at costs ranging from $4.4 to $6.7 million.[5] However, all such flood control and water conservation plans soon became low priorities as the War Department began to divert most of its resources into preparation for World War II.

The war effort changed the socio-economic composition of northern San Diego County. The two major flood control and water conservation projects were delayed, but of more importance was the Department of Navy purchase of Rancho Santa Margarita y Las Flores in 1942. This action altered the future of Oceanside dramatically. Bordering the city on the north, this sprawling 143,000-acre parcel of land, stretching twenty miles in length and as much as ten miles in width, became the site of the U.S. Marine Corps training base, Camp Joseph H. Pendleton — named for a Marine Corps general who had recently died and had devoted the last ten years of his life to the establishment of a training base in San Diego County. On 25 September 1942, a veritable city of Marine Corps trainees and other military personnel took up residence a few miles from formerly isolated Oceanside. The obvious impact of the base was the acceleration of Oceanside's economic and population growth, as the city responded to meet the demands of something resembling an overnight boom town.[6]

The coming of Camp Pendleton affected the people of Oceanside in other ways as well. The base commander at Pendleton believed that, as a Marine Corps training establishment, it was essential to have a facility where amphibious operations could be simulated, and also a harbor where actual maneuvers could originate. Through the same emergency provisions of the War Powers Act of 1941, whereby Department of the Navy lawyers had purchased the rancho from its reluctant owners, the Marine Corps began advanced planning for construction of a harbor somewhere along its twenty-three-mile Pacific Coast shoreline.[7]

The Navy's Eleventh District of the Bureau of Yards and Docks located in San Diego conducted a hasty survey of possible sites for the basin in early 1942. Upon choosing a lagoon site lying between the San Luis Rey and Santa Margarita rivers, the bureau began drawing up specific construction specifications. The bureau report pointed out that this site (about one mile from Oceanside's northern limits) would require the least amount of initial dredging and be less costly to expand if necessary. Moreover, the report stated: "The channel entrance was chosen with regard to the possible effect on the harbor of the littoral sand drift."[8] In reality, the exigencies wrought by the Japanese attack on Pearl Harbor and fear of an enemy invasion on the California coast figured strongly in this survey and report, which was produced in less than two months.

Anxious to move along with construction, Brigadier General Joseph C. Fegan, the first Commandant of Camp Pendleton, forwarded the bureau report to Colonel Edwin C. Kelton, District Engineer of the Los Angeles Corps of Engineers office, and asked for his assessment of the site. Kelton's response of 11 April 1942 was prefaced with the statement: "It must be understood that, because of the incomplete data and the short time allowed for the study, it constitutes a well-considered opinion only." His opinion included probabilities that the dominant sand movement at the harbor entrance would be downcoast, but no one in the Corps ventured a speculation of how much annual movement there would be in any particular period of time. Given that sand movement would be primarily downcoast, Kelton commended the site because of its location north of the principal Oceanside beach nourisher, the San Luis Rey River. Kelton wrote that this factor "should reduce probability of excessive downcoast erosion." However, he also pointed out that the harbor would interrupt downcoast movement from the Santa Margarita River, the other principal Oceanside sand supplier.[9]

Because of the potential for sand accretion in the harbor entrance and erosion downcoast, the Corps did not recommend that the harbor be built at the site suggested by the Bureau of Yards and Docks. Yet if the Marine Corps chose to build the harbor there despite this, the Corps of Engineers offered some recommendations to improve its potential performance. Rather than building straight "arrowhead jetties," Corps officials suggested constructing ones which would be widely separated at the shore and reach their narrowest point at the entrance channel. This, they believed, would help to dispel wave action by allowing them to expand inside the harbor. They also recommended that the material dredged to create the harbor be placed immediately downcoast "to prevent very short term erosion effects." Finally, they suggested that the basin be expanded if financially possible to include 500 feet of low-lying, flood-prone land north of the planned boundary, for it would "prove of immense benefit and...eliminate a constant source of annoyance."[10]

The reservations of Kelton and the Corps did little to deter the Marines in the heat of wartime necessity. As one observer remembered, when a Camp Pendleton official was warned about the potential of this site for shoaling and interruption of sand to downcoast beaches, his response was "we have a war to fight, we need the harbor, and we'll worry about the consequences after the war."[11] "Without much reference to anybody else," another individual recalled, the Marine Corps finalized plans for the harbor, and construction by a private contractor began in May 1942. The Marines did follow the Corps' recommendation that the jetties narrow toward the entrance, although not as much as suggested. They also expanded the basin according to recommendations to 900 by 1,700 feet, with an outer jetty on the north of 2,035 feet, and one on the south of 1,300 feet. Del Mar Boat Basin, as it was named, became operational on 15 December 1942, at an original construction cost of $2.72 million.[12] Thereafter, the Marine

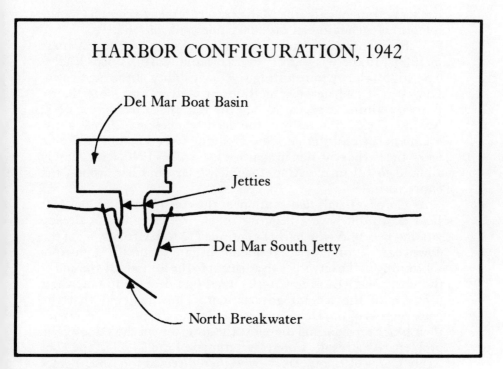

HARBOR CONFIGURATION, 1942

Del Mar Boat Basin

Jetties

Del Mar South Jetty

North Breakwater

Corps began using the boat basin for a variety of amphibious training maneuvers to be employed in actual combat in the South Pacific theatre of the Second World War. Yet, shortly after the harbor became operational, extensive sand accretion began to reduce the entrance channel depth.

By July 1944, depth measurements in the Del Mar Boat Basin revealed that the entrance channel had shoaled to 14 feet at the Mean Lower Low Water level (MLLW), and had narrowed to 50 feet in width. The harbor entrance at that depth was "virtually unnavigable" for anything but the smallest military vessels. In that month, the first episode in a long series of periodic maintenance dredging began at the boat basin. By the end of the summer, as a result of extensive dredging conducted for the Marines by a private contractor, the entrance channel was again operational at a depth of 20 feet (MLLW) and a width of 190 feet. To everyone's dismay, but to the surprise of few in the Corps of Engineers, the entrance channel was shoaled to the point of unnavigability again after winter storms in the 1944-1945 season. This time, in order to use the harbor entrance again, the Marines were forced to contract for the removal of an additional 219,000 cubic yards of sand.[13]

With preparations for a possible invasion of the Japanese mainland in the works in 1945, Navy and Marine Corps leaders gave high priority to restoring the navigability of the boat basin. However, it had never actually been used in any more than a limited training capacity. When the war ended in August 1945, Marine Corps' interest in the facility declined significantly. Maintenance costs for periodic dredging were so prohibitive that when the harbor shoaled in again in December 1946, it was simply allowed to fill in, creating a semicircular sand bar around the entire basin.[14]

As Corps officials had cautioned, the construction of Del Mar Boat Basin did have a negative impact on Oceanside's already eroding beach. As the harbor continued to trap virtually all of the downcoast littoral drift, residents began to notice a distinct shortening of the city's beach adjacent to the Strand. By the end of the war, the Oceanside City Council had decided to take their problem to the federal government. They believed that the construction of the Del Mar Boat Basin was the primary cause for their beach erosion, and therefore the government should solve the problem. As a result, Congress authorized the Chief of the U.S. Army Corps of Engineers — who then directed the Los Angeles District Office — to look into the issue of responsibility for Oceanside's eroded beach. Meanwhile, the city hired a private contractor, Charles T. Leeds (a former Los Angeles District Engineer) to prepare a report on the impact of the Camp Pendleton harbor on erosion to the south of it.[15]

Members of the Oceanside City Council were interested in more than just beach restoration. The council, in conjunction with the San Diego County Postwar Planning Department, also contracted Leeds to conduct a study of the possibility of building a civilian small-craft harbor somewhere along the county's north coast. The Marine Corps harbor had caused, in the council's opinion, the severe beach erosion that was beginning to damage the tourist economy; yet the harbor construction had also sparked the idea that the area south of that facility might make an excellent civilian harbor. A small-craft harbor and ancillary businesses could generate an unprecedented economic boon in Oceanside. Since a harbor already existed there and had operated with some success, city officials began a quest to secure a civilian facility possibly sharing the same channel entrance. The Leeds report, issued in August 1946, reached conclusions which fit perfectly into the city's plans. Leeds argued that there should be harbors along the California coast at no greater than thirty- to forty-mile intervals. At that time, no harbor existed from San Diego Harbor to Newport Beach in Orange County, a distance of about ninety miles. He also stated that the current population and projected growth justified the construction of a civilian harbor in northern San Diego County. In his opinion, there were three prime locations for the harbor, but the site of the Camp Pendleton boat basin was the most economical and beneficial to the residents of the area.[16]

When Congress directed the Corps to investigate beach erosion at Oceanside, it also authorized a "post-war planning study" with the intent of assessing feasibility for civilian harbor construction on the California coast. Issued on 30 June 1947, the report to the Chief of Engineers declared that in northern San Diego County construction of a civilian harbor at Camp Pendleton would cost less than at any other potential site. Moreover, it argued that the Camp Pendleton site would "concentrate beach erosion problems in one location, resulting in the maintenance of a navigable channel at all times and permitting the full use of the harbor by the Marine Corps." Oceanside thus received a second important endorsement for its planned harbor, but the report ended with a discouraging footnote that since the Marine Corps opposed "joint occupancy of Camp Pendleton Harbor," the Corps of Engineers could not proceed with a survey for construction there.[17]

Marine Corps officials had opposed any civilian use of Del Mar Boat Basin since its construction. They were perhaps even more adamantly against the construction of an adjacent non-military harbor. City officials had made several futile attempts since 1946 to persuade the Marine Corps to at least consider their plans. As one individual remembered: "They were always rebuffed in any attempt to discuss acquisition of Marine Corps property as a harbor site."[18] Virtually any site that Oceanside officials considered for joint use of the entrance required the use of Marine Corps land purchased in the Rancho Santa Margarita acquisition. City planners had to persuade the Marines to relinquish some land north of Oceanside before any further action could be taken.

The situation remained stalemated over Marine Corps opposition until 1949. By this time the boat basin, unnavigable since the end of 1946, had shoaled to a depth of one-to-three feet (MLLW) and was little more than an artificial lagoon. At low tide, a large sandbar over 100 feet long was clearly visible in the entrance channel. Early in the year, a new commander, General Clifton B. Cates, took charge of Camp Pendleton, and was immediately distressed over the condition of the harbor. Shortly after his arrival, Oceanside officials made another bid for the joint harbor complex. More receptive than past commanders, and anxious to restore Del Mar Boat Basin to operation, Cates listened to their plan with interest. His enthusiasm for the idea was reflected in a surprise memorandum to the Chief of Engineers on 28 April 1949, which stated that the Department of the Navy had reached "the inescapable conclusion that the interests of the Marine Corps may best be served by combining its requirements with those of the community, [and that] the former disapproval... has been reconsidered by the Commandant of the Marine Corps."[19] This surprising reversal in the Marine Corps' position on sharing a harbor entrance was due in large part to the persistence of the Oceanside City Council, the change in command at Camp Pendleton, as well as the ever-shallower and now useless Del Mar Boat Basin.

The city's efforts to affix the burden of responsibility for local beach erosion came to fruition when Leeds issued his report in October 1949, entitled "Effects of Shore Erosion and Accretion Adjacent to Camp Pendleton Boat Basin Harbor." The report cited the construction of the harbor jetties as being entirely responsible for the severe erosion occurring on Oceanside's beach, declaring that therefore it was up to the federal government to rectify the situation. Anxious to restore the beach, Oceanside officials submitted the Leeds report to the Corps of Engineers in Los Angeles for review. A short time later, Corps officials announced their agreement with the findings, but did not concur that it was a federal responsibility to restore the beach. In 1946, Congress authorized federal participation in shore protection projects on publicly-owned property, but limited government expenditure to no more than one-third the entire cost. Oceanside officials were therefore faced with funding two-thirds of what promised to be a very expensive beach restoration project. Fully aware that their city was incapable of producing that much money, they chose instead to lobby Congress for a change in the law or for an exception to it in Oceanside's case.[20]

The Leeds report also furthered the city's quest for a small-craft harbor. Because thousands of cubic yards of dredged material would be needed for deposition on Oceanside beach, it suggested the basin for a small-craft harbor could be dug in the process of meeting that requirement. Both city and Corps officials found this idea of accomplishing two tasks with one project appealing. The prospect also made the Oceanside harbor site easily the least expensive of the possibilities for northern San Diego County.[21]

The Corps of Engineers held a public meeting on 4 October 1949 concerning the harbor proposal and beach erosion problems at Oceanside. Representing the Marine Corps at the meeting was Brigadier General O.T. Pfeiffer, who expressed his support of the plan to share the harbor entrance channel with the city. His principal interest, however, was the reopening of Del Mar Boat Basin. Pfeiffer stated, "the only way Marines can be skilled in amphibious operations is to be where they can operate boats. The need for our boat harbor at Camp Pendleton, therefore, goes to the primary purpose for which there are Marines."[22]

This meeting generated the first organized public sentiment about both the harbor and beach erosion issues. Several individuals rose to endorse the harbor concept, while the Federated Sportsmen of San Diego County issued a formal letter encouraging the Corps to proceed with development. That organization even offered to provide statistics which would prove the economic feasibility and immense benefits that the proposed harbor "would bestow on the sportsmen of Southern California, and fishermen, both sport and commercial."[23]

After praise for the harbor idea died down, the meeting then turned to the much more volatile erosion issue. Several individuals angrily demanded that the government do something to restore the beach. The local American Legion post urged the Corps of Engineers "to take immediate action to prevent further damage to the beach and its installations." The acting adjutant of the post, Max McComas, then presented photographic evidence of what he believed to be the results of the boat basin jetty construction on Oceanside beach, and an eye-witness account of the erosion. He closed with an analogy: the Navy had borrowed binoculars from citizens in a time of crucial wartime need, which had now been returned or replaced. "We of Oceanside," McComas declared, "in effect cheerfully loaned our beach to help win the war. Now we respectfully request our government to give it back by replacing the sand that we would have normally acquired were it not for the Camp Pendleton jetty and harbor."[24] Most of those who decried the beach erosion wanted the harbor removed altogether. Yet if it remained, they demanded that the federal government somehow keep a constant supply of sand on the beach to the south. For both Oceanside city leaders and the Corps of Engineers, the meeting had been an eye-opening experience. The intensity of public interest surprised every government official involved.

The two actions which citizens advocated made city officials determined to accomplish both harbor development and beach maintenance. As a result of the recent Marine Corps acquiescence to a joint harbor, they pushed ahead with feasibility and design studies, while intensifying their congressional lobbying effort to have their beach erosion problem considered apart from the existing law limiting federal assistance to one-third of the total cost. Such efforts resulted in congressional authorization in 1949 for the Corps of Engineers to initiate studies to make an actual determination of the federal share in the cost of beach restoration at Oceanside. The Corps also began conducting studies into harbor improvements at Camp Pendleton with expansion under consideration.[25] By 1950, these studies were all underway; however, the progress was slowed in 1951, when the escalating Korean conflict diverted funds away from civil projects. The hope that Oceanside would finally get both its small-craft harbor and solutions to its beach erosion was brighter as the new decade began, yet many clouds still remained on the horizon.

NOTES

[1]Report, "Oceanside: A Case Study," undated, 1979, Beach Erosion Shore Protection file, 1979, Los Angeles District, U.S. Army Corps of Engineers, Box 1 of 1, Record Group 77/ Federal Records Center number 81-0015, National Archives, Laguna Niguel, CA. Hereinafter cited as LNNA RG 77/(federal records center number) Box number/number; John Pethick, *An Introduction to Coastal Geomorphology* (Somerset, England: Edward Arnold Publishers, 1984), pp. 9-11; U.S. Army Engineer District, "Enclosures to Accompany Survey Report, Flood Control, San Luis Rey River, California," 16 Sept. 1940, Oceanside and Camp Pendleton Historical file, LNNA RG 77/64A-0951 Box 1/4. Hereinafter cited as Enclosures, San Luis Rey River, Oceanside and Camp Pendleton Historical file, LNNA RG 77/64A-0951 Box 1/4; Report, "Oceanside Beach Erosion," undated, ca. 1977, Oceanside Beach Erosion Study file, 1976-1977, LNNA RG 77/80-0018 Box 7/8. Leeds, Hill, and Jewett, *Shore Protection Small-Craft-Harbor Development in the Oceanside-Camp Pendleton Area, California* (Los Angeles: Leeds, Hill, and Jewett, Inc., 1955), p. 6.

[2]Enclosures, San Luis Rey River, Oceanside and Camp Pendleton Historical file, LNNA RG 77-64A-0951 Box 1/4; U.S. Army Engineer District, "Shore Protection Report on Preliminary Examination of Harbor at Camp Pendleton, California," 1 Feb. 1950, Oceanside Preliminary Examination file, LNNA RG 77/79-0001 Box 1/13. Hereinafter cited as Shore Protection Report, 1950, Oceanside Preliminary Examination file, LNNA RG 77/79-0001 Box 1/13.

[3]U.S. Army Engineer District, "Report on Survey Flood Control, Santa Margarita River and Tributaries, California," 20 April 1944, Santa Margarita River file, LNNA RG 77/83-0004 Box 4/20. Hereinafter cited as Flood Control, Santa Margarita River, LNNA RG 77/83-0004 Box 4/20; U.S. Engineer District, "Preliminary Examination Report: Flood Control, Santa Margarita River and Tributaries, California, 19 April 1939, Santa Margarita River file, LNNA RG 77/83-0004 Box 4/20. Hereinafter cited as Preliminary Examination, Santa Margarita River, Santa Margarita River file, LNNA RG 77/83-0004 Box 4/20.

[4]*Ibid.*

[5]Enclosures, San Luis Rey River, Oceanside and Camp Pendleton file, LNNA RG 77/64A-0951 Box 1/4; The Bonsall reservoir would have forestalled the need to import water for the region at a high cost from probably the Colorado River. The plan fell victim to World War II budgetary constraints.

[6]In 1940, northern San Diego County had a population of 12,742. The estimated population for 1970, according to the Corps, was about 30,000. See *ibid.;* Flood Control, Santa Margarita River, Santa Margarita River file, LNNA RG 77/83-0004 Box 4/20; William J. Herron, Jr., *An Oral History of Coastal Engineering Activities in Southern California, 1932-1981* (Los Angeles, CA: U.S. Army Engineer District, forthcoming) p. 8-5; Paolo E. Coletta, ed., *United States Navy and Marine Corps Bases, Domestic* (Westport, CT: Greenwood Press, 1985), p. 572.

[7]*Ibid.; First War Powers Act,* 55 Stat. 838 (1941); U.S. Army Engineer District, "History of the Camp Pendleton Boat Harbor Construction," taken from Shore Protection Report, 1950, Oceanside Preliminary Examination file, 1950, LNNA RG 77/79-0001 Box 1/13.

[8]*Ibid.*

[9]Coletta, *United States Navy and Marine Corps Bases,* p. 574; U.S. Army Engineer District, "History of the Camp Pendleton Boat Harbor Construction," taken from Shore Protection Report, 1950, Oceanside Preliminary Examination file, 1950, LNNA RG 77/79-0001 Box 1/13.

[10]Colonel Edwin C. Kelton, Los Angeles District Engineer, to Commanding General, Amphibious Corps, Pacific Fleet, Camp Elliot, San Diego County, California, subj: Small-craft harbor, Oceanside, California, Oceanside Project Cost Estimates file, 1946-1961, LNNA RG 77/80-0034 Box 18/20; Herron, *Oral History,* pp. 8-1, 8-3, 8-5.

[11]*Ibid.,* p. 8-5.

[12]*Ibid.*, p. 8-1; Leeds, Hill, and Jewett, *Shore Protection and Small-Craft-Harbor Development*, p. 28; "History of Camp Pendleton Boat Harbor Construction," taken from Shore Protection Report, 1950, Oceanside Preliminary Examination file, 1950, LNNA RG 77/79-0001 Box 1/13.

[13]*Ibid.*, Charles T. Leeds, *Possible Reconstruction of Entrance of Boat Basin, Camp Joseph H. Pendleton* (Los Angeles, CA: 1944), *passim.*

[14]*Ibid.*, Leeds, Hill, and Jewett, *Shore Protection and Small-Craft-Harbor Development*, p. 28; Herron, *Oral History*, p. 8-5.

[15]Charles T. Leeds, *Effects of Shore Erosion and Accretion Adjacent to Camp Pendleton Boat Harbor* (Los Angeles, CA: 1949); Anthony F. Turhollow, *A History of the Los Angeles District, U.S. Army Corps of Engineers, 1898-1965* (Los Angeles: U.S. Army Engineer District, 1975), p. 105.

[16]A.T.W. Moore, Los Angeles District Engineer, to Division Engineer, South Pacific Division, San Francisco, CA, subj: Preliminary examinations at Camp Pendleton and Santa Monica harbors, 29 April 1947, Camp Pendleton Harbor file, 1946-1974, LNNA RG 77/80-0033 Box 6/20; Charles T. Leeds, *Small-Craft Harbor Possibilities in Northern San Diego County* (Los Angeles: Leeds, Hill, and Jewett, Inc., 1946), *passim*; Leeds, Hill, and Jewett, *Shore Protection and Small-Craft-Harbor Development*, p. 38; The other site mentioned principally was the Agua Hedionda Lagoon to the south of Oceanside.

[17]*River and Harbor Act of 1945*, 59 Stat. 32 (1945); U.S. Congress, House, *An Act Authorizing Construction, Repair, and Preservation of Certain Public Works of Rivers and Harbors, and for Other Purposes*, Pub. L. 79-525, 79th Cong., 2d sess., H.R. 6407, *passim;* Report to the Chief of Engineers, U.S. Army, by the District Engineer, Los Angeles, "Preliminary Examination of the Coast of Southern California with a View of the Establishment of Harbors for Light-Draft Vessels," summarized in *ibid.*, pp. 10, 39; Minutes of a public meeting held at Oceanside, California, 1 Oct. 1963, Oceanside file, 1961-1962, LNNA RG 77/84-0018 Box 7/8. Hereinafter cited as Minutes, Oct. 1963, Oceanside file, 1961-1962, LNNA RG 77/84-0018 Box 7/8.

[18]Herron, *Oral History*, p. 8-9.

[19]*Ibid.;* W.P.T. Hill, Commandant of the Marine Corps, to Chief of Engineers, Department of the Army, subj: Conversion of boat basin to a small-boat harbor, Camp Pendleton, 28 April 1949, Camp Pendleton Harbor file, 1946-1974, LNNA RG 77/80-0033 Box 6/20.

[20]Leeds, *Effects of Shore Erosion, passim;* Turhollow, *A History of the Los Angeles District*, p. 105; U.S. Congress, House, *An Act Authorizing Federal Participation in the Cost of Protecting Shores of Publicly Owned Property*, Pub. L. 79-727, 79th Cong., 2d sess., 1946. See also 60 Stat. 1056 (1946); U.S. Congress, House, *An Act to Amend the Act entitled "An Act Authorizing Federal Participation in the Cost of Protecting the Shores of Publicly Owned Property*, "Pub. L. 84-826, 84th Cong., 2d sess., 1956. See also 70 Stat. 702 (1956).

[21]Turhollow, *A History of the Los Angeles District*, p. 105.

[22]Leeds, Hill, and Jewett, *Shore Protection and Small-Craft-Harbor Development*, p. 28.

[23]Hal S. Morgan, Executive Secretary, Federated Sportsmen of San Diego County, to Colonel W.D. Luplow, Los Angeles District Engineer, subj: small-craft harbor development, 1 Oct. 1949, Camp Pendleton Harbor file, 1946-1974, LNNA RG 77/80-0033 Box 6/20.

[24]American Legion, Joseph G. McComb Post, 146, to Los Angeles District, Corps of Engineers, subj: Beach erosion at Oceanside, CA, 20 Sept. 1949, Camp Pendleton Harbor file, 1946-1974, LNNA RG 77/80-0033 Box 6/20; Shore Protection Report, 1950, Oceanside and Camp Pendleton Historical file, LNNA RG 77/64A-0951 Box 1/4.

[25]Report, "Major Expenditures for Oceanside Harbor, California," 20 Feb. 1964, Camp Pendleton Harbor file, 1946-1974, LNNA RG 77/80-0034 Box 18/20.

CHAPTER II

Toward a
Civilian-Military Harbor

As a result of the events of late 1949, both Oceanside and Army Corps of Engineers officials believed strongly in continuing plans to establish a civilian harbor at Del Mar Boat Basin. By 1950, the economically attractive prospects of a small-craft harbor had influenced Oceanside public opinion to the point of enthusiastic support of the idea. City officials then began to grapple with a host of unanswered questions concerning acquisition of government land, plan feasibility, and jurisdiction if the joint military-civilian complex materialized. In the meantime, they sought a solution to the city's ever-narrowing beaches. Now congressionally mandated to study the possibilities of establishing a small-craft harbor somewhere in northern San Diego County, the Corps began to explore the problem. The individuals working on this study were aware, however, that establishment of a harbor in this region of the southern California shoreline would severely challenge the technological capabilities of coastal engineering. The critical shoaling problems experienced at the Marine Corps installation had demonstrated graphically that harbor design in this open-ocean setting required special consideration for both technical and economic feasibility.

For the Corps of Engineers, economic feasibility depended exclusively on navigation considerations. However, a corps report of 1 February 1950 tied solutions for Oceanside's eroded beaches to plans for future harbor construction. Basic in this plan was the provision that all dredged material from north of Oceanside be placed on the city's beaches. The engineers pointed out that data concerning littoral movement in the Oceanside cell were yet "too meager" to draw conclusions, but they believed the current theory that called it "a wave-cut seacoast in a state of equilibrium" to be fallacious. This theory held that there was only a slight annual north to south movement within the cell. However, observations at Camp Pendleton had shown that during 1949 there was actually a net upcoast drift. Moreover, there had been almost no erosion immediately south of the harbor. Although they did suggest that littoral drift was consistently upcoast (as had been observed in 1949), they argued that because of the area's exposure to southerly and southwesterly swells coming unbroken from thousands of miles, it was erroneous to assume that the Oceanside cell was in a state of equilibrium.[1] The primary purpose of this examination of littoral movement was to determine the level of federal responsibility for Oceanside's beach erosion. However, the engineers conducting these investigations began to discover how fundamental sand movement was to the condition of the beaches.

The findings of this report influenced progress on harbor development and beach restoration for years to come. The "complete littoral barrier" that had formed around Del Mar Boat Basin was now allowing north-south movement to replenish the beach directly south of the harbor, but the engineers believed that it might be responsible for erosion between one-half and one mile downcoast. To restore the beach at Oceanside, they believed that the harbor had to be removed entirely. If restored or enlarged, the report stated, "the plan for shore maintenance would probably include a mechanical system for sand bypassing littoral drift across the harbor inlet."[2] At that time, sand bypassing was not a clearly-defined concept; nonetheless, the Corps had suggested such a concept as a means of maintaining Oceanside beach and keeping the harbor navigable as early as 1950. The engineers concluded that beach erosion at Oceanside "may be due wholly or in part" to the Camp Pendleton jetties, and that any plan for correction should include considerations for both harbor improvement and shore protection, and the maintenance of both. Surveys should be conducted to assess those plans, and the federal government should pay for them.[3]

While those studies were beginning, an emergency situation arose in Oceanside. Powerful swells from the South Pacific accelerated erosion along the city's beach during the first half of 1950. Hardest hit was an area between Witherby Street on the south end of town and Wisconsin Avenue, four blocks south of the pier. Concerned that any additional high seas could undermine that part of the Strand and damage structures behind it, city officials appealed to their federal representatives. On 20 June 1950, Colonel Earl E. Gesler, the president of the Corps' Beach Erosion Board, having heard about the problem from Congressman Clinton McKinnon of California, telephoned Colonel Walter P. Luplow, the Los Angeles District Engineer. Luplow explained that he was fully aware of the erosion problem. The Corps did have plans to dredge about one million cubic yards of sand from Del Mar Boat Basin's shoaled-in harbor entrance channel and place it on Oceanside's beach. However, this could not take place until funds became available, and at present there was no money appropriated for emergency work at Oceanside. Luplow recommended that the Corps be given permission to dredge about half of the one million cubic yards and place it at the pier, but added that he could do nothing until authorized.[4]

In May, Luplow had met with city officials to discuss remedial measures for the beach. In addition to sand deposition, they also talked about building groins (stone walls built perpendicular to the shore extending at varying lengths seaward) at each end of the beach to trap sand inside them. As a shore protection measure, they also discussed the possibility of constructing a seawall (a rock wall built parallel to the shore at points of extreme erosion) in order to break the waves before they hit the Strand or buildings behind it. Luplow recommended against both of these because he believed that groins would only serve to further interrupt littoral movement, while seawalls were unsightly, obstructed access, and did nothing to restore the beaches. What Oceanside residents and lawmakers viewed as an emergency made them grow quickly impatient with the Corps of Engineers. This impatience was substantially a result of a general misunderstanding of the Corp's position in the decision-making process. Without congressional approval, the Corps could take no action to mitigate Oceanside's immediate erosion problem. Studies were underway, and Luplow carefully reminded critics that investigations which were rushed in order to find a quick solution were often fatally flawed. Moreover, Camp Pendleton harbor experience amply illustrated that in this particular coastal setting hasty actions were extremely ill-advised.[5]

Erosion-causing storms occurred again in the winter of 1950-51. Despite the Oceanside City Council's efforts to get remedial work done, nothing had happened by the spring of 1951. In June, Corps representatives ventured to Oceanside to inspect the damage wrought by recent high waves. On a 280-foot segment of the beach front three blocks south of the pier, the street had been mostly undermined, and the waves had damaged some structures behind it. The city was forced to take remedial measures on its own after this episode, and at the time of the Corps' inspection workers were feverishly building a 1,500-foot stone wall from quarry rock in front of the worst-damaged area. By pouring concrete over the stones at times of low tide, the city's Superintendent of Streets, Ernest Taylor, reported that the seawall was holding despite continued large wave activity. Meanwhile, other workers labored to repair damaged sewer lines which ran under the Strand. Taylor also informed Corps officials that two small groins which the city had built the previous winter to satisfy local property owner demands for an anti-erosion measure had proven to have contributed in a minor way to the erosion damage." Taylor had opposed the construction of these small 50-foot groin structures placed at Wisconsin Avenue and 600 feet downcoast from that street because of his suspicion that they would be of "little value." In the following year, the City Council approved the lengthening of both groins, rather than their removal as Taylor recommended. The Corps observers noted that the current revetment work appeared to be adequate, barring an abnormally large wave episode, but reminded Taylor that there was still no federal funding appropriated for corrective work at Oceanside.[6]

The nature of littoral movement in the Oceanside cell continued to perplex all those involved in shore protection and harbor navigation. Corps personnel knew that without lengthy observations of that movement, they could not draw up designs for either harbor construction or beach nourishment. In 1951, they asked the city's cooperation in making observations, and hoped that this would help determine the rate and direction of littoral movement.[7] Marine Corps officials at Camp Pendleton, anxious to reopen their harbor to meet the exigencies of the developing Korean conflict, finally prevailed upon the Navy in 1952 to approve funding for a study of harbor modifications to be conducted by the Corps of Engineers. In this $25,000 study authorized in August of that year, the Marines requested that the Corps determine the direction and rate of littoral drift, the impact of the harbor on adjacent beaches, and possible modification of the jetties to reduce shoaling. The Marine Corps also wanted the Corps of Engineers to assess the feasibility for a sand bypassing system in the Del Mar Boat Basin.[8]

The emphasis on littoral movement in the Oceanside cell yielded quick results. In March 1953, the Corps submitted a report to the Marines which observed that Oceanside beach in only two years had lost 2.5 million cubic yards of sand partially because of "upcoast movement into Camp Pendleton bulge [the accretion south of the harbor], and downcoast movement out of the area."[9] Reports such as these were beginning to reveal that drift in the Oceanside littoral cell was still quite unpredictable, and only through years of observation could accurate calculations be made. Therefore, all Corps recommendations during this period were prefaced with the disclaimer that there had not been sufficient observation of the coastal geomorphology. However, the Corps did observe with some confidence that without modifications to Del Mar Boat Basin any deposition of sand on Oceanside's beach would make its way inexorably into the entrance channel of the harbor, and thus "complete a costly cycle of artificial sand redistribution against opposing natural forces, and dredging could easily become a monthly operation."[10]

The report finally presented the Marine Corps with three modification plans, each of which called for extensive breakwater alterations. One of those, which the Marine Corps ultimately adopted with modifications, called for a 900-foot extension seaward of the north jetty; and for another 1,400-foot extension parallel to the shoreline. The south jetty, in Corps officials' opinion, should be restructured to angle in toward the north jetty end (a feature which they also recommended before the initial harbor construction) to allow waves to expand inside the turning basin, and to minimize the length of pipe needed if sand was ever bypassed under the entrance channel. The Corps estimated that with this configuration, maintenance dredging of about 500,000 cubic yards from the harbor would be required about every five years.[11]

The Interim Report, as it was entitled, increased tensions between the federal government and Oceanside, not because of its content, but because of its classification. Commissioned by the Marine Corps, the report was not a public document and therefore not distributed. When city officials learned of its existence and asked the Corps for copies, they were incensed to receive word that it was unavailable. James Dunham, one of the federal engineers working on Oceanside, had explained this to Ernest Taylor, and had given a general description of the report's content in early June 1953, but city officials wanted to have it in their possession. The Los Angeles District Engineer, Colonel William R. Shuler, was therefore obliged to describe the report to Taylor in some detail in a letter written later that month. Shuler explained, however, that he could not forward the document to the city; the Navy would have to release it to Oceanside.[12]

Equally upsetting to Oceanside officials was the fact that there had recently been a joint federal-state-county inspection of beach erosion in San Diego County, and Oceanside was not visited because of time constraints. In response to city complaints, U.S. Congressman James B. Utt of California wrote a terse letter to the Assistant Chief of Engineers for Civil Works, declaring: "The people of Oceanside are very much concerned with their erosion problem, and I respectfully urge that every consideration be given to it."[13] Dimming the prospects further for a solution to erosion problems, came the announcement that because of severe budget constraints imposed by the Korean War and President Dwight Eisenhower's domestic austerity program, funding for the Corps study of harbor improvement and shore protection at Oceanside-Camp Pendleton had been removed.[14]

Oceanside's vigorous protest of these events prompted the Corps of Engineers to hold a private meeting with the mayor and other city officials in hopes of clarifying the situation. Representing the Corps, James Dunham explained the current budget constraints to the chagrin of city officials who wanted solutions to beach erosion, progress on harbor construction, or both. On the question of the city's building of additional groins, Dunham said the Corps did not recommend it. Citing an old coastal engineering axiom, he stated, "a groin does not make a grain of sand. By this we mean that the placing of groins will not result in building a beach if there is not sufficient sand movement; also, if a groin does catch the moving sand on one side, it will starve the beach on the opposite side." While none of the Corps personnel present recommended groin construction, they added that they would not oppose the structures unless they interfered with navigation. When asked how much funding would be needed to restart the Corps study, Dunham estimated $30,000, but gave little promise that money would come soon from the federal government. After the meeting, Oceanside officials began to appeal again to their congressmen to have their city included in the cooperative study on beach erosion that was being conducted and from which their town had been omitted.[15]

While they were successful in including Oceanside in the cooperative study, problems remained in actual physical progress on erosion and harbor improvement. The city desperately needed the deposition of sand from the harbor on its beaches, but even Marine Corps plans for that action had been delayed by President Eisenhower's curbs on domestic spending. Harbor improvements for Del Mar Boat Basin had begun to be considered in concert with the building of a civilian facility. Therefore, budget managers in Washington, D.C., regarded any such Marine Corps proposals as civil projects "not in accord with the President's program." The Marines grew increasingly frustrated because they were unable to acquire funds to dredge a harbor which at that time would have served only a military purpose. When the Navy's Office of Public Works at San Diego announced that, rather than adopting the Corps' recommendation for harbor improvements, the facility would be maintained through continuous dredging, the Marines again asked the District Engineer for advice. Los Angeles District Engineer Colonel Arthur H. Frye, Jr., responded that this cost-cutting measure would probably result in more expense to the Navy within a decade than the Corps' plan would. The history of dredging the harbor in its current configuration demonstrated clearly the necessity of removing at least 100,000 cubic yards bimonthly to keep it open. Moreover, the current harbor design often did not afford safe dredging or navigation conditions and, in Frye's opinion, should be modified rather than continually maintained.[16] Through 1953, 1954, and into 1955, such fiscal constraints kept both of Oceanside's goals, as well as the Marine Corps' desire for an operable harbor, unresolved.

The Corps' beach erosion control report issued in April 1955 furthered tensions between the city and the federal government. City officials had no dispute with the findings in the *Cooperative Study of Oceanside, Ocean Beach, Imperial Beach, and Coronado, San Diego County, California* which advocated the placement of about 900,000 cubic yards of dredging material on Oceanside's beach. What they did find objectionable was the apparent reversal of the Marine Corps which would allow the material to come from the small-craft harbor site southeast of Del Mar Boat Basin. The report stated clearly that officials at Camp Pendleton "could foresee no need to the Marine Corps for a larger boat basin as compared to the loss of about 32 acres of fast land."[17]

This came as surprising and disappointing news to those in

Oceanside who believed that the Marine Corps supported not only their desires for beach restoration, but also for an adjoining civilian harbor. Newly-elected Mayor Howard Richardson complained bitterly to Senator William Knowland in Washington, D.C., about the recent turn of events; Knowland consequently directed his questions about the issue to the Corps. As he and Oceanside officials soon discovered, the rehabilitation of Camp Pendleton harbor had recently returned to being "strictly a Navy and Marine Corps problem."[18] Budgetary constraints were again at the root of these problems. The Marine Corps wanted above all other considerations to make the harbor operable, and thus were willing to go along with Navy plans to dredge the entrance channel and maintain it constantly — if it would get the harbor open. Because of its lower initial costs in comparison to other alternatives, the Navy still viewed this plan as the most economical despite Corps contentions to the contrary. Oceanside again appeared to be alone with its problems.

At this opportune time, the city of Oceanside's long-range plans began to yield results. In November 1955, Leeds, Hill, and Jewett, the consulting firm commissioned by the city in 1949, submitted its report on shore protection and small-craft harbor development in the Oceanside area. The firm released the report in time for consideration in a committee of the California state legislature concerned with marine affairs and harbor development. The committee endorsed the "Chain of Harbors Concept," first mentioned in a 1947 Corps report on small-craft facilities on the California coast. The concept suggested that coastal shelters should be spaced no more than thirty to fifty miles apart for a number of safety and economic reasons. At that time, no civilian harbor existed between Newport Beach and San Diego Harbor, a distance of ninety statute miles. The report pointed out that Oceanside was almost exactly equidistant from those two harbors.[19] The Leeds, Hill, and Jewett study made an impressive bid for a small-craft harbor at Oceanside. The forty-five-page report contained a wealth of scientific and demographic data, as well as endorsements from the U.S. Coast Guard and the National Beach Erosion Board, both of which arrived unequivocably at the conclusion that a civilian harbor was needed badly in northern San Diego County — and that Oceanside was the most logical and economical place to build one.[20]

HARBOR CONFIGURATION, 1958

←——— Del Mar Boat Basin

——— Del Mar South Jetty extension

North Breakwater extension

Still hampered by budget constraints, the Marine Corps at Camp Pendleton continued efforts to work within the Navy guidelines to reopen the harbor. In 1958, the Navy began construction on a version of the Corps' recommended improvements to the harbor breakwaters. This amounted to lengthening the north breakwater by 2,300 feet (one-third of the extension in line with the outer arm, and the other two-thirds angling roughly paralled with the shoreline), and the south jetty by 300 feet. While giving some additional protection from shoaling, the lengthened breakwaters further aggravated erosion downcoast and provided only short use of the harbor before the new entrance was also unnavigable. However, Corps officials believed that this design would best suit the small-craft harbor expansion if it took place.[21] The Marines remained uninterested in, or at least unenthusiastic over the plan for sharing an entrance channel with the city during the construction of the breakwater extensions. However, when the harbor again shoaled in little more than one year later, they were faced with the same problem anew.

Thereafter, a number of factors began to move in favor of Oceanside. Most important was the increasing cooperation among the people interested in arriving at a solution. Three individuals were particularly instrumental during the late 1950s in efforts to make the small-craft harbor and shore protection at Oceanside a reality. For the Corps of Engineers, William Herron of the Los Angeles District Beach Erosion Section began to coordinate affairs for the federal government in its relations with Oceanside. He continued a pattern of steady and able direction of the Corps' role in Oceanside established by the retiring James Dunham. Also instrumental in this effort were newly-elected Mayor Erwin Sklar and a consulting engineer for the city employed by Leeds, Hill, and Jewett, Omar Lillevang. Already a self-made millionaire, upon his election Sklar made his mayoral goals the establishment of a harbor for Oceanside and the restoration of its beaches. "A very dynamic person who believed in direct action," Sklar turned all of his energies and personal resources into these goals. He had "no patience with bureaucratic red tape," and traveled frequently to Washington, D.C. and Sacramento to expedite any needed legislative matters. Moreover, Sklar developed a good relationship with the commandant of Camp Pendleton, and approached him directly about Marine Corps recalcitrance toward the joint military-civilian harbor. Sklar's success in Washington was augmented significantly by the strong support of Congressman Utt, an advocate of the Oceanside harbor plan. Lillevang had been working for the city in recent years, developing an engineering study of the harbor design. By 1959, he was completing an elaborate plan which included a layout of the harbor in relation to Del Mar Boat Basin, taking into consideration both wave action and littoral movement. Sklar, Lillevang, and Herron all agreed that the harbor was a good idea. They also agreed that although the Corps had studies underway for harbor feasibility, federal fiscal constraints would likely require the city to finance the construction of the facility alone.[22]

With these well-defined plans at hand, Sklar approached the Marines. In an impromptu meeting with the new commandant at Camp Pendleton, Major General Reginald H. Ridgely, he asked: "General, why is it we can never get the time of day from you people when we want to talk about a harbor? You don't even know what we want to do and yet you say we can't do it." Unprepared for such a direct approach, the startled commandant invited Sklar to come to Camp Pendleton and show him the city's plans. At the meeting, Lillevang revealed his layout of the harbor, and Ridgely expressed his favor toward it, but he told those present that any approval would be contingent on the assurance that it would not interfere with Marine Corps operations. Sklar assured him that the city would begin a thorough investigation of proposed harbor operations with critical comments from the Los Angeles District Corps office.[23]

Five months later, Lillevang and Herron met with the Marines at Camp Pendleton to present their completed plan. It seemed to address most of the Marines' concern about boat traffic and interference with operations, and Herron gave a favorable assessment from the Corps' perspective. The Marines agreed that the Corps of Engineers should move forward and prepare a technical review of Lillevang's plan, and then draw up a draft of an interim report of potential harbor designs.[24]

Sklar's leadership, Lillevang's technical expertise, and Herron's advisory and liaison skills fueled momentum toward the joint military-civilian small-craft harbor. Sklar coordinated matters with his city council, drawing up a resolution establishing intent to build a harbor, and placing a bond initiative to fund it before the city's voters. His aggressive style succeeded again and again in averting bureaucratic logjams, and expedited progress. Lillevang continued to fine-tune specific design and configuration for the harbor, while keeping in close contact with the Los Angeles District. Herron meanwhile directed the Corps' review of Oceanside's harbor design and, in October 1958, issued an interim report of findings to the Marine Corps. The report endorsed both the concept and plan, arguing that the harbor would be beneficial to all parties concerned. While the Marines and the Navy considered these recommendations, Los Angeles District Engineer Colonel Carroll T. Newton continued momentum for Oceanside by successfully transferring $13,000 in fiscal year 1959 funds from another harbor study in order to finish the "urgently needed" Camp Pendleton-Agua Hedionda Lagoon harbor and shore protection study.[25]

The Corps had remained as active on the issue of beach erosion near Oceanside as fiscal restraints would allow. After the 1946 mandate to assess the extent of beach erosion caused by military structures at Oceanside, the Corps prepared an extensive report and submitted it to Congress in 1956. The report argued that in the Oceanside area, federal responsibility for damages to the beach and structures downcoast of Del Mar Boat Basin might exceed one-third of the cost for repair and restoration.[26] As a result, Congress authorized the Corps to conduct further studies to determine the extent of federal aid which should be appropriated for restoration "without regard to limitations of federal law applicable to beach erosion control."[27]

While the Corps completed this study, beach erosion at Oceanside grew worse. Congressman James Utt, at the urging of Mayor Sklar, guided an emergency bill through Congress which appropriated $289,000 for beach erosion control in San Diego County. Meanwhile, the Navy came to the immediate rescue of Oceanside in carrying out its planned harbor modifications. From April 1957 through May 1958, its dredging operations from the new entrance channel placed 800,000 cubic yards of badly-needed sand on Oceanside beaches, thereby protecting exposed sewer lines and the frontage street from damage. Unfortunately, the harbor modifications not only failed to prevent shoaling, they were unsuccessful in arresting erosion as most of the dredged sand made its way back into the harbor within one year.[28] That amount of upcoast movement was a surprise even to careful observers of littoral drift, and reinforced the belief that at best the phenomenon was unpredictable.

Despite the uncertain impact that an even larger harbor would have on the city's beaches, residents voted overwhelmingly in favor of the bond issue for the small-craft facility. The positive aspects of the harbor far outweighed its drawbacks, and the momentum that had begun nearly a decade before increased dramatically in the late 1950s. Anticipation that the Corps' equity study, scheduled for release in 1960, would place the majority of responsibility for beach restoration on the federal government helped to allay some of the city's fears about erosion. If the harbor was constructed along Lillevang's guidelines, the site would also be the "borrow pit" for material to deposit on the city's beaches. Therefore, shore protection and small-craft harbor development would be accomplished in one operation. This feature helped the city acquire a one-million-dollar loan from the California Division of Small Craft Harbors to assist in the cost of building the harbor.[29]

While many of the Corps' engineers had reservations about harbor expansion at Oceanside because of the potential impact to downcoast beaches, they now believed that the benefits outweighed the negative aspects. A harbor already existed north of Oceanside, and legislators, government officials, and the public demanded construction of a new civilian facility somewhere in northern San Diego County. Rather than disrupt another section of the coast with another system of structures, the engineers agreed that it would be more judicious to modify and expand Del Mar Boat Basin. Keeping erosion problems caused by harbor structures concentrated in one area, they believed, was sound coastal management. Moreover, a majority of the people in Oceanside wanted the harbor built there. Coastal engineers would simply have to find ways to keep the beach to the south intact at the same time. Thereafter, Sklar and Lillevang undertook the potentially difficult task of acquiring the land needed for the borrow pit and the harbor. Willing to use his own personal wealth to expedite matters, Sklar took his cause to the nation's capital on several occasions in 1959 and 1960. With Lillevang there to outline the technical aspects of the project, they set out to persuade the Secretary of the Navy to relinquish 67 acres to Oceanside for dredging material and for a harbor. A major obstacle to this was the fact that military reservations were excluded by law from sale or lease. After a number of long sessions with lawyers in the Navy Department, Oceanside officials realized that if the Marine Corps declared those 67 acres of Camp Pendleton "surplus to its needs," the Department of the Interior would then acquire title to the land. Interior could then sell the land with the proviso that it be used for public recreation. Moreover, Interior could sell the land to the city at fifty percent of its appraised value if used for recreational purposes. As a result of these careful negotiations, Oceanside acquired the Marine Corps land at a cost of only $177,500. Two factors weighed heavily in the Marine Corps reversal: the current Del Mar Boat Basin breakwater design had proven to be inadequate to retard shoaling. The Marines hoped that a new design would keep the harbor navigable for longer periods. Moreover, they knew that with the jointly-maintained entrance channel, there would be another party to share equally in the cost of maintaining navigability. At the same time, the city negotiated successfully the acquisition of an additional 33 acres of privately-owned land. The two parcels of land comprised what would become the Oceanside Small-Craft Harbor.[30]

In early 1960, the Corps in Los Angeles held a conference on federal cost-sharing of beach restoration at Oceanside. William Herron, who had directed the study for the Corps, explained to the conference, which included representatives from the State Department of Water Resources, that intergovernmental cooperation was essential in dealing with Oceanside's problem. Moreover, shore protection could result from the harbor construction. After examining the collected data on Oceanside, all the conferees agreed that federal responsibility would most likely be one hundred percent, and "any material dredged to maintain the harbor should be placed on the downcoast beach at no local cost." They also agreed that the required shore protection — probably about 1.5 million cubic yards of material — must be impounded from northward drift by a groin on the north end of Oceanside beach. According to Herron, the groin was a "necessary modification" to harbor improvement, for without it the sand placed on the beach would drift back into the harbor just as it had in 1958 and 1959. Furthermore, if and when the small-craft harbor was constructed, the groin would become part of the south jetty of that facility. Later that month, the Division Engineer in San Francisco approved the study. Three months later the Corps' Beach Erosion Board also approved it.[31]

During the summer of 1960, the Corps, the California Department of Water Resources, and the City of Oceanside began to work out an agreement on responsibilities for pursuing a beach erosion control project at Oceanside. As Congress reviewed the Corps' findings on beach erosion, Oceanside officials secured advances from the State of California for part of the expense of the cooperative beach erosion control project. This was in anticipation that federal funds would reimburse the city in the event of the government's acceptance of full responsibility. In efforts to secure full federal responsibility, California Senator Thomas Kuchel introduced a bill into the U.S. Senate in August 1960 that called for a federally-funded beach erosion project for Oceanside. "By reasons of the exigencies of the military situation in that area," Kuchel announced on the Senate floor, "there has been, I regret to say, a considerable beach erosion problem arise near the City of Oceanside, a problem recognized by the Department of Defense."[32] Congress authorized the project in September.

The rush to get the erosion project underway was prompted by the dangerously narrowing beach which many believed might be further undermined by the coming winter storms. Unfortunately, the waves did not wait until the winter season to do their damage. Late in July, a tropical disturbance in the South Pacific sent

Oceanside waterfront, 1960, after the beach was destroyed by
wave action.

unusually powerful erosive waves to Oceanside's exposed beach.
During this event, an area north of the pier extending to the city's
northerly boundary—which had been losing sand all year—
became completely denuded, exposing sewer lines and uncovering
the foundations of the street pavement. The sand escarpment
which protected the Strand had shrunk to a precarious eight feet in
width, and waves threatened to damage the pavement itself. Unable
to wait for federal funding, the city began emergency rock hauling
on 31 July without obtaining authorization from the Corps of
Engineers. The following day, city officials dispatched a fleet of
earth-moving vehicles which began hauling sand from the proposed small-craft harbor site to the northern beach in the hope of
averting the collapse of both the sewer pipes and the Strand.[33]

Oceanside City Engineer Alton Ruden believed strongly that
the measures were necessary, although they were not yet authorized by the Corps of Engineers. Congress had approved the beach
erosion control project in September 1960, but the city's beach
could not await funding that still had to go through appropriations.
For six days in August, earth-movers rolled unceasingly during

low tide from the borrow pit to the beach, placing 17,000 cubic yards of material on the most critically-eroded spots. Yet the southern swell continued into September. Late in the month sand hauling had begun again with the city paying for another 23,720 cubic yards of fill. During this haul, Ruden wrote Herron to apprise him of the situation and the city's current action. "We are proceeding under the assumption," Ruden stated, "that this movement of sand, as well as the one concluded six weeks ago, will be authorized and included in the beach erosion control project expected to start soon."[34]

The city's willingness to take matters into its own hands in this situation was indicative of the manner in which Oceanside officials had dealt with problems in the past, and would continue to do in the future. The Oceanside city government was in fact the driving force in both harbor and beach restoration plans. The severe erosion problems threatened into October. Ernest Taylor, City Manager for Oceanside, appealed to the Corps to expedite in any way possible the authorized beach erosion project and attached a report on the recent emergency written by Ruden. In closing, Ruden reported with exasperation: "If the severe Southern swell does not stop within one or two days, it appears that we will be unable to save either the sewer or the Strand." Fortunately for the city, the large southern swells ceased by November 1960.[35]

Confident that they would be reimbursed for their work and fearful of new erosion, city officials continued to contract the hauling of additional sand from the borrow pit and small-craft harbor site. By the end of 1961, two separate haulings had placed more than 481,000 cubic yards onto the badly-eroded beach. During the 1961 hauling, Corps personnel cautioned that unless the city took steps to prevent the upcoast drift which had caused the fall 1960 emergency, the sand would soon be gone. They recommended that the city arrange for the construction of a groin at the north side of the San Luis Rey River mouth to intercept the upcoast drift. Oceanside responded by financing the construction of a 500-foot groin which did indeed prevent some upcoast drift, thereby protecting the north Strand for a brief period.[36]

Once the city sold $4.5 million in revenue bonds for the harbor, most of the obstacles were cleared for completion of the beach erosion project and construction of the small-craft facility. To assure that they would receive the best interest rate for the bonds, Sklar and other city officials traveled to Chicago and New York in order to familiarize underwriters of the value of the small-craft harbor. Simultaneously, the city launched a three-week "Invest in Oceanside" campaign, urging residents to invest one dollar in order to buy the first $1,000 bond. Thereafter, city officials turned their efforts to seeking reimbursement for the money spent in battling the 1960 emergency. When the bill for reimbursement became law on 29 March 1961, they were successful in that attempt as well. The legislation authorized the Secretary of the Army to reimburse the city for its efforts to save structures along its beach. The law also provided almost $1.5 million in federal funds for shore protection at Oceanside.[37] This represented another victory for the strong-willed Oceanside City Council.

The reimbursement, however, proved to be a point of contention between the Corps and the city. The statute contained the proviso that the city's claim to reimbursement be subject to the approval of the Chief of Engineers. While the Chief approved the city's claim in the first three dredging episodes, the fourth, occurring between 15 August and 8 December 1961, carried a much higher per cubic yard cost than the others. The city had hired a different contractor for this haul, and the cost to the city was 57 cents per cubic yard as opposed to 23.5 cents for the third contract. Upon assessing the claim, the Chief of Engineers argued that in light of the fact that the Corps had recently let a contract for the remainder of the dredging at a cost of 38.4 cents per cubic yard, the city should be reimbursed for total yardage at that rate only. Since the federal government was assuming the responsibility for this, and it would fall into the harbor development phase of the project, there was little choice in the matter. The net loss of $78,000 left city officials disgruntled, but resigned to the decision.[38]

Although the borrow pit which was to become the small-craft harbor site had been deepening since mid-1960, formal ground-breaking for the facility did not take place until 6 February 1961. A project nearly seventeen years in the making was now officially under way. City officials had prevailed through a long series of obstacles — including an ongoing condemnation suit of private property adjacent to the harbor site — in their quest to build a recreational harbor.[39]

Erwin Sklar's ability to influence politicians again paid off for Oceanside when he secured, with help of William Herron and Jack Coe of the California Department of Water Resources, an advance for funding of the beach erosion control project from the

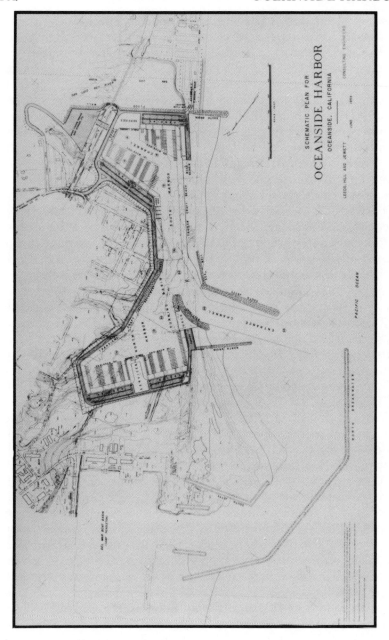

Oceanside Small-Craft Harbor design, June 1959.

state in 1961. Now also the president of the newly-formed Oceanside Small-Craft Harbor District, Sklar continued his all-out lobbying effort to expedite both development of the marina and protection of the beach. With the support and advice of Herron and Coe, Sklar went to Sacramento after passage of the federal beach erosion act in 1961. The law, in their opinion, would not appropriate funds quickly enough to provide for maximum efficiency and economy in the ongoing beach restoration. While $675,000 became available in 1962, the bulk of the federal money for restoration would not be appropriated until fiscal year 1963. By that time, the volatile waves might again remove the recently-placed sand unless additional measures were taken. City officials had fought hard but unsuccessfully in Washington to have all the money appropriated earlier. Convinced of the necessity of somehow advancing funds to the Corps so that it could complete the erosion project, they traveled to the state capitol asking for a special hearing before the assembly. Thanks to Sklar's lobbying efforts and the sponsorship of area assemblymen, a successful bill was introduced under provisions of the California Water Code which authorized the advance of state funds, interest-free, for Oceanside to forward to the Corps of Engineers. Thus the State Department of Water Resources, in August 1961, advanced the city $1.221 million for that purpose.[40] This unprecedented action in which a state advanced funds for a future federal project was indicative of the political acumen and resolve that Oceanside officials demonstrated.

With fiscal 1962 funds, Corps officials took steps to protect Oceanside's beach, prevent harbor shoaling, and create an essential component of the small-craft facility. The engineers accomplished these three goals in one effort: the construction of what would become the small-craft harbor south jetty. Completed in 1961, this 1,000-foot stone wall worked in conjunction with the Camp Pendleton north breakwater to form the new harbor entrance channel. This was an integral part of the plan developed by city engineers and modified and refined by Corps personnel. In 1962, the Corps built a 710-foot groin whose longitudinal top elevation closely followed the hydrographic contours. The seaward-most end of the groin had a top elevation of about 13 feet (MLLW). In subsequent years this groin settled into the bottom and became known as the submerged groin. The funds advanced by the state of California allowed the Corps to contract dredging of 2.2 million

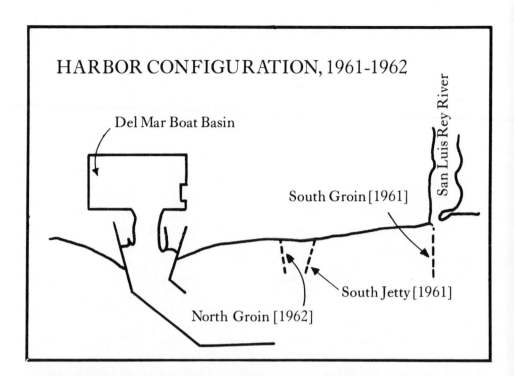

HARBOR CONFIGURATION, 1961-1962

Del Mar Boat Basin

San Luis Rey River

South Groin [1961]

South Jetty [1961]

North Groin [1962]

Beach restoration, 1961-62.

cubic yards of material from both the harbor site and the entrance channel of Del Mar Boat Basin.[41] During the harbor construction period, the Corps of Engineers deposited sand from the Camp Pendleton boat basin entrance channel and fill from the harbor excavation site, while the city used a portion of its harbor funds to dredge the inlet to the proposed facility. By February 1963, nearly four million cubic yards of new material lay on Oceanside beach.[42]

Members of the Oceanside Small-Craft Harbor District predicted optimistically at groundbreaking that the marina would be ready for partial use by the fall of 1962. Two factors made this prediction inaccurate. First, they had not sufficiently considered the impact of weather on the construction schedule. Second, they had not foreseen that the Corps' dredging contractor in the entrance channel would experience nearly two months of down time. The contractor, Standard Dredging Company of New York, had been the lowest bidder for the work and by law was therefore offered the job. On 22 June 1962, while operating in open seas around the entrance channel, the main pump motor on the Standard dredge burned out. One month later, Oceanside City Manager Franklin Lilley complained to the District Engineer in Los Angeles that dredging had stopped, and this was creating a twofold problem. With the coming of another storm season, Oceanside was left with a beach that was still largely unprotected. "We had anticipated," Lilley stated, "that by this time a large portion of our beach would have been restored. If this were so, we would be well protected against normal storms." He also expressed concern that such delays would postpone the harbor opening, and asked when the dredging would resume. About two weeks after Lilley's inquiry the barge returned after being repaired at Long Beach, and the company resumed dredging. This delay — coupled with the fact that Standard, through poor scheduling, had dredged in waters protected by the north breakwater during the calmest weather period of the year — not only retarded progress on the harbor, but also kept the beach partially exposed to winter waves. This forced Standard to dredge during the height of the storm season and involved the Corps in litigation with the company lasting until the late 1960s.[43]

As harbor construction neared completion, Oceanside Small-Craft Harbor District officials faced new challenges. Unlike harbors that were built entirely with federal funds, the Oceanside facility would present a host of maintenance and jurisdictional problems to the city when completed. The Harbor District board believed that it had solved most of the potential problems in sharing the entrance channel with the Marine Corps, but in the summer of 1962 the directors began to deal with the issue of maintenance. As the harbor opened and its slips began to fill to capacity, they predicted that the District would eventually be able to meet its expenses and turn a profit. Until that time, however, the directors worried that the harbor would operate at a loss, and they would be unable to meet the cost of maintenance dredging at even the most optimistic intervals of necessity.

Sklar's leadership as president again proved instrumental as the board prepared to head off this problem. He drafted a letter to Los Angeles District Engineer Colonel William T. Bradley that outlined the virtues and benefits of the harbor to both citizens and the government, and appealed to the federal government to take on the responsibility of maintaining the navigation features there. As the Oceanside harbor would provide anyone who wished to use it all of the facilities offered in a federally-built marina, and the Corps had approved the construction design, he argued: "it appears logical that favorable consideration may be given to the assumption of the maintenance responsibility for the general navigation facilities by the Federal Government." Sklar and the directors hoped that the Corps would include navigation feasibility in an ongoing study of navigation in the Camp Pendleton-Agua Hedionda Lagoon area. (This was a revival of the study first authorized in 1948, but terminated when Oceanside decided to develop its own harbor.) While awaiting an answer from the Corps, the directors hired Omar Lillevang of Leeds, Hill, and Jewett to prepare a design study of the navigation features of the harbor to present to the federal government.[44]

The proposal presented somewhat of a problem for the Los Angeles District because there was no authorization to maintain the harbor. There was, however, a precedent established when the Corps assumed navigation responsibility at Pascagoula Harbor in Mississippi in 1961. Lee R. Henning, the Acting Chief of the Engineering Division in Los Angeles, wrote the Division Engineer in definite support of the idea. He cited the savings that the city had rendered to the government by taking on the harbor construction and combining it with the beach erosion project, and also pointed out that this harbor was vital to both the Marine Corps and recreational users throughout southern California. Moreover, he added in closing: "Mr. Sklar . . . has informed me that he plans a personal visit to OCE in the near future to further discuss the Harbor District's request for Federal assistance." In October 1962, the Division Engineer recommended to the Office of the Chief of Engineers that the feasibility study be authorized at once.[45]

Because of Sklar's initiative and lobbying, the quality of Lillevang's report submitted on 8 March 1963, and a favorable recommendation after the review by Herron and the Shore Protection Section, Congress received a report in 1965 that endorsed the Corps' assumption of navigation responsibilities wholeheartedly. In October, as a part of the Rivers and Harbors Act of 1965, Congress authorized federal responsibility for maintenance of the Oceanside and Camp Pendleton harbor entrance, and also directed that all dredged material be placed on the downcoast beaches.[46]

The Oceanside Small-Craft Harbor opened officially in June 1963. The new facility that eventually offered 600 rental slips was a triumph for the city, the state, and the federal government. The initiative belonged primarily to city officials such as Sklar and Lillevang, but their efforts would have been futile if not for the assistance and cooperation of elected officials, those who worked closely on the project from state government, and the Los Angeles District of the Corps of Engineers. As Herron remembered, "all were in favor of the harbor." All of their concerted efforts were required to bring the harbor to reality. Cooperation of the Marine Corps and the Department of the Navy was also essential in moving the project forward. When the need arose for a restricted zone which would exclude civilian vessels, the city, the Corps, and the Marines again cooperated in achieving this quickly and efficiently.[47]

The joint military-civilian harbor was at last a reality, and an immediate success as slips rented quickly. Moreover, the millions of cubic yards of fill placed on the beach to the south restored it to its pre-war condition. Oceanside city officials had aggressively pursued a plan which they believed would benefit a broad spectrum of social and economic groups in southern California, including the Marine Corps at Camp Pendleton. At the same time, coastal experts with the Corps of Engineers, recognizing the popular demand for a civilian facility in northern San Diego County, gave their endorsement and assistance in the planning and construction of Oceanside Small-Craft Harbor. Not only would there be a

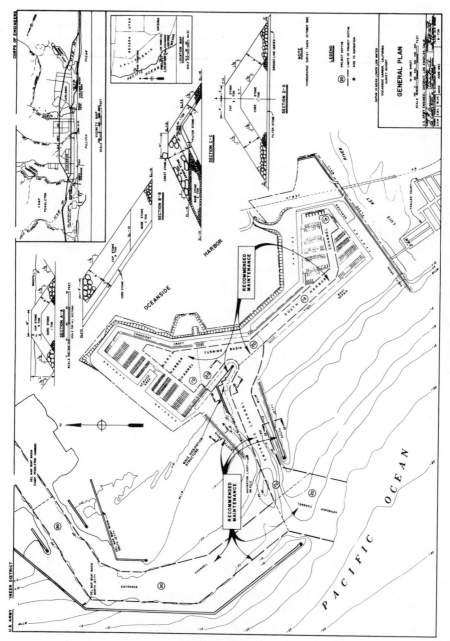

Oceanside Harbor General Plan, 1963.

Aerial view of Oceanside Harbor and the Del Mar Boat Basin, 1963.

better-designed harbor, downcoast erosion would remain concentrated in an area which already had breakwater disruption.
Moreover, the harbor construction would result in beach restoration at the site of the most extreme erosion. The city of Oceanside
had both its harbor and its beach, and the Marine Corps again had
a useable boat basin. Through the early and mid-1960s nearly
everyone was happy with the situation at Oceanside.

NOTES

¹Report, "Shore Protection Report on Preliminary Examination of Harbor at Camp Pendleton, California," Los Angeles District, U.S. Army Corps of Engineers, 1 Feb. 1950, Oceanside and Camp Pendleton Historical file, LNNA RG 77/64A-0951, Box 1/4.

²*Ibid.* The authors of the report believed that after about two years, the sand had built up sufficiently around the harbor jetties to nourish the beach on the south end of Oceanside.

³*Ibid.* The authorization for the survey from the Chief of Engineers came with the acceptance of a federal cost estimated at $53,000. See Brigadier General W.D. Potter, Acting Assistant Chief of Engineers for Civil Works, to Division Engineer, South Pacific Division, subj: Survey of Harbor at Camp Pendleton Harbor, CA, file, 1946-74, LNNA RG 77/80-0033 Box 6/20.

⁴Division Engineer, South Pacific Division, to President, Beach Erosion Board, Washington, D.C., subj: Camp Pendleton Harbor with a View to Shore Protection, 20 June 1950, Camp Pendleton Harbor, CA, file, 1946-74, LNNA 77/80-0033, Box 6/20. For a complete history of the Beach Erosion Board, see Mary-Louise Quinn, *The History of the Beach Erosion Board, U.S. Army, Corps of Engineers, 1930-1963* (Fort Belvoir, VA: U.S. Army Corps of Engineers, Coastal Engineering Research Center Miscellaneous Report, 77-9, 1977).

⁵*Ibid.;* General J.S. Bragdon, Acting Chief of Engineers, to Senator William F. Knowland, subj: Beach erosion, Oceanside, 20 July 1950, Camp Pendleton Harbor, CA, file, 1946-74, LNNA RG 77/80-0033 Box 6/20; Report, "Design Analysis and Cost Estimates: Plans of Protection for Oceanside," Los Angeles District, U.S. Army, Corps of Engineers, Oceanside and Camp Pendleton Historical file, LNNA RG 77/64A-0951 Box 2/4.

⁶Lt. Col W.R. Shuler, Los Angeles District Engineer, to Brig. Gen. C.H. Chorpening, Asst. Chief of Engineers for Civil Works, subj: Storm damage to Strand at Oceanside, 11 June 1951, Camp Pendleton Harbor, CA, file, 1946-74, LNNA RG 77/80-0033 Box 6/20.

⁷Lt. Col. J.G. Jones, Acting Chief of Engineering Division, Los Angeles District, to Ernest Taylor, Supt. of Streets, Oceanside, CA, subj: Flourescent sand experiments, 2 Mar. 1951, Camp Pendleton Harbor, CA, file, 1946-74, LNNA RG 77/80-0033 Box 6/20; Lt. Col. John R. Jannarone, Los Angeles District to E. Taylor, subj: Beach erosion observations, 6 Dec. 1951, Oceanside Project Cost Estimates File, 1946-61, LNNA 77/80-0034 Box 18/20.

⁸Interview, William J. Herron, Jr. (Taped answers to questions sent by author), Sun City, AZ, 8 April 1986. Hereafter cited as Herron interview; Report, "Letter Interim Survey Report on Harbor Entrance Improvement, Camp Pendleton, CA," Los Angeles District, U.S. Army, Corps of Engineers, Camp Pendleton Harbor-Del Mar Boat Basin File, 1955, LNNA RG 77/83-0001 Box 8/20.

⁹*Ibid.*

¹⁰*Ibid.*

¹¹*Ibid.;* The plan recommended in the report was similar to a design already in use in Santa Barbara Harbor, CA.

¹²Col. W.R. Shuler to E. Taylor, subj: Camp Pendleton Harbor report, 12 June 1951, Camp Pendleton Harbor, CA, file, 1946-74, Oceanside, LNNA RG 77/80-0033 Box 6/20.

¹³Brig. Gen. C.A. Chorpening, to U.S. Congressman James B. Utt, subj: Cooperative beach erosion inspection which bypassed Oceanside, 17 July 1953, Oceanside Project Cost Estimates file, 1946-61, LNNA 77/80-0034 Box 18/20.

¹⁴Minutes, Notes in Connection with a Conversation with U.S. Engineers, 30 July 1953, Camp Pendleton Harbor, CA, file, 1946-74, LNNA 77/80-0033 Box 6/20. Oceanside officials tried unsuccessfully to secure this document for two years. See Charles T. Leeds, Leeds, Hill, and Jewett, Consultants, to Frank Lilley, Administrative Officer, Oceanside, subj: Acquisition of Interim Report, 28 June 1955, Camp Pendleton Harbor, CA, file, 1946-74, LNNA RG 77/80-0033 Box 6/20.

¹⁵Minutes, Notes in Connection with a Conversation with U.S. Engineers, 30 June 1953, Camp Pendleton Harbor, CA, file, 1946-74, LNNA RG 77/80-0033 Box 6/20; R.O. Eaton, Beach Erosion Board, to Brig. Gen. Warren T. Hannum, California Dept. of Natural Resources, subj: Lack of funding for a beach erosion study, 19 Aug. 1953, Oceanside Project Cost Estimates file, 1946-1961, LNNA RG 77/80-0034 Box 18/20; F. Lilley to William Herron, Jr., Shore Protection Section, Los Angeles District, U.S. Army, Corps of Engineers, subj: Beach erosion study, 18 March 1955, Oceanside Project Cost Estimates file, 1946-61, LNNA RG 77/80-0034 Box 18/20.

¹⁶Col. Arthur H. Frye, Jr., Los Angeles District Engineer, to District Public Works Officer, Eleventh Naval District, San Diego, CA, Del Mar Boat Basin Improvements, 8 July 1954, Camp Pendleton Harbor, CA file, 1946-74, LNNA 77/80-0033 Box 6/20; W.M. Brown, San Diego District Naval Public Works Officer, to Los Angeles District Engineer, subj: Del Mar Boat Basin improvements, 1 July 1954, Camp Pendleton Harbor, CA file, 1946-74, LNNA RG 77/80-0033 Box 6/20; Lt. Col. Robert N. Schwartz, Executive Officer, U.S. Army Corps of Engineers, to San Diego District Naval Public Works Officer, subj: Del Mar Boat Basin improvement, 17 Jan. 1955, Camp Pendleton Harbor, CA, file, 1946-74, LNNA RG 77/80-0033 Box 6/20.

¹⁷Report, "Beach Erosion Control Report on Cooperative Study of Oceanside, Ocean Beach, Imperial Beach, and Coronado," Los Angeles District, U.S. Army, Corps of Engineers, (11 April 1955), Oceanside and Camp Pendleton Historical file, LNNA RG 77/64A-0951 Box 2/4.

¹⁸Howard T. Richardson, Mayor, Oceanside, CA, to U.S. Senator William F. Knowland, subj: Oceanside beach erosion problems, 16 Sept. 1955, Oceanside Project Cost Estimates File, 1946-61, LNNA RG 77/80-0034 Box 18/20; Brig. Gen. E.C. Itschner, Assistant Chief of Engineers for Civil Works, to Sen. Knowland, subj: Oceanside beach erosion measures, 3 Nov. 1955, Oceanside Project Cost Estimates file, 1946-61, LNNA RG 77/80-0034 Box 18/20; Col. A. Frye to Charles R. Crull, City Engineer, Oceanside, subj: Harbor maintenance, 31 May 1956, Camp Pendleton Harbor, CA, file, 1946-74, LNNA RG 77/80-0033 Box 6/20.

¹⁹See "Joint Interim Committee of the California State Legislature on Marine Affairs and Bay Area Development to the 1955 General Session of the Legislature," for a discussion of the Chain of Harbors concept; California State Legislature, *An Act Relating to the Development of Small-Craft Harbors and Waterways by the State Lands Commission*, California Assembly Bill 2939 (1955); Report, "Preliminary Examination Report, Coast of Southern California, with a View to the Establishment of Harbors for Light-Draft Vessels, (30 June 1947), Los Angeles District, U.S. Army Corps of Engineers, Report Bibliography, Oceanside Harbor-River Improvement Survey file, LNNA RG 77/83-0006 Box 1/12; Herron interview.

²⁰Leeds, Hill, and Jewett, *Shore Protection and Small-Craft Harbor Development in the Oceanside-Camp Pendleton Area, California* (Los Angeles: Leeds, Hill, and Jewett, Inc., 1955), pp. i, ii, iii-iv, 20-26, 31, 34, 38, 42-43.

²¹Herron, *Oral History*, p. 8-6; Moffat and Nichol, Engineers, *Experimental Sand Bypass System at Oceanside, California: Phase I Report: Data Collection and Analysis* (Los Angeles: Moffat and Nichol, 1983), p. 1-11; Report, Resumé of Camp Pendleton Situation, Los Angeles District, U.S. Army, Corps of Engineers, 17 June 1963, Oceanside file 1961-62, LNNA RG 77/84-0018 Box 7/8. Hereafter cited as Camp Pendleton resumé.

²²Herron interview.

²³Herron *Oral History*, pp. 8-9, 8-11; Maj. Gen. R.A. Ridgely, U.S. Marine Corps, Camp Pendleton, to Erwin Sklar, Mayor, Oceanside, CA, subj: Marine Corps position on a joint military-civilian harbor, 4 Feb. 1958, Camp Pendleton Harbor, CA, file, 1946-74, LNNA RG 77/80-0033 Box 6/20.

²⁴W. Herron to Los Angeles District Engineer, memorandum, subj: Camp Pendleton Harbor Study, 14 July 1958, Camp Pendleton Harbor, CA, file, 1946-74, LNNA RG 77/80-0033 Box 6/20.

[25]Oceanside City Council, "Resolution of Necessity and of Intent and Capability of the City of Oceanside to Establish and Operate a Harbor," 7 Aug. 1958, Camp Pendleton Harbor, CA, file, 1946-74, LNNA RG 77/80-0033 Box 6/20; Herron interview; Report, "Interim Report on Feasibility of Locating a Proposed Recreational Harbor Entrance in the Lee of the Extended Breakwater at Del Mar Boat Basin, Camp Pendleton, California," Los Angeles District, U.S. Army, Corps of Engineers, Oct. 1958, Camp Pendleton Harbor-Del Mar Boat Basin File, 1955, LNNA RG 77/83-0001 Box 8/20; Col. C.T. Newton, Los Angeles District Engineer, to Division Engineer, South Pacific Division, 9 Dec. 1958, subj: Transfer of funds for continuation of Camp Pendleton-Agua Hedionda Lagoon harbor and shore protection study, 9 Dec. 1958, Camp Pendleton Harbor, CA, file, 1946-74, LNNA RG 77/80-0033 Box 6/20; Chief, Engineering Division, Los Angeles District, to San Francisco District Engineer, subj: Authority to transfer funds to Camp Pendleton study, 29 Mar. 1959, Oceanside Project Cost Estimates File, 1946-61, LNNA RG 77/80-0034 Box 18/20.

[26]See U.S. Congress, House, *Report of the Chief of Engineers on Beach Erosion, Vicinity of Oceanside, CA*, Pub. L. 84-520, 84th Cong., 2d sess., 1956, for a discussion of this problem.

[27]*Federal Assistance Act for Beach Erosion Control*, 72 Stat. 304 (1956).

[28]U.S., Congress, Senate, *An Act Authorizing the Construction, Repair, and Preservation of Certain Public Works on Rivers and Harbors for Navigation, Flood Control, and Other Purposes*, Pub. L. 85-500, 85th Cong., 2d sess., 1958, S. 3910, *passim*; Moffat and Nichol, Engineers, *Experimental Sand Bypass System at Oceanside, California: Phase I Report: Data Collection and Analysis*, p. 1-11; Leeds, Hill, and Jewett, *Beach Erosion at Oceanside, California, and Compensatory Grant of Federal Land* (Los Angeles: Leeds, Hill, and Jewett, 1959), *passim*. (Located in Oceanside Beach Nourishment file, 1959-60, LNNA RG 77/84-0018 Box 6/8.)

[29]Oceanside City Council, "Resolution of Necessity and of Intent and Capability of the City of Oceanside to Establish and Operate a Harbor, #58-59," 10 Sept. 1958, Oceanside Beach Nourishment file, 1959-60, LNNA RG 77/84-0018 Box 6/8; Oceanside City Council, "Resolution Adopting Schematic Plan of Oceanside Harbor and Directing that a Request be Made to the Federal Government for the Land Necessary Therefore, #58-68," 10 Sept. 1958, Oceanside Beach Nourishment file, 1959-60, LNNA RG 77/84-0018 Box 6/8; Herron, *Oral History*, p. 8-11.

[30]Leeds, Hill, and Jewett, *Beach Erosion at Oceanside, passim*; Adm. F.A. Bantz, Asst. Sec. of Navy, to E. Sklar, 14 Jan. 1959, subj: Navy position on sharing joint military-civilian harbor entrance, 14 Jan. 1959, Oceanside Project Cost Estimate file, 1946-61, LNNA RG 77/80-0034 box 18/20; Herron, *Oral History*, p. 8-11; Herron interview; History of Project, Oceanside, Anthony Turhollow personal files, Los Angeles District, U.S. Army, Corps of Engineers. Hereafter cited as Turhollow history.

[31]Memorandum for the record from W. Herron, subj: Conference on Oceanside equity study, 11 Feb. 1959, Oceanside Beach Nourishment file, 1959-60, LNNA RG 77/84-0018 Box 6/8; W. Herron to Los Angeles District Engineer, subj: Groin construction at Oceanside, undated 1960, Oceanside Beach Nourishment file, 1959-60, LNNA RG 77/84-0018 Box 6/8; Los Angeles District Engineer to South Pacific Division Engineer, 25 Feb. 1960, subj: Cooperative beach erosion control study of coast of San Diego County, 25 Feb. 1960, Oceanside Beach Nourishment file, 1959-60, LNNA RG 77/84-0018 Box 6/8; F.J. Hortig, California State Lands Commission, to City of Oceanside, subj: Permit approval for groins, seawall, jetty, and revetment, 25 Feb. 1960, Oceanside Project Cost Estimate file, 1946-61, LNNA RG 77/80-0034 Box 18/20.

[32]California Department of Water Resources to F. Lilley, City Manager, Oceanside, subj: Agreement between the Dept. and the City for construction of beach erosion control project, 3 Aug. 1960, Oceanside Beach Nourishment file, 1959-60, LNNA RG 77/84-0018 Box 6/8; Los Angeles District Engineer to South Pacific Division Engineer, subj: Oceanside's ability to finance the needed groin for beach erosion control, 21 Sept. 1960, Oceanside Beach Nourishment file, 1959-60, LNNA RG 77/84-0018 Box 6/8; Oceanside City Council, "Resolution Specifying City Responsibilities in Federal Beach Erosion

Control Project, #60-105," Oceanside Beach Nourishment file, 1959-60, LNNA RG 77/84-0018 Box 6/8; U.S. Congress, Senate, Sen. Thomas Kuchel speaking in favor of *A Bill to Provide Beach Erosion Control in San Diego County*, S. 3838, 86th Cong., 2d sess., 12 Aug. 1960, *Congressional Record* 106: 16247; Request for Construction of Beach Erosion Control Project at Oceanside, California from Walter G. Schulz, Chief Engineer, Division of Design and Construction, 2 Aug. 1960, Oceanside Beach Nourishment file, 1959-60, LNNA RG 77/84-0018 Box 6/8; H.W. Thompson, Chief, Engineering Division, Los Angeles District, to John R. Teerink, California Department of Water Resources, subj: Beach erosion control project, 10 Aug. 1960, Oceanside Beach Nourishment file, 1959-60, LNNA RG 77/84-0018 Box 6/8; F. Lilley to J. Teerink, subj: Cost sharing of beach erosion control project, 15 Aug. 1960, Oceanside Beach Nourishment file, 1959-60, LNNA RG 77/84-0018 Box 6/8; J. Teerink to Los Angeles District Engineer, subj: Transmittal of approval of cooperative beach erosion control project, 15 Sept. 1960, Oceanside Beach Nourishment file, 1959-60, LNNA RG 77/84-0018 Box 6/8; 106 *Cong. Rec.*, 16247.

[33] Alton Ruden, City Engineer, Oceanside, to W. Herron, subj: Emergency measures in response to severe beach erosion, 30 Sept. 1960, Oceanside Beach Nourishment file, 1959-60, LNNA RG 77/84-0018 Box 6/8.

[34] *Ibid.*; F. Lilley to Los Angeles District, subj: Emergency measures to erosion, Sept. 1960, Oceanside Beach Nourishment file, 1959-60, LNNA RG 77/84-0018 Box 6/8; E. Taylor to Los Angeles District, subj: Photographs of Oceanside beach, 10 Oct. 1960, Oceanside Beach Nourishment file, 1959-60, LNNA RG 77/84-0018 Box 6/8.

[35] *Ibid.*; E. Taylor to Los Angeles District, subj: Emergency beach erosion measures, 10 Oct. 1960, Oceanside Beach Nourishment file, 1959-60, LNNA RG 77/84-0018 Box 6/8; A. Ruden to W. Herron, 14 Nov. 1960, subj: Expenditures for emergency work at Oceanside, Corresp. and Rpts., Oceanside Beach Erosion Control file, 1960, LNNA RG 77/84-0018 Box 6/8.

[36] Record of Emergency Placement of Sand on Oceanside Beach, undated 1960, Oceanside file, 1961-62, LNNA RG 77/84-0018 Box 7/8; Lt. Col. John Oswalt, Jr., Los Angeles Deputy District Engineer, to South Pacific Division Engineer, subj: Oceanside beach erosion, 20 Oct. 1960, Oceanside Project Cost Estimates file, 1946-61, LNNA RG 77/80-0034 Box 18/20; Col. William T. Bradley, Los Angeles District Engineer, to South Pacific Division Engineer, subj: Construction of beach erosion control project, 19 Oct. 1960, Oceanside Project Cost Estimates file, 1946-61, LNNA RG 77/80-0034 Box 18/20; Larry M. Bagley and Dana Hield Whitson, "Putting the Beach Back at the Oceanside: A Case Study of Locally Initiated Beach Restoration," *Shore and Beach* (Oct. 1982), p. 24.

[37] *San Diego* (California) *Union* (30 March 1961); U.S. Congress, Senate, *An Act to Authorize Certain Beach Erosion Control of the Shore in San Diego County, California*, Pub. L. 87-9, 86th Cong., 2d sess., 1961, S. 307, *passim* (The Chief of Engineer's report on this law is contained in U.S. Congress, House, H.D. 456, 86th Cong., 2d sess., 1961); Elvis J. Stahr, Jr., Secretary of the Army, to David E. Bell, Director, Bureau of the Budget, subj: Enactment of S. 307, 24 Mar. 1961, Oceanside file, 1961-62, LNNA RG 77/84-0018 Box 7/8; W. Herron to Los Angeles District Engineer, subj: Shore protection works at Oceanside, 2 Dec. 1960, Oceanside Project Cost Estimates file, 1946-60, LNNA RG 77/80-0034 Box 18/20; Lt. Col. J. Oswalt to J. Teerink, 2 Dec. 1960, subj: Combining beach erosion and harbor development projects, Oceanside Cost Estimates File, 1946-1973, LNNA RG 77/80-0034 Box 18/20; Turhollow history.

[38] *Beach Erosion Control Authorization Act*, 75 Stat. 18 (1961); A.V. Potter, Chief, River and Harbor Planning Section, Los Angeles District, to Audit Branch, subj: City claim for reimbursement of emergency erosion work, 12 Apr. 1962, Oceanside file, 1961-62, LNNA RG 77/84-0018 Box 7/8.

[39] *Oceanside* (California) *Blade-Tribune* (20 Jan., 9 Feb. 1961).

[40] Herron interview; Chief, Planning and Reports Branch, Los Angeles District, U.S. Army, Corps of Engineers, to Comptroller of the Army, subj: Beach erosion control project dredging, 6 Nov. 1961, Oceanside Project Cost Estimates file, 1946-73, LNNA RG 77/80-

0034 Box 18-20; Maj. Gen William F. Cassidy, Director of Civil Works, Office of the Chief of Engineers, to Comptroller of the Army, subj: Acceptance of contributed funds for Oceanside beach erosion control project, 17 Aug. 1961, Oceanside file, 1961-62, LNNA RG 77/84-0018 Box 7/8; H.W. Thompson, Chief, Engineering Division, Los Angeles District, to South Pacific Division Engineer, subj: Civil works appropriations for fiscal 1963, 29 Sept. 1961, Oceanside General file, 1961-69, LNNA RG 77/80-0034 Box 18/20; Turhollow history.

[41]Maj. Gen. W. Cassidy to Comptroller, 17 Aug. 1961; H. Thompson to South Pacific Division Engineer, 29 Sept. 1961; Bidding contract: Dredging near Oceanside, 21 Nov. 1961, Oceanside General file, 1961-69, LNNA RG 77/84-0018 Box 7/8.

[42]Report, "Survey Report on Oceanside Harbor (Camp Pendleton), California to the Chief of Engineers," Los Angeles District, U.S. Army, Corps of Engineers, 20 Feb. 1964, Oceanside Project Cost Estimates file, 1946-61, LNNA RG 77/80-0034 Box 18/20; Minutes, Public Meeting at Oceanside on Proposed Survey Report for Navigation, 1 Oct. 1963, Oceanside General file, 1961-69, 1960s, LNNA RG 77/84-0018 Box 7/8. Hereafter cited as Minutes, 1 Oct. 1963.

[43]Turhollow history; E. Taylor to Los Angeles District Engineer, 26 July 1962, subj: Beach erosion and delay in dredging, Oceanside Shore Protection file, LNNA RG 77/84-0018 Box 7/8; Edward Koehm, Chief, Engineering Division, Los Angeles Army Engineer District, to F. Lilley, 13 Aug. 1962, subj: Dredge malfunction, Oceanside Shore Protection file, LNNA RG 77/84-0018 Box 7/8; Herron interview; See Dredging Logbooks, Oceanside 1962-63, Oceanside Harbor Log, Mar.-Nov. 1962, LNNA RG 77/70-1819 Box 299212, for a day-by-day account of Standard's work.

[44]Resolution of Oceanside Small-Craft Harbor District, 14 Aug. 1962, Oceanside Project Cost Estimates file, 1946-61, LNNA RG 77/80-0034 Box 18/20; E. Sklar, President, Oceanside Small-Craft Harbor District, to Los Angeles District Engineer, subj: Federal assumption of navigation maintenance at Oceanside Harbor, 13 Aug. 1962, Oceanside General file, 1961-69, LNNA RG 77/80-0034 Box 18/20; Minutes, 1 Oct. 1963.

[45]Lee R. Henning, Acting Chief, Engineering Division, LAD, to South Pacific Division Engineer, subj: Recommendation for federal assumption of maintenance of navigation features at Oceanside, 20 Sept. 1963, Oceanside file, 1961-62, LNNA RG 77/84-0018 Box 7/8.

[46]Omar Lillevang, Leeds, Hill, and Jewett, to Los Angeles District Engineer, 8 March 1963, subj: General navigation features, Oceanside Harbor Cost Estimates file, 1946-73, LNNA RG 77/80-0034 Box 18/20; Herron interview; Report, "Survey Report for Navigation of Oceanside Harbor, Oceanside (Camp Pendleton), California, June 1963, Los Angeles District, U.S. Army, Corps of Engineers, Rpt. Bibliography file, LNNA RG 77/83-0006 Box 1/12; U.S. Congress, House, *Oceanside Harbor, Oceanside (Camp Pendleton), California: An Interim Survey*, Pub. L. 89-298, 89th Cong., 1st sess., 1964, H.D. 76, *passim*; William J. Herron, "Periodic Maintenance Starts at Oceanside Harbor," *Southwest Builder and Contractor* (March 1966), (draft copy).

[47]Resolution of the Oceanside Small Craft Harbor District Furnishing Assurances of Local Cooperation," undated 1965, Oceanside General file, 1961-69, LNNA RG 77/80-0034 Box 18/20; Report, "Review by the State of California on Proposed Survey Report of the Chief of Engineers, Department of the Army, on Navigation, Oceanside Harbor, Oceanside (Camp Pendleton), California, 18 June 1964, Camp Pendleton Harbor, CA, file, 1946-74, LNNA RG 77/80-0033 Box 6/20; Rental brochure for Oceanside Small Craft Harbor, undated 1963, Oceanside file, 1961-62, LNNA RG 77/84-0018 Box 7/8; Camp Pendleton resumé; Report, Navigation Regulations Naval Restricted Area, Camp Pendleton Boat Basin, California, U.S. Marine Corps, 12 Nov. 1963, Oceanside file, 1961-62, LNNA RG 77/84-0018 Box 7/8; Maj. Sheldon Biles, Assistant Los Angeles District Engineer, to South Pacific Division Engineer, 12 Nov. 1963, subj: Restricted area at Camp Pendleton Boat Basin, Oceanside file, 1961-62, LNNA RG 77/84-0018 Box 7/8.

CHAPTER III

Intergovernmental Relations and Environmental Regulations

While the Oceanside Small-Craft Harbor provided immediate recreational and commercial benefits to northern San Diego County residents and visitors, it also created new problems — and exacerbated old ones for the City of Oceanside and the Corps of Engineers. Slip spaces in the harbor were rented quickly as both pleasure craft owners and commercial fishermen took advantage of this highly-demanded harbor complex. Once fully operational, the harbor soon met the rental expectations of its architects. In order to meet the demands of the boaters, ancillary businesses such as service stations, restaurants, motels, and equipment sales and rental stores opened. It appeared that Oceanside at last had the facility that would help the city sustain economic prosperity. Still, the Oceanside project was not without problems.

Material from the harbor excavation site caused an immediate issue. Located between the Santa Margarita and San Luis Rey rivers, the material was composed predominantly of fine sand and silt from river erosion. However, it also contained a substantial percentage of cobbles — three-to-six-inch diameter stones washed from inland floods, and buried with the silt. Earlier in the century, the excavation site had actually been an operating gravel quarry. Constant fears about erosion on the southern part of Oceanside beach prompted an agreement between city and Corps officials to place most of the excavation material there. By early 1964, however, most of the sand had disappeared while the cobbles remained. The stones had formed drifts along the surf line, and extended from there well out into the water at low tide. In reporting this situation to William Herron of the Los Angeles District, City Engineer Alton Ruden lamented: "Naturally, the people living

A solitary beachgoer sits among the cobbles, 1977.

near and using this portion of the beach are very unhappy about
the concentration of cobbles and have been constantly attempting
to have them removed." In spite of these complaints, Ruden
believed that the cobbles prevented erosion and therefore should
not be removed. He asked for the Corps' advice on the issue.[1]

There was concern among Corps officials about the concentration of cobbles at Oceanside. They had hoped, as Ruden did, that
the sand would fill in around the cobbles. However, as they learned,
the powerful ocean currents at Oceanside had until then only
removed any material lighter in weight than the cobble. Since the
beach fill had occurred only ten months before, Assistant Los
Angeles District Engineer Major Sheldon Biles advised Ruden
"that any removal of cobbles at the present time would be
premature." Biles believed that two adjustments were occurring at
Oceanside beach. First, the slope of both the surf and tide zones
was undergoing change because of the recent beach nourishment;
and secondly, the accelerated movement of sand was occuring

because of the newly-forming slopes on the restored beach. Until these adjustments were completed, Biles argued, the cobbles should remain undisturbed "except by natural forces, for a year or so, and then remedial measures could be developed if so warranted." He also agreed with Ruden that the cobbles probably did retard erosion, and might still attract and hold more sand.[2]

Property owners along Oceanside beach were much less willing to be patient. In March 1964, an article in the *Los Angeles Times* highlighted the cobble problem and the citizen response. The Corps received many letters of protest, one of which posed the question to Biles: "[I] wonder if you would be interested in spending your vacation on a beach where it is impossible to get to the water?" In response to the protests, city officials sent bulldozers to the beach to push some of the cobbles out to sea. Ruden opposed this action because of his fears that it would leave the beach even more vulnerable to erosion than it was already. When the Corps supported his contentions, Ruden was able to persuade the City Council to stop the bulldozers despite public pressure to get rid of the cobbles.[3]

The problem was fast becoming a political one for the presiding Oceanside City Council. With elections coming on 16 April, their opponents were making political hay by blaming the current members of the council for bringing about the cobble problems. Despite expert recommendations, the council was hard-pressed to find quick solutions to the cobble problem.[4]

Not only was the cobble issue flaring, the nagging problem of erosion continued to plague the city. The nearly four million cubic yards of material placed on the beach at Oceanside in 1962 and 1963 was disappearing rapidly. This was occurring despite the construction of a groin designed to hold the sand in place, and the recent completion of the beach sandfill project. Coastal engineers familiar with Oceanside had predicted since the 1940s that the beach there would require periodic nourishment. However, they did not anticipate after completion of the restoration project that the beach erosion problem would arise again so soon. The eroding beach revealed the dilemma of coastal engineers working at Oceanside: the beach needed to be maintained for a variety of good reasons, but a simple sandfill operation, no matter how large, provided little more than temporary relief in this setting. Solutions to erosion problems at Oceanside therefore required more elaborate and more costly structural or renourishment measures that would probably test the limitations of existing technology.

The rapid disappearance of sand at Oceanside indicated that there was not only downcoast and upcoast littoral drift, but also offshore losses. The powerful currents at Oceanside sometimes stripped the sand from the beaches, pulling it to sea. At other times the currents pushed sand against the groin at the north end of the beach, or southward down the coast. This longshore transport of littoral material spelled the revival of another nagging problem. Continuing a cycle that had first been created with the construction of Del Mar Boat Basin in 1942, the sand from Oceanside beach again made its way back north, around the groin and into the joint military-civilian harbor entrance channel. Southerly transport, carried around and through the north harbor breakwater, contributing further to shoaling.

Soundings taken along the southward face of the north breakwater in May of 1964 revealed that the harbor depth there had fallen from twenty to ten feet (MLLW) since the last dredging. Later soundings showed that the entire entrance channel was shoaling to the point that the largest Marine Corps craft would not be able to travel through during low tide.[5]

By the spring of 1965, individuals such as Oceanside Harbor Superintendent Harold B. Snyder were becoming fearful of a potentially dangerous navigation situation. As the tourist season approached, Snyder believed that the chances of boating accidents would increase because of the shallow water. In May, he reported to the Los Angeles District that recent soundings taken by a commercial fisherman at the end of April indicated a very shallow area just off the north groin of the civilian harbor. Snyder estimated that near this groin there could be little more than five to seven feet of water at low tide. "The seriousness of this problem cannot be overstressed," he warned. "Every effort will be made by the staff to alert the boatmen and to instruct them whenever possible, but as the summer draws closer, more and more boats will be in the water on the weekends and the task will be more difficult." The Harbor District was so concerned about this extreme shallow area that it contracted a small dredging operation in August 1965. By the end of the month, about 111,000 cubic yards of sand were removed from around the toe of the groin.[6]

Corps officials had been assessing the situation at Oceanside since the 1964 reports of shoaling. One measure which they believed should be taken was the extension of the groin at the mouth of the San Luis Rey River. Most of the sand which had left Oceanside beach since 1963 had in fact traveled around the toe of that structure on its way to the entrance channel. Another additional measure, which they knew that city officials would oppose, was to place dredged material taken from the entrance channel on beaches to the north of the harbor breakwaters. This would undoubtedly result in less shoaling and lengthen the periods between maintenance dredging; but the severe erosion taking place on the beach to the south mandated that the sand be deposited there.[7]

As the engineers knew, the surging ocean turned Oceanside Harbor into a powerful suction pump when conditions were right, and the placement of the dredged sand back on the beach to the south simply restarted the cyclical pattern. Yet they were also aware of the political interest in maintaining Oceanside's beach. The Corps was squarely in the unenviable position of being pressured to spend tax dollars on a measure that would undoubtedly result in more future expenditures to do the same thing over again. However, other measures which might bring more lasting relief from harbor shoaling and erosion would require lengthy feasibility study and tremendous construction costs. Meanwhile, the engineers were faced with the immediate problems of an unnavigable harbor and an eroded beach. Oceanside was becoming a Pandora's Box for the Corps of Engineers.

As of the summer of 1965, harbor maintenance at Oceanside was still not the Corps' responsibility. The Chief of Engineers had recommended in his report to Congress that the Corps assume maintenance of the navigation features of the harbor, and most believed that the bill proposed for this would soon become law. However, that did not occur until October 1965. In the meantime, Los Angeles District personnel prepared for maintenance on the assumption that it soon would be mandated. They apprised the Marine Corps of the recent soundings and recommended that the Navy earmark $250,000 to cover one-half of the estimated cost of the dredging which would most likely take place during the spring of 1966. The Marines at Camp Pendleton were acutely aware of the shoaling problems. During the year they had learned of damage to some of their tank landing ships and discovered that vessels with 15-foot drafts could operate in the harbor only at high tide. Therefore, they were most interested in having the harbor dredged as soon as possible. Although funding had to await passage of the

1965 Omnibus Rivers and Harbors Act in October, both the Corps and the Marines planned cost-sharing on the assumption that not only would the money be available, but also that the engineers would take over navigation responsibilities for the Harbor District. If the bill passed as written, it would mean that the Marines and the Corps of Engineers would divide equally the estimated cost of the $500,000 dredging bill. To help the Corps prepare plans and specifications for the dredging, the Marines advanced $12,500 to the Los Angeles District even before the legislation was proposed.[8]

When Congress approved the Rivers and Harbors Act in October 1965 with the provision for federal navigation maintenance responsibility at Oceanside, it came as welcome news to the Small-Craft Harbor District Board. The District had had a role in its passage and in approval of the additional provision to reimburse it for the August dredging. Mayor Erwin Sklar again traveled to the nation's capital during the congressional subcommittee meetings, and in his own direct fashion lobbied for reimbursement. He also fought to ensure that the Corps of Engineers would assume navigation responsibility for the harbor entrance channel and that sufficient funding would be appropriated for maintenance dredging. Despite the harbor's immediate success, slip-rental revenues and taxes were insufficient to provide the District with funding for the cost of maintenance dredging. Superintendent Snyder was anxious to get the dredging underway also, because shallow water remained even after the District's dredging operation along the north groin in August. Shoaling damaged several large boats during the year, resulting in a dramatic increase in insurance rates for craft using the harbor. Snyder hoped that the maintenance dredging, now planned for early 1966, would convince the companies to bring the rates down again. By the end of 1965, the Utah Construction and Mining Company had secured the contract to dredge an estimated 450,000 cubic yards of sand from the joint facility. Shortly thereafter, the Harbor District adopted new resolutions of cooperation and responsibilities with the federal government for operation of the small-craft facility.[9]

When the Corps and the Marines split the cost of maintenance dredging, it demonstrated the high degree of cooperation that was developing in regard to the Oceanside Harbor complex. The joint military-civilian facility was becoming a benchmark of cooperative inter-governmental relations. The common interests of an aggressive city government and responsible federal agencies were best being served by such a heightened level of cooperation. Usually working on the state level, the Corps was in this instance collaborating with a local government, and at the same time serving both civilian and military interests. The Corps of Engineers was emerging not only as one of the cooperating federal agencies, but also as a liaison between the various levels of government.

In the meantime, the Los Angeles District's problems with Standard Dredging Company (the firm that had experienced two months of down time because of a motor burnout while dredging in Del Mar Boat Basin in 1962) arose again. In 1963, Standard issued a claim for a change order calling for the Corps to pay an additional $450,000 due to the fact that abnormal sea conditions had resulted in several weeks of down time, forced the extension of dredging pipelines, and done damage to equipment. Corps personnel believed the claims were "without merit," for if Standard had remained on the contract schedule, it would not have been forced to dredge during the winter storm season. Moreover, the Corps considered the company's equipment claims "grossly exaggerated" in regard to actual value of replacement costs. In Corps officials' opinion, Standard had brought on its own problems and furthermore delayed both beach restoration and harbor development at Oceanside. Therefore they refused to pay Standard's claim and issued a counter-claim to that effect.[10]

The claims remained unsettled until 1969, when they finally reached the Corps of Engineers Board of Contract Appeals. After hearing testimony, the chairman of the appeals board rejected Standard's claim that Oceanside was a "unique harbor entrance." The decision upheld the Corps' contention that the company's problems were brought on entirely by poor management and operation. Despite the Standard Dredging delays, the company managed to dredge more than 684,000 cubic yards between March and April 1966, all of which was placed on the beach to the south of the harbor. Everyone concerned hoped that the sand would stay on the beach longer this time, but few had reason to believe it would.[11]

In addition to working out new safety measures with the Corps, such as a shortening and exposure of the north groin, Oceanside Small-Craft Harbor District officials were becoming interested in modifying the harbor to accommodate additional boats. The board, realizing that additional slip spaces would bring more revenue, hoped to gain Corps approval for their plans. Such approval was required now that the federal government was maintaining the navigation features of the harbor. While the Corps was considering the idea, the Oceanside City Council adopted a resolution for harbor expansion which would be put to a vote of the people on 2 August 1966. In the meantime the council went to work on drawing up specific harbor plans. When ninety percent of the voters approved the measure, the council urged the Corps to conduct a feasibility study for harbor expansion.[12]

Other problems interrupted momentum on harbor expansion in late 1966. Since the need for dredging had arisen earlier than expected in 1965, Corps personnel had been conducting periodic sand tracing experiments at Oceanside to learn more about littoral movement there. From these tests, they estimated that before the harbor construction in 1942, approximately 1.3 million cubic yards of sand had oscillated back and forth annually with a net downcoast flow of 150,000 to 200,000 cubic yards. Extremely fine sand of about 1.8 millimeters in diameter was most prevalent and also highly subject to wave motion. They came to the inescapable conclusion that at least 33 percent of the harbor shoaling came from around the south jetty of the civilian facility, and therefore major modifications would be required to solve the problem. As an immediate step to keep the harbor operable, they recommended that maintenance dredging be conducted annually rather than biannually. With these facts in mind, Los Angeles District Engineer Colonel Norman Pehrson informed Oceanside officials he recommended that a three-year $150,000 study be conducted to assess the feasibility of harbor design modification and expansion.[13]

Since the next scheduled dredging would not be until 1968, city officials were faced with two pressing problems as the tourist season of 1967 loomed closer. The harbor was again experiencing shoaling. Soundings that spring revealed that in some places the channel was only six to seven feet deep at low tide. Not only was this a problem for the larger Marine Corps vessels using the entrance channel, commercial sport fishermen who ran regular trips were finding it increasingly difficult to maintain their schedules with the sanding problem. The Oceanside Small-Craft Harbor District predicted disparingly that revenues would drop from $245,000 in the year before to around $220,000 in 1967. Once again, Erwin Sklar, president of the board of directors of the district, took matters into his own hands. He traveled to

Washington, D.C., to confer with congressmen and other officials "about permanent remedies to the yacht basin's silting woes." While there, he apprised Marine Corps leaders in the Pentagon of the shoaling situation at the joint harbor facility. Meanwhile, Los Angeles District people such as William Herron and Charles Fisher of the Coastal Resources Branch were attempting to expedite dredging by exploring ways to provide funding for both the Corps' and the Marines' share of the cost. While these matters were pending, another boat grounded in the harbor on 9 May. A few days later the harbor was officially closed.[14]

Oceanside's second major problem in 1967, beach erosion, could be solved by elimination of the harbor shoaling. From dredging, the city would obtain the sand needed once again to restore a beach which was experiencing in some places worse erosion than in 1962. In mid-June Los Angeles District awarded a $200,000 dredging contract to Shellmaker Incorporated of Newport Beach, California.[15] Meanwhile, the harbor closing touched off hostilities within the Board of Directors of the Harbor District. One of the directors, Max McComas, criticized the others for not acting sooner, and predicted that the harbor would not open until 1 September at the earliest.[16]

The condition of Oceanside's beaches rekindled citizens' wrath in 1967. A report on beach erosion issued by the Corps in June noted: "The beach between the pier and Wisconsin Avenue was restored in March-April 1966 with dredge spoil. . . however, wave action has again stripped the beach exposing cobbles from the groin at the mouth of the San Luis Rey River downcoast to Loma Alta Creek." The major cause for the rapid erosion in May and June 1967—as well as for the extreme harbor shoaling—was a powerful tropical storm that swirled off the southern tip of the Baja peninsula for several days. The storm sent strong upcoast waves to unprotected Oceanside, quickly transporting the fine beach sand to the harbor entrance channel. These facts did little to placate property owners along the Strand who blamed the Corps of Engineers for their woes. Al Hollenstein, president of the Motel Mile Beach Association (an organization of shorefront property owners in Oceanside) complained bitterly in letters to President Lyndon Johnson, and California Senators George Murphy and Thomas Kuchel. To Kuchel, he declared "[t]he Army Corps of Engineers oversaw the building of a harbor in Oceanside, and ruined our beaches," while to Murphy he complained: "How about protecting these valued resources from the ill-advised engineering and inexcusable execution of the Federal government itself?"[17]

The Deputy Chief of Engineers wrote a reply to the Motel Mile Association letter for President Johnson. His office also recommended that someone from the Los Angeles District make a trip to Oceanside to meet with the association. The District Engineer determined that Herron would be the best diplomat in this potentially tense situation, and sent him there for a meeting on 27 July. In the meeting, marked by several "angry outbursts," the association presented a plan—drawn up by one of its members who also happened to be an engineer—which called for the construction of a system of timber groins along the beach. This, he believed, would solve both the cobble and sand erosion problem in one action. Herron pointed out the Corps' skeptical position on groins as a means of sand replenishment, and also cautioned that the costs would be prohibitive. He informed the association that the Corps had no authority or funding presently to deal with beach erosion there. Hollenstein then charged erroneously that the federal government had diverted millions of dollars to build the harbor at the expense of beach restoration, and instead of replenishing the beach with quality fill, the Corps had dumped tons of cobbles from the excavation site. The meeting ended with Herron succeeding in convincing the association that the Corps was sympathetic to Oceanside's problem. However, the members remained disillusioned with all of the governmental agencies involved at Oceanside.[18]

Through the remainder of 1967, the city and the Corps grappled with erosion and shoaling problems. During July, Shellmaker dredged nearly 180,000 cubic yards of sand from the entrance channel, the harbor reopening shortly afterwards. The Corps awaited funding for the harbor improvement study, and in the meantime received authorization to reimburse the city for all emergency maintenance dredging conducted since August 1965. As an anti-cobble measure, the city proposed late in the summer that the rocks be exchanged for sand transported from an inland site. A private contractor had approached the city with the idea, and the council passed a resolution to test the process. Los Angeles District engineers, after assessing the proposal, told city officials that they did not recommend the substitution, but at the same time made no objections to it. They held that the cobbles, while a recreational nuisance, were still acting as an erosion deterrent, and would eventually disappear naturally into the beach. After testing proved the idea economically infeasible, the city abandoned the plan.[19]

By the beginning of 1968, the Oceanside Harbor complex was again experiencing serious shoaling problems. Most of the shoaling had occured in September 1967, when a "Chubasco" (a typhoon originating in Mexico) moved north and resulting wave action disintegrated underwater sand bluffs near Oceanside, and forced the loose material into the harbor entrance. As a result of this, Oceanside officials pressed the Corps to compress the three-year navigation study into one which could be completed in a few months. On 3 January, a hostile *San Diego Union* editorial called for the government to expedite the "rapid and effective funding and treatment" of Oceanside's problem.[20]

City officials had also been taking matters into their own hands. In February, the engineering firm of Leeds, Hill, and Jewett presented a shoaling study of the harbor funded by the Harbor District in 1967. The report concluded that while maintenance dredging had been successful at times in keeping the entrance channel open, additional measures were necessary for dependable navigation conditions. It recommended that dredging in the entrance channel be extended further seaward, but more import-antly advocated the enlargement of the entire channel by extension and improvement of the jetties. During that month, the Oceanside Small-Craft Harbor District also received a $500,000 loan that Erwin Sklar had negotiated from the California Department of Harbors and Watercraft. The loan was to fund extension of the south breakwater and San Luis Rey River groin according to a harbor improvement plan developed for Oceanside in 1967 by the engineering firm of Moffatt and Nichol of Los Angeles.[21] Anxious to find a solution to the shoaling problem, the Corps had already been reviewing the Moffatt and Nichol plan. By the time the state loan came through Corps officials were ready to endorse it. When the city formally requested that the Corps be the contractor for the work, Herron assured them that the agency "would cooperate 100 percent in coordinating the two projects [groin and jetty construction] to attain a maximum effective program."[22]

In hopes of restoring adequate channel depths by the beginning of the summer season, the Corps expedited the commencement of the 1968 maintenance dredging. On 26 March, Shellmaker, Incorporated, began working in the entrance channel, this time dredging a total of 433,900 cubic yards, all of which was placed on the beach to the south. The civilian harbor, closed since the first of the year, opened for business again in late April. Meanwhile, Silberberger Construction Company of Vista, California, which received the Corps' contract award, began work on the groin and jetty extensions for an agreed fee of $350,580.[23] Thus at the same time, two costly projects were underway at Oceanside, both with the intent of keeping the harbor open and safe. While few questioned the value of the facility and the efficacy of its construction, no one predicted that its maintenance costs would continue to be so significant.

Los Angeles District personnel had been drawing up a preliminary report on the larger navigation study being done on Oceanside during this time. They held a public meeting in June 1968 to present their findings, which included a tacit endorsement of harbor expansion plans prepared for the city by Moffatt and Nichol. Corps officials also announced that they were considering federal reimbursement to the Harbor District for the revetment work.[24] This was an issue soon to cause friction between the Corps and the city, as the former was mandated to assess the value of the revetment work over a period of years before reimbursing the latter. Harbor District officials wanted speedy reimbursement, which the Corps could not grant. Caught between the constraints of federal regulations and the demands of local governments and private citizens, the Corps again assumed an unpopular but unavoidable position.

At the meeting, hostile citizens again had a chance to voice their opinion about the Corps' extensive study of the Oceanside problems. From cobbles to erosion, the Corps received the blame and the citizens' anger. The president of the Motel Mile Association issued a statement that characterized the current and future attitude of many in Oceanside by asserting, "[F]urther time for study of the beach erosion problem is not warranted...and immediate action should be taken."[25] Such pressure had forced the city to undertake a number of measures which had rendered only temporary and expensive relief. Before taking any additional steps, Corps officials wanted to study the situation at Oceanside more thoroughly.

The combination of dredging and the city's breakwater improvements did prove beneficial in the short term. In September 1968, soundings revealed that the harbor entrance channel was maintaining a depth of twenty feet despite a period of southwesterly swells that washed away much of Oceanside beach. At the end of 1968, channel depths were still sixteen to twenty-two feet, and new Harbor Superintendent E.A. Sandling thought the city's revetment work, completed in June, primarily responsible. He was confident that annual maintenance dredging by the Corps of Engineers would assure a safe and navigable harbor. The district had been upgrading the harbor facilities in anticipation of better times. Guest slips now were among the most luxurious in southern California, offering accommodations such as electricity and water, and nearby recreational facilities. Boaters from throughout the region began to take full advantage of the new facility, and by November 1968 the harbor was completely full for the first time in its history.[26]

Despite the recent success of the harbor, the District Board of Supervisors knew they would have difficulty repaying the loan from the state for the revetment work. They had already approached the Corps with the idea of reimbursement, but during 1968 had received little encouragement that this would occur, even though the Engineers had endorsed the projects. Congress had recently placed strict controls on all cash expenditures for the Corps. With this in mind, city officials traveled to Washington, D.C., to lobby for their cause. Firmly convinced that the work had proven to be a benefit to the federal government, they argued strongly that it had already saved money by reducing the need for any emergency dredging, and would continue to do so in the future. Mayor Howard Richardson enlisted the support of Califor•.ia Congressman James Utt, who brought the issue before the Senate Public Works Committee. Utt and Richardson then approached the Office of the Chief of Engineers in the hope of gaining support. When the Chief issued a favorable report to be presented to the Senate committee, it marked another triumph for the lobbying efforts of Oceanside.

This favorable report on reimbursement did not come without considerable reservations within the Office of the Chief of Engineers. The Oceanside issue raised questions about the precedent which might be established in reimbursing a local government for a project that had not received congressional authorization. Some Corps officials were concerned that other local governments might also choose to resort to the "private relief bill technique," rather than first securing approval as directed by law. Through the "private relief bill technique," a local government planned and built a project on the speculation of convincing lawmakers that a reimbursement was warranted because of its economic benefit to the federal government. Only strong lobbying on the part of the Oceanside city government, and the Los Angeles District's opinion that this was an exceptional case, secured the Chief of Engineers' endorsement for reimbursement.[27]

With the next scheduled maintenance dredging came a new controversy. In March 1969, the Corps announced plans to perform the routine work at an estimated cost of $500,000. Compared to previous years, the need for dredging was minor. Harbor depths had fallen to twelve feet at low tide—well above previous shoaling episodes. However, this meant that Marine Corps LSTs which had a draft of fourteen feet could not navigate the harbor at low tide periods. In mid-July, Shellmaker, Incorporated again set up its dredge in the harbor and its discharge pipes along the city's beach. As this occured, a number of property owners along the beach began to protest to the city council and the Corps. They argued that dredging during the height of the tourist season damaged business, and urged the Corps to delay such operations until the winter. The problem for the Corps was "essentially one of financing," as District Engineer Norman Pehrson explained to one of the residents. In Pehrson's opinion, the best time to dredge, from an engineering point of view, was between October and December when wave conditions are best. However, recent appropriations curbs placed on Corps projects by Congress delayed funding for this particular dredging operation. Nonetheless, citizen protests of the dredging were strong enough that the Oceanside Small-Craft Harbor District passed a resolution urging the Corps to dredge only in the winter months in the future.[28]

The dredging itself went according to plan, as Shellmaker removed 353,000 cubic yards from the channel under the terms of a new bidding arrangement, whereby the contractor submitted a bid based on how much sand would be removed for a set price. During the operation, the Corps discovered that the city's 1968 revetment created an unexpected effect. Instead of merely impounding sand, the "dog-leg" extension created an eddy current which sent upcoast sand seaward. This had the effect of transferring the sand shoal to the southern corner of the approach channel. Although downcoast winter waves now renourished the beach to the south, the work had not retarded harbor shoaling but had moved it to another part of the entrance channel.[29] As deliberations continued on reimbursement to the city for the work, this knowledge figured strongly in the Corps officials' opinion about benefits to the federal government.

Despite the fact that the city's revetment work had changed the shoaling characteristics in the entrance channel, the Oceanside Small-Craft Harbor District was experiencing its best year ever in 1969. With the harbor operating at capacity and improved prospects for meeting the obligations of the $500,000 state loan for revetment work, the Board of Directors took advantage of the good times to make a bid for expansion. The directors were motivated partially by "an unprecedented boom" in use. Not only were there 592 boats docked in the 570-boat-capacity harbor on Easter weekend, there was currently a waiting list of 200 boat owners. Harbor District officials viewed expansion as the only way to make the harbor self-supporting in the future. Even if the harbor remained at capacity, it would continue to operate in a deficit situation at current rental rates for many years to come. Moreover, Oceanside residents were currently assessed a tax to meet any deficits left by the harbor operation—an unpopular law at best. The Board developed two plans for expansion: one modest, and the other grandiose. The first, which would cost an estimated $150,000, provided for an additional forty slips to be built within the existing harbor perimeter. The board hoped this project would be financed through city taxes; and then additional revenues would permit a reduction of those taxes in the coming years. While one member believed that 130 to 200 additional slips were possible within the current basin, others believed that more than 40 to 50 would "strangle the harbor."[30]

The elaborate expansion plan included the construction of an outer harbor seaward from the present south jetty. Essentially, this would double the size of the harbor and provide hundreds of new slip spaces. This was the plan which the board believed would make the harbor self-supporting. The Corps of Engineers had been considering this plan and others similar to it in a navigation study being conducted on Oceanside Harbor. With the expenditure freeze on federal water projects in 1968, funding for the study had been placed on hold. Oceanside officials now lobbied for

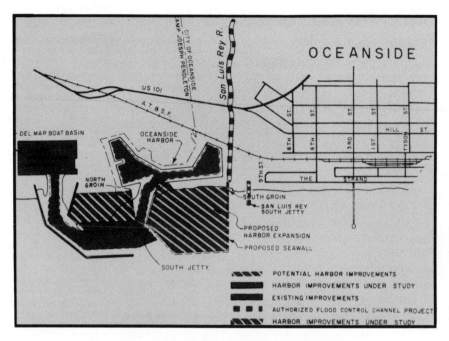

Potential harbor improvements, 1969.

congressional funding to resume the study. In October 1969, they succeeded, and the Corps received $95,000 to resume studies on both harbor improvement and beach erosion at Oceanside.[31]

The restart of the Oceanside navigation study presented some new issues for the Los Angeles District engineers. Not only were they to assess reimbursement to the city for the 1968 revetment work, as well as navigation and beach erosion, but also the feasibility of harbor expansion for both pleasure and military use. The Marine Corps at Camp Pendleton now wanted to install a new LST facility in Del Mar Boat Basin. The harbor would therefore have to accommodate vessels up to 525 feet in length. Moreover, the U.S. Coast Guard announced plans to berth an 84-foot cutter in the north part of the civilian complex. As Corps personnel began to review the situation, two problems soon surfaced. Expansion plans which called for creation of an outer basin southwest of the existing complex would mean the loss of the harbor beach, which had become one of the most popular in the Oceanside vicinity. Lying between the south groin and south jetty of the harbor, the beach remained wide and sandy at times when downcoast beaches experienced severe erosion. With excellent breaking waves, it also was one of the most extensively used surfing beaches in San Diego County. The loss of this thirty-acre public beach could easily be a stumbling block to any expansion plans. The expansion would also narrow the channel and the mouth of the San Luis Rey River. Some in the Los Angeles District expressed apprehensions about the possible sand accretion and flood control hazards that this might present.[32]

The issues raised by harbor expansion soon became troublesome for the Corps and the city. Any significant enlargement of the complex would have to take place southwest of the harbor. The Corps had conducted preliminary examinations to assess the feasibility of expanding the harbor to the north at the beach area between the civilian and military facilities, but the Marine Corps opposed the idea based on their proposed use of that area. To the east and south were harbor facilities, streets, and the San Luis Rey River, thus ruling out any development in those directions. The Harbor District viewed the plan as necessary to its economic future, and therefore believed that residents would be supportive. Most people in the Los Angeles District supported the plan on the general principle that there was demand for more slip spaces, and that the complex should be run as profitably as possible. However, the Corps had reservations about any plan which carried such a risk of flood damage and which removed public beach acreage. Therefore, there was wide speculation throughout the South Pacific Division whether the navigation study, which was assessing expansion, should be combined with a beach erosion investigation of the same area. The idea had been suggested as a streamlining and cost-cutting measure. However, as the Deputy Division Engineer assessed the situation: "It would appear to the public somewhat paradoxical that we are destroying one beach with one project and trying to enhance beach with another adjacent project."[33]

Federal studies at Oceanside and all other coastal projects undertaken by the federal government came suddenly under the provisions of the most sweeping piece of environmental legislation in American history: the National Environmental Policy Act (NEPA), signed into law on 1 January 1970. Congress had approved the law to assure present and future generations an environment that was healthful, safe, and aesthetically pleasing. The law required that all federal projects be evaluated with regard to their environmental consequences. To accomplish this, a "lead agency" (usually the federal agency planning the project) prepared an Environmental Impact Statement (EIS). This document would be reviewed in draft form by all interested organizations and the public. After comment and public review, the draft EIS would be finalized with appropriate modificatins and would be used to guide modifications to engineering designs.[34]

For the Corps of Engineers, NEPA meant that additional manpower and resources were needed. The Los Angeles District created an environmental section to grapple with the vagaries of the complex new law. Production of the EIS became a major concern, and the Corps transferred many of its personnel to prepare them. The problems that many people in the Corps anticipated with Oceanside's harbor expansion plans were amplified when considered in the context of NEPA assessment. One positive aspect of this investigation was that, rather than the initially anticipated loss of beach, the restructuring of the south jetty and groin would create a sand accretion area which the city would maintain. As a result, there would only be a net loss of three acres of public beach. The Corps and city hoped that this would positively influence officials of the Department of the Interior and the State Department of Parks and Recreation, both of which had expressed doubts about the project because of public beach loss. However, as the environmental assessment of the project began, doubts about its economic and ecological feasibility persisted.[35]

Modification of the breakwater system of the Oceanside complex without expansion became a more pressing issue when the Marine Corps submitted a report on its new amphibious craft. The new vessels had a 21.5-foot draft when fully loaded, and Corps of Engineers personnel estimated that the seaward end of the entrance channel would now have to be dredged to a depth of thirty feet (MLLW). It would also be necessary to move the north beach berm line shoreward at least 400 feet, so that the huge craft could maneuver in the turning basin. If this were done, the entire north beach would require stone revetment. The Oceanside Harbor District had been awaiting this action anxiously since 1969. Breaking waves in the harbor had threatened structures in the harbor and on land. The board was also pressuring the Corps to do something about the submerged groin which resulted in the loss of a pleasure craft in the summer of 1970. Yet all of these measures had to await funding from the Department of the Navy before the Corps could begin study and design.[36]

While deliberations and analyses continued on harbor enlargements and modifications, the familiar problem of shoaling arose again in the fall of 1970. On 30 November, H.E. McNabb, superintendent for the Oceanside Harbor District, wrote Ronald Weiss, project engineer for the Corps Oceanside Navigation Study, to apprise him of the recent soundings. "While I dislike hollering 'wolf' or being an alarmist," McNabb warned, "it would be my estimate that if the build-up continues at present rate, this Harbor will be closed in ninety days unless some immediate remedial action is taken."[37] Since the harbor depths had held sufficiently through mid-1970, the Corps had cancelled its dredging for that year. By the time of McNabb's letter, the Corps had already scheduled funding for maintenance dredging for fiscal 1971, and had received a discharge permit from the California Regional Water Quality Control Board. When the harbor suddenly shoaled in during the fall, the Corps opened bids for the contract early in 1971, yet this meant that the work did not begin until 23 April.[38] Dredging during the winter months when the chances of storm waves were the greatest had proven disastrous to Standard Dredging Company nearly a decade before. The current contractor, Shellmaker, refused to make the same mistake. When completed on 30 July, however, the operation had again taken place during two months of the peak tourist season, and the beach-front property owners complained loudly.[39] This was an unusual circumstance, but the Corps clearly had provoked local ire.

Preparations also took longer for this dredging operation since the work now fell under the provisions of NEPA. One specific requirement which applied at Oceanside was sand compatibility. Material deposited on the beach now had to be compatible in size and composition with material already on the beach. This actually presented less of a problem at Oceanside than at other dredging sites; very little sand remained on the beach there as the Corps prepared for the 1971 maintenance dredging. Although the Harbor District was experiencing its best times yet in the late 1960s and early 1970s, erosion and cobble problems continued to plague residents to the south. During these years, Los Angeles District personnel fielded a variety of hostile complaints. Most concerned the condition of the beach—some general and others specific in nature. One individual complained not only to the District Engineer, but also to President Richard Nixon that the

Corps was deliberately neglecting to place dredged material on the beach fronting his property. That area was, however, a private beach. Others complained that the Corps was placing material in the wrong parts of the public beach. Still others protested that the Corps was "studying things to death," and found the length of time taken for producing a solution to the erosion and cobble problems "ridiculous."[40]

The Corps of Engineers had indeed been studying the Oceanside problems painstakingly. The Los Angeles District's careful study was prompted by two factors: fiscal constraints and a reluctance to find a quick technological or structural "fix" for Oceanside. While funding had resumed during the late 1960s, many people working on solutions were hesitant to build structures without thorough study. Structures had been one of the primary causes for beach erosion, and the installation of additional ones for sand entrapment was not without risk. Because structural measures had worked at other places on the southern California coast did not mean they would necessarily work at Oceanside. Moreover, structures could have an adverse impact on beaches downcoast. For such reasons the Corps had chosen not to combine the navigation and beach erosion studies when funding resumed.

By late 1971, the Los Angeles District shore protection section was ready to present three plans along with a "do nothing" alternative to the Oceanside Harbor District and interested public. Ronald Weiss from the Los Angeles District explained that the rivers which empty into the Pacific near Oceanside had not supplied sufficient sand during the past few decades, and this along with littoral interruption from the harbor breakwaters had resulted in an average yearly loss of about eight feet of beach. He added that the erosion would have been worse in recent years had it not been for the presence of the controversial cobbles. Weiss then began to explain the Corps' three alternatives for erosion along one mile of public beach fronting the city. The first was a system of five 500-foot groins built perpendicular to the shore about 1,000 feet apart. Periodic sand nourishment would occur between the groins. The second plan called for the construction of rock barriers about 1,000 feet offshore spaced in line 500 feet apart. This system would be nourished initially with about 500,000 cubic yards of sand. A third plan would continue to place dredging sand and additional material from inland on the beach with no structures built.[41]

After hearing Weiss's presentation, the Harbor District came to a quick decision on the favored plan. Despite the fact that the offshore submerged breakwaters carried an estimated price tag of slightly less than $1.5 million (at least 25 percent of which the city would have to pay) most present at the meeting supported it. According to Weiss, the barriers would remain three feet under water at low tide, and provide excellent surfing (except at low tide) while creating a new fish habitat. He also explained that the barriers would probably have less effect on downcoast beaches than groins. When asked about the effects of the barriers on maintenance dredging of the harbor, Weiss said that was still uncertain, but any plan must be compatible with studies being conducted on harbor expansion.[42] Both Oceanside and Corps officials wanted to find solutions to beach erosion as soon as possible. These plans were a positive step in that direction, but everyone knew that actual implementation was years away.

Meanwhile the Oceanside navigation study, congressionally-mandated in 1967, had run into the barrier of new environmental constraints. The Corps had been refining the plan to build an outer harbor to the southwest since 1968, since it had proven to be the only viable location for expansion of the small craft facility. When NEPA forced an environmental impact statement to be prepared for the project, at least one alternative site had to be selected for the project. Corps personnel chose what they considered beforehand to be an unfeasible alternative: land between civilian and military facilities which belonged to the Marine Corps. As they began to assess the impact of destruction of the beach and lagoon area—and the restructuring of the mouth of the San Luis Rey River—it became clear that ecological considerations would not allow expansion to occur southwest of the civilian harbor. The only alternative remaining brought them into direct confrontation with the Marines.[43]

The Marines at Camp Pendleton were clearly upset about this alternative when they met with the Corps in July 1972. Since this land was not available, the Marines questioned why the Corps had prepared such a plan as an alternative at all. Weiss and Ferdinand Wagner of the Los Angeles District explained the impossibility of development to the southwest, and pointed out that encroachment on Marine Corps property represented the only alternative at the present. They also noted that the plan was prefaced with the statement: "In the event the North Beach Area becomes excess to the Military Requirements," and were aware that at present the land was not available. Still interested in modifying the harbor to accommodate the new class of larger amphibious vessels, the commandant of Camp Pendleton told Weiss and Wagner that the Marines were in the process of securing funding for the Corps of Engineers to draw up design plans. He gave little encouragement that the Marine Corps would approve any further encroachment on its property.[44]

By late 1972, the more immediate problem of shoaling emerged again. In November, the harbor entrance channel depth was down to eleven feet in places. The City Council of Oceanside urged the Corps to resume dredging as soon as possible, not only because of harbor depths, but also to have the work done by Memorial Day 1973 (the official beginning of the tourist season). The Corps was ready to begin in the fall, but more extensive environmental rules postponed the work. The Office of the Chief of Engineers was now requiring an EIS for dredging projects, and divers were at work in Oceanside Harbor to prove that this operation would not have a "negative impact" on the ecology of the ocean floor. While Oceanside dredging proved environmentally sound and thus did not require an EIS, the delay meant that dredging did not begin until June 1973.[45]

By the end of 1972, even more environmental restraints were placed on coastal development with the passage of federal and state laws. The U.S. Congress early in the year passed the Coastal Zone Management Act, which called for development of a comprehensive plan for all of the nation's shorelines. The provisions of the act allowed federal grants so that each coastal state could develop its own plans and establish an organization for regulation. In California, voters also approved Proposition 20, the State Coastal Zone Conservation Act, on 7 November 1972. The act provided that "no development within a thousand yards inland from the mean tide could take place without a permit from one or more coastal commissions." The act also provided for the establishment of six regional and one statewide Coastal Commission to review and issue such permits.[46] In the future, these laws assured that any coastal development would be more closely regulated than ever before.

Many issues remained unresolved in Oceanside as this new array of federal and state environmental legislation went into effect. Beach erosion solutions that called for structures would undoubtedly come under close scrutiny. Likewise, harbor modification and expansion would have to be considered within the constraints of state and federal legislation. The Corps of Engineers continued to expand and refine its environmental assessment capabilities to meet the challenges and demands of the new laws. However, the delays that environmental concerns caused in operations like maintenance dredging further tested the patience of residents of Oceanside, and contributed greatly to strained relations between the city, local residents, and the Corps. Meanwhile, the recurrent problems of beach erosion and harbor shoaling continued.

NOTES

[1]Gerald G. Kuhn and Francis P. Shepard, *Sea Cliffs, Beaches, and Coastal Valleys of San Diego County: Some Amazing Histories and Some Horrifying Implications* (Berkeley, CA: University of California Press, 1984), p. 55; Interview, author with Ronald Weiss. Los Angeles, CA, 2 April 1986. Hereafter cited as Weiss interview; Alton Ruden to W. Herron, subj: cobbles, 21 Jan. 1964, Oceanside General file, 1961-69, LNNA RG 77/80-0034 Box 18/20.

[2]Maj. Sheldon Biles to A. Ruden, subj: cobbles, 26 Feb. 1964, Oceanside General file, 1961-69, LNNA RG 77/80-0034 Box 18/20.

[3]*Los Angeles Times* (6 Mar. 1964); W.F. Linnett to Maj. S. Biles, subj: beach conditions, 1 Apr. 1964, Oceanside file, 1964-66, LNNA RG 77/84-0018 Box 6/8; Maj. S. Biles to W. Linnett, subj: concern about beach conditions, 9 Apr. 1964, Oceanside file, 1964-66, LNNA RG 77/84-0018 Box 6/8.

[4]Memorandum for the Record from W. Herron regarding *Los Angeles Times* article of 6 Mar. 1964, 17 Mar. 1964, Oceanside file, 1964-66, LNNA RG 77/84-0018 Box 6/8; Herron interview.

[5]Edward Koehm to E. Sklar, subj: harbor depths, 30 Jul. 1964, Oceanside General file, 1961-69, LNNA RG 77/80-0034 Box 18/20.

[6]Harold B. Snyder to Board of Directors, Oceanside Small Craft Harbor District, subj: harbor shoaling, 3 May 1965, Oceanside General file, LNNA RG 77/80-0034 Box 18/20.

[7]Memorandum for Navigation Section from Hugh Converse regarding authorized review survey of Oceanside Harbor, undated 1965, Oceanside Navigation file, 1966-70, LNNA RG 77/84-0018 Box 3/8.

[8]L.C. Coxe to Commandant, Camp Pendleton, subj: Del Mar Boat Basin entrance, 2 Jul. 1965, Camp Pendleton, CA, file, 1946-74, LNNA RG 77/80-0033 Box 6/20; *Los Angeles Times* (13 Jul. 1965); South Pacific Division Engineer to Office of the Chief of Engineers, subj: summer storm at Oceanside, 28 Aug. 1965, Oceanside General file, 1961-69, LNNA RG 77/80-0034 Box 18/20; Memorandum from Col. John A.B. Dillard to Los Angeles District, subj: availability of dredging equipment for Oceanside, 27 Jul. 1965, Oceanside General file, 1961-69, LNNA RG 77/80-0034 Box 18/20; U.S., Congress, House, *An Act Authorizing the Construction, Repair, and Preservation of Certain Public Works on Rivers and Harbors for Navigation, Flood Control, and Other Purposes*, Pub. L. 89-298, 89th Cong., 1st sess., 1965, H.D. 76, p. 1092; *Omnibus Rivers and Harbors Act of 1965*, 79 Stat. 1073, 1965, Title III, Sec. 301; U.S. Army, Corps of Engineers, *Water Resources Development by the U.S. Army Corps of Engineers in California, 1977* (Washington, D.C: Government Printing Office, 1978), p. 33-1; U.S. Congress, House, *Oceanside Harbor, Oceanside (Camp Pendleton), California*, H. Doc. 76, 89th Cong., 1st sess., 1965, p. 1.

[9]*Ibid.;* H. Snyder to W. Herron, subj: insurance rates at Oceanside Harbor, 4 Nov. 1965, Oceanside file, 1964-66, LNNA RG 77/84-0018 Box 6/8; Memorandum for the Record to Los Angeles District on dredging funding for Oceanside, 6 Apr. 1965, Oceanside General file, 1961-69, LNNA RG 77/80-0034 Box 18/20; Memorandum for the Record from Maj. Robert Ojendyk regarding fonecon with E. Sklar, 12 Aug. 1965, Oceanside General file, 1961-69, LNNA RG 77/80-0034 Box 18/20; Transfer of Funds from Marine Corps to Corps of Engineers, 30 Nov. 1965, Oceanside file, 1964-66; LNNA RG 77/84-0018 Box 6/8; E. Koehm to South Pacific Division Engineer, subj: maintenance dredging, 1966, 1 Jan. 1966, Oceanside file, 1964-66, LNNA RG 77/84-0018 Box 6/8; Abstract of Construction bid, Utah Construction Company, 1 Feb. 1966, Oceanside file, 1964-66, LNNA RG 77/84-0018 Box 6/8; Southwestern District, U.S. Navy, to Commandant, Camp Pendleton, subj: Marine Corps share of dredging costs, 4 Apr. 1966, Oceanside General file, 1961-69, LNNA RG 77/80-0034 Box 18/20; Col. J. Dillard to Commander, Southwest Division, Naval Facilities Engineering Commission, subj: dredging schedule for fiscal 1968, 3 June 1966, Oceanside General file, 1961-69, LNNA RG 77/80-0034 Box 18/20; City of Oceanside Resolution 66-14, 14 Sept. 1966, Oceanside Navigation file, 1966-70, LNNA RG 77/84-0018 Box 3/8; City of Oceanside Resolution 66-161, 9 Nov. 1966, Oceanside Navigation file, 1966-70, LNNA RG 77/84-0018 Box 3/8.

[10]Col. J. Dillard to Standard Dredging Company, subj: claim for change order, 12 Feb. 1965, Oceanside file, 1964-66, LNNA RG 77/84-0018 Box 6/8; Col. J. Dillard to South Pacific Division Engineer, subj: Standard Dredging claim, 10 Sept. 1965, Oceanside file, 1964-66, LNNA RG 77/84-0018 Box 6/8; Col. J. Dillard to Director, Southwest Division, Bureau of Yards and Docks, 14 Mar. 1966, Oceanside file, 1964-66, LNNA RG 77/84-0018 Box 6/8, also in Camp Pendleton Harbor, CA, 1946-74, LNNA RG 77/80-0033 Box 6/20; Decision before the Corps of Engineers Board of Contract Appeals, 1 Apr. 1969, Oceanside file, 1967-68, LNNA RG 77/84-0018 Box 7/8; Herron interview.

[11]Moffatt and Nichol, *Sand Bypass Study, Phase I*, p. 1-12.

[12]Harriette Treadwell to Oceanside Small Craft Harbor District, subj: proposed harbor expansion, 18 July 1966, Oceanside General file, 1961-69, LNNA RG 77/80-0034 Box 18/20; H. Snyder to W. Herron, subj: proposed future slip development, 15 Jul. 1966, Oceanside General file, 1961-69, LNNA RG 77/80-0034 Box 18/20; F. Lilley to Col. J. Dillard, subj: removal of part of the north groin of small craft harbor, 14 Jul. 1966, Oceanside General file, 1961-69, LNNA RG 77/80-0034 Box 18/20.

[13]Col. Norman Pehrson to Commander, Southwest Division, Navy Bureau of Yards and Docks, subj: sand tracing at Camp Pendleton, 31 Jan. 1967, Oceanside Sand Transfer Study file, 1967, LNNA 77/79-0001 Box 1/13, also in Oceanside Navigation file, 1966-70, LNNA RG 77/84-0018 Box 3/8; Col. N. Pehrson to South Pacific Division Engineer, subj: Oceanside's request for additional federal harbor study, 28 Mar. 1967, Oceanside General file, 1961-69, LNNA RG 77/80-0034 Box 18/20; Senator George Murphy to Lt. Gen. William Cassidy, subj: Oceanside Harbor problems, 22 Mar. 1967, Oceanside General file, 1961-69, LNNA RG 77/80-0034 Box 18/20.

[14]Gen. Lewis Fields to Los Angeles District, subj: funding for maintenance dredging of Del Mar Boat Basin, 21 Apr. 1967, Camp Pendleton Harbor, CA, 1946-74, LNNA RG 77/80-0033 Box 6/20; Memorandum for the Record from W. Herron regarding Oceanside maintenance dredging, 12 May 1967, Camp Pendleton Harbor, CA, 1946-74, LNNA RG 77/80-0033 Box 6/20; *Oceanside Blade Tribune* (24 Mar. 1967); *Los Angeles Times* (4 May 1967); *San Diego Union* (14 June 1967). Hereafter referred to as *OBT, LAT,* and *SDU.*

[15]Memorandum for the Record from Herron, 12 May 1967, Camp Pendleton Harbor, CA, 1946-74, LNNA RG 77/80-0033 Box 6/20; *SDU* (25 May, 16 June 1967).

[16]*SDU* (25 May 1967); Anthony Mauricio to Department of Small Craft Harbors, Washington, D.C., subj: Oceanside Harbor shoaling, 1 June 1967, Oceanside General file, 1961-69, LNNA RG 77/80-0034 Box 18/20.

[17]U.S. Army Engineer District, *Beach Erosion Control Report on Cooperative Study of Southern California, Cape San Martin to Mexican Boundary* Appendix IV, Final Report, (June

1967), p. 33; Al Hollenstein to Sen. G. Murphy, subj: beach erosion at Oceanside, 11 July 1967, Oceanside General file, 1961-69, LNNA RG 77/80-0034 Box 18/20; A. Hollenstein to Sen. T. Kuchel, subj: beach erosion at Oceanside, 11 July 1967, Oceanside General file, 1961-69, LNNA RG 77/80-0034 Box 18/20; *OBT* (30 July 1967).

[18] *Ibid.*, and (28 Jul. 1967); Maj. Gen. F.J. Clarke to A. Hollenstein, subj: beach erosion at Oeanside, 21 July 1967, Oceanside General file, 1961-69, LNNA RG 77/80-0034 Box 18/20.

[19] Moffatt aned Nichol, *Sand Bypass Study, Phase I*, p. 1-12; Col. James Irvine, Jr., to A. Mauricio, subj: dredging at Oceanside Harbor, 26 June 1967, Oceanside General file, 1961-69, LNNA RG 77/80-0034 Box 18/20; Col. N. Pehrson to Commandant, Camp Pendleton, subj: reimbursement to Oceanside for emergency dredging, 11 July 1967, Oceanside General file, 1961-69, LNNA RG 77/80-0034 Box 18/20; F. Lilley to W. Herron, subj: replacement of cobbles with sand, 15 Aug. 1967, Oceanside General file, 1961-69, LNNA RG 77/80-0034 Box 18/20; E. Koehm to F. Lilley, subj: sand substitution, 22 Aug. 1967, Oceanside General file, 1961-69, LNNA RG 77/80-0034 Box 18/20.

[20] James Dunham to Oceanside Small Craft Harbor District, subj: reasons for severe shoaling in Sept. 1967, 25 Jan. 1968, Oceanside General file, 1961-69, LNNA RG 77/80-0034 Box 18/20; *SDU* (27 Dec. 1967, 3 Jan. 1968).

[21] Leeds, Hill, and Jewett, Inc., *Shoaling Study, Oceanside Small Craft Harbor* (Los Angeles: Leeds, Hill, and Jewett, 1968), *passim;* F. Lilley to Col. N. Pehrson, subj: Harbor modification plans, undated 1968, Oceanside General file, 1961-69, LNNA RG 77/80-0034 Box 18/20; *SDU* (20 Feb. 1968); Report, "Engineering, Economics, and Financial Feasibility Review, $500,000 Construction Cost," California Department of Harbors and Watercraft, Feb. 1968, Oceanside Beach Erosion file, 1967-71, LNNA RG 77/84-0018 Box 6/8; E.A. Curtis to E. Sklar, subj: State loan agreement with Oceanside, 23 Feb. 1968, Oceanside Beach Erosion file, 1967-71, LNNA RG 77/84-0018 Box 6/8.

[22] W. Herron to Los Angeles District Engineer, subj: Harbors and Watercraft meeting, 19 Feb. 1968, 20 Feb. 1968, Oceanside General file, 1961-69, LNNA RG 77/80-0034 Box 18/20; Col. N. Pehrson to South Pacific Division Engineer, subj: Oceanside Harbor improvements, 29 Feb. 1968, Oceanside General file, 1961-69, LNNA RG 77/80-0034 Box 18/20; E. Sklar to N.W. Sprow, subj: Acceptance of loan from State, 27 Mar. 1968, Oceanside Beach Erosion file, 1967-71, LNNA RG 77/84-0018 Box 6/8; City of Oceanside Resolution, 27 Mar. 1968, Oceanside General file, 1961-69, LNNA RG 77/80-0034 Box 18/20.

[23] Moffatt and Nichol, *Sand Bypass Study, Phase I*, p. 1-12; *SDU* (27 Mar., 20, 26 Apr., 23 May 1968); Report, "Progress, Camp Pendleton, Oceanside Harbor Maintenance Dredging," Shellmaker, Inc., 24 Apr. 1968, Oceanside file, 1967-68, LNNA RG 77/84-0018 Box 7/8.

[24] Notice of Public Hearing on "Review Report for Oceanside Harbor," and on "Survey Report of the Shores between the Santa Margarita River and the Agua Hedionda Lagoon, San Diego County, California," 29 May 1968, Oceanside General file, 1961-69, LNNA RG 77/80-0034 Box 18/20; Notes on presentation made by E.A. Sandling on behalf of the Oceanside Small Craft Harbor District at Public Meeting, 27 June 1968, Oceanside General file, 1961-69, LNNA RG 77/80-0034 Box 18/20.

[25] Minutes of Public Meeting, 27 June 1968, Public Hearing, Oceanside Harbor, to accompany Review Report, LNNA RG 77/84-0018 Box 3/8.

[26] *OBT* (18 Sept. 1968); *SDU* (24 Sept., 16 Nov., 12 Dec. 1968).

[27] See Memorandum for the Record from Charles Fisher in regard to a conversation with OCE, 9 Jan. 1969, Oceanside General file, 1961-69, LNNA RG 77/80-0034 Box 18/20; *River and Harbor Act of 1968*, 82 Stat. 731, 1968, Title III, Sec. 215; Cong. J. Utt to George Fallon, subj: Federal reimbursement to Oceanside for revetment work, 24 Jan. 1969, Oceanside General file, 1961-69, LNNA RG 77/80-0034 Box 18/20; *OBT* (10 Apr. 1969).

[28] *SDU* (27 Mar., 12 June, 25 July 1969); Col. N. Pehrson to Brunswig Sholars, subj: dredging periods, 14 July 1969, Oceanside General file, 1961-69, LNNA RG 77/80-0034

Box 18/20; *Vista* (California) *Press* (30 July 1969); Oceanside Small Craft Harbor District Resolution 69-5, 11 June 1969, Oceanside General file, 1961-69, LNNA RG 77/80-0034 Box 18/20.

²⁹*SDU* (12 June 1969); Col. N. Pehrson to South Pacific Division Engineer, subj: Harbor shoaling, undated 1969, Oceanside General file, 1961-69, LNNA RG 77/80-0034 Box 18/20; Herron interview.

³⁰Frank Leon to Oceanside Small Craft Harbor District, subj: Request to audit State loan for harbor improvement, Oct. 1968, Harbor Computations, Oceanside Operation and Maintenance, 1969-70, LNNA RG 77/84-0018 Box 6/8; *SDU*, (12 June, 4 July 1969).

³¹*Ibid.*, (30 Apr., 8 July 1969); *OBT* (4, 9 Oct. 1969). Oceanside officials also succeeded in acquiring a $300,000 loan from the state if needed for emergencies. See *SDU* (14 Aug. 1969).

³²*Ibid.*, (28 Nov., 1969); Memorandum for the Record from Orville Magoon regarding a Phase I conference on Oceanside Navigation Study, 29 Dec. 1969, Oceanside General file, 1961-69, LNNA RG 77/80-0034 Box 18/20; Los Angeles District Engineer to South Pacific Division Engineer, subj: OceansideNavigation Study, 25 June 1970, Oceanside, CA, file, 1970-73, LNNA RG 77/80-0034 Box 18/20; Col. Richard Erlenkotter to Los Angeles District Engineer, subj: Oceanside Navigation Study Phase I conference, 10 Feb. 1970, Oceanside CA, file, 1970-73, LNNA RG 77/80-0034 Box 18/20.

³³*Ibid.*; Weiss interview; E. Koehm to South Pacific Division Engineer, subj: Oceanside Beach Erosion Control project, 10 June 1970, Oceanside CA file, 1970-73; LNNA RG 77/80-0034 Box 18/20.

³⁴U.S. Army Engineer District, *History of Navigation and Navigation Improvements of the Pacific Coast* (Washington: GPO, 1983), p. 110; Elaine Moss, ed., *Land Use Controls in the United States: A Handbook on the Legal Rights of Citizens* (New York: Dial Press, 1977), pp. 18-36; U.S. Army Engineer District, *Digest of Water Resources Policies and Authorities*, EP 1165-2-1, 30 June 1983.

³⁵Larry Bagley to Ronald Weiss, subj: Harbor expansion, 18 Nov. 1970, Oceanside CA, file, 1970-73, LNNA RG 77/80-0034 Box 18/20; Notes taken at meeting with the Corps of Engineers, State Department of Parks and Recreation, and Department of the Interior, 22 Dec. 1970, Oceanside CA, file, 1970-73, LNNA RG 77/80-0034 Box 18/20.

³⁶Memorandum for Shore Protection File from R. Weiss regarding modification of Oceanside Harbor to Accommodate the 1179 Class LSTs, 18 Dec. 1970, Oceanside CA, file, 1970-73, LNNA RG 77/80-0034 Box 18/20; H.E. McNabb to C. Fisher, subj: Problems with submerged groin, 7 July 1970, Oceanside CA, file, 1970-73, LNNA RG 77/80-0034 Box 18/20; H. McNabb to Commander U.S. Coast Guard in Long Beach, subj: hazards of submerged groin, 7 July 1970, Oceanside CA, file, 1970-73, LNNA RG 77/80-0034 Box 18/20.

³⁷H. McNabb to R. Weiss, subj: Harbor shoaling, 30 Nov. 1970, Harbor Computations, Oceanside Operation and Maintenance, 1969-70, LNNA RG 77/84-0018 Box 6/8.

³⁸Col. Robert Malley to Commander, Southwest Division, Navy Bureau of Yards and Docks, subj: Maintenance dredging, 16 Jan. 1970, Oceanside CA, file, 1970-73, LNNA RG 77/80-0034 Box 18/20.

³⁹*Ibid.*; F. Lilley to Col. R. Malley, subj: dredging during tourist season, 10 Apr. 1970, Oceanside CA, file, 1970-73, LNNA RG 77/80-0034 Box 18/20; Col. Paul Loop to South Pacific Division Engineer, subj: Dredging surveys, 21 Sept. 1970, Oceanside CA, file, 1970-73, LNNA RG 77/80-0034 Box 18/20; E. Koehm to South Pacific Division Engineer, subj: Dredging Policies and Practices, 21 Apr. 1970, Oceanside CA, file, 1970-73, LNNA RG 77/80-0034 Box 18/20; Discharge Permit from California Regional Water Quality Control Board, 15 Dec. 1970, Oceanside CA, file, 1970-73, LNNA RG 77/80-0034 Box 18/20; Report, "Dredging," Shellmaker, Inc., 30 July 1971, Oceanside Operation and Maintenance, 1971-74, LNNA RG 77/84-0018 Box 6/8; E. Koehm to Chief, Construction Division, Los Angeles District, subj: Maintenance dredging, 1 Apr. 1971, Oceanside CA, file, 1970-73, LNNA RG 77/80-0034 Box 18/20; H. McNabb to Los Angeles District

Engineer, subj: Public relations and dredging, 13 Aug. 1971, Oceanside CA, file, 1970-73, LNNA RG 77/80-0034 Box 18/20; Weiss interview.

[40]Col. S.J. Black to Sen. G. Murphy, subj: Inland dams upsetting the ecological balance, 30 Apr. 1970, Harbor Computations, Oceanside Operation and Maintenance, 1969-70, LNNA RG 77/84-0018 Box 6/8; G. Bennett to Col. R. Malley, subj: Beach erosion, 17 June 1971, Oceanside CA, file, 1970-73, LNNA RG 77/80-0034 Box 18/20; B. Sholars to Pres. Richard Nixon, subj: Dredge deposition, 3 Aug. 1970, Oceanside CA, file, 1970-73, LNNA RG 77/80-0034 Box 18/20; D.K. Tooker to Los Angeles District Engineer, subj: Dredge deposition, 15 May 1969, Oceanside General file, 1961-69, LNNA RG 77/80-0034 Box 18/20; E. Koehm to L. Hirschler, subj: Beach erosion, 5 Nov. 1971, Oceanside CA, file, 1970-73, LNNA RG 77/80-0034 Box 18/20; Roy Breyer to Pres. R. Nixon, subj: Beach erosion, 14 Apr. 1971, Oceanside CA, file, 1970-73, LNNA RG 77/80-0034 Box 18/20; Weiss interview; B. Sholars to E. Koehm, subj: Length of time taken for studies, 22 Apr. 1971, Oceanside CA, file, 1970-73, LNNA RG 77/80-0034 Box 18/20.

[41]Interview author with Donald Spencer. Los Angeles, CA, 29 Apr. 1986. Hereafter cited as Spencer interview; Report, "Proceedings of the Environmental Workshop held at Oceanside," 17 Nov. 1971, Oceanside Beach Erosion file, 1972-75, LNNA RG 77/84-0018 Box 3/8. Hereafter cited as Proceedings, 17 Nov. 1971; SDU (9 Dec. 1971); Memorandum for Shore Protection File from R. Weiss in regard to Beach Erosion Control Study meeting, 18 Nov. 1971, Oceanside Beach Erosion file, 1972-75, LNNA RG 77/84-0018 Box 3/8. Hereafter cited as Weiss memorandum, 18 Nov. 1971; Weiss interview; OBT (18 Nov. 1971).

[42]Proceedings, 17 Nov. 1971; SDU (9 Dec. 1971); Weiss memorandum, 18 Nov. 1971; Weiss interview; OBT (9 Dec. 1971).

[43]Col. N. Pehrson to South Pacific Division Engineer, subj: Survey for Oceanside Navigation Study, 10 Oct. 1969. Oceanside General file, 1961-69, LNNA RG 77/80-0034 Box 18/20 Box 18/20; Report, "Preliminary Proposed Expansion of Del Mar Boat Basin (Plan II Map of Plan)," Nov. 1971, Camp Pendleton Harbor, CA, 1946-74, LNNA RG 77/80-0033 Box 6/20; Memorandum for the Record, Los Angeles District in regard to a meeting between the Corps of Engineers and the Marine Corps at Camp Pendleton, 11 July 1972, Del Mar Basin file, 1972-76, LNNA RG 77/84-0018 Box 7/8.

[44]Ibid.: Memorandum for the Record from R. Weiss regarding expansion of Del Mar Boat Basin entrance to accommodate new 1179 LSTs, 18 Oct. 1972, Camp Pendleton Harbor, CA, 1946-74, LNNA RG 77/80-0033 Box 6/20.

[45]City of Oceanside Resolution 72-18, 25 Oct. 1972, Oceanside Operation and Maintenance, 1971-74, LNNA RG 77/84-0018 Box 6/8; SDU (27 Oct. 1972); Weiss interview; Moffatt and Nichol, Sand Bypass Study, Phase I, p. 1-12.

[46]Moss, Land Use Controls, pp. 2-3, 115-116, 306; Gregory Graves and Sally Simon, eds., A History of Environmental Review in Santa Barbara County, California (Santa Barbara: Graduate Program in Public Historical Studies, 1980), p. 65.

CHAPTER IV

The Search for
Permanent Solutions

Coastal experts in the federal, state, local, and private sectors working at Oceanside were well aware by the early 1970s that the present method of battling erosion and shoaling was ineffective. In the past ten years, between two and three million cubic yards of sand had been dredged from the harbor entrance and placed on Oceanside beach only to return and continue a persistent and costly cycle. Maintenance dredging of the harbor had occurred on an average every eighteen months since the small craft facility opened. In each event, the Corps of Engineers directed the contractor to place all of the dredged material on Oceanside beach to the south. After some dredging episodes, the sand remained on the beach for several months. However, one storm system or merely an unusual wave event could, and often did, strip most of the sand from the beach and deposit a good deal of it in the harbor entrance channel. While most people wanted a more lasting solution to the two problems than periodic dredging, progress on most of those plans was stymied by new environmental considerations, and by a reluctance on the part of coastal engineers to apply additional technology to remedy what was largely a man-made problem. The forces of nature had been disrupted by the construction of the harbor jetties, and were clearly at odds with the two human objectives of keeping sand out of the harbor and on the beach to the south.

As the Corps prepared for the next round of maintenance dredging in February 1973, actual long-term solutions to shoaling, harbor overcrowding, and erosion appeared distant and perhaps unfeasible. Nonetheless, both the beach erosion and navigation studies continued. Corps personnel also awaited the results of radioisotope sand tracing experiments conducted at Oceanside in January 1973. They hoped that the study of the movement of radioactive sand being analyzed at the Corps' Coastal Engineering Research Center in Fort Belvoir, Virginia, would help in their harbor breakwater design modifications. This would enable them to finalize the navigation study which was already in its advanced stages. Meanwhile, they contracted for the removal of nearly 435,000 cubic yards of sand from the ever-shallowing harbor entrance channel. As Los Angeles District Project Leader Ronald Weiss summarised the current operation: "It's the most expeditious way of handling the situation until we get something better."[1]

Los Angeles District personnel believed they had come up with something better when they did complete the Oceanside navigation study in October 1973. In the report, the Corps considered six plans for expansion and modification of the existing small craft facility. The first called for expansion at the mouth of the Santa Margarita River, but this approach involved high flood risks, endangered a river estuary and nesting habitat for the endangered California least tern, and sited the project within the boundaries of Marine Corps Base Camp Pendleton, too far from the original harbor for efficient operation. A second location (already discussed in the last chapter) was at the North Beach area between the existing military and civilian facilities. Camp Pendleton personnel had not changed their minds since 1972 about prohibiting construction at that location. A third possibility (also mentioned in the last chapter) was the original expansion plan of the City of Oceanside. Environmental considerations diminished the feasibility of this plan on the ground that it would necessitate diversion of the San Luis Rey River, thus destroying both an estuary and wildlife habitat. This plan also carried the onus of having a high probability of structural damage in the event of a flood on the river.

Two other possible sites were at the Buena Vista and Agua Hedionda lagoons south of the city. Both of these locations were environmentally sensitive; and both were too distant from the existing harbor to be economically feasible.[2]

The Corps therefore placed its faith in a another plan which seemed to have the least amount of environmental and jurisdictional conflict. Members of the Los Angeles District hoped this plan would solve the problems of harbor expansion, channel improvement, and the recurrent shoaling problem. The small craft harbor would be expanded seaward from the south half of the

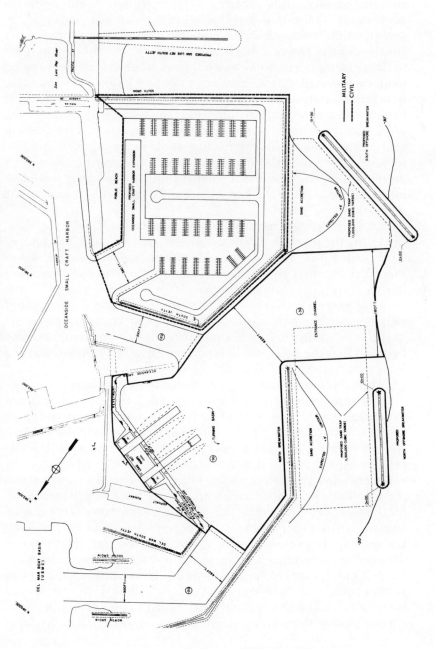

Corps of Engineers harbor improvement plans, 1973.

existing facility, thus creating a basin which could berth an additional 1,200 boats. Extensive breakwater additions and re-design would make this plan possible. The Corps proposed the construction of two offshore breakwaters, one of 1,000 feet parallel to the existing north breakwater, and another of 1,500 feet angled in an east-west direction seaward of the new basin. Between these new breakwaters and the existing modified ones, Corps personnel believed that sand traps would form, thus diverting much of the sand which formerly choked the harbor entrance. The existing south jetty of the small craft harbor would be lengthened by 1,000 feet and joined with the south groin, thereby creating the needed protection for the new basin. In addition, another jetty would be built at the mouth of the San Luis Rey River to divert sand to the new south sand trap.[3]

Acting District Engineer Lieutenant Colonel John Metlios, unveiling the plan at a public meeting at Oceanside on 30 October 1973, called it the most reasonable alternative. He pointed out to those present that this proposal would eliminate the hazardous harbor entrance, create an additional fifty acres of harborside land, increase recreational boating enterprises, provide a quiet water beach inside the new basin, and most importantly, improve the harbor's capability to be self-supporting. As for financing, Metlios believed that the costs would be shared equally by the federal and local governments.[4]

While most at the meeting supported the Corps idea, a number of questions were raised. Most concerned the impact that the expansion would have on the beach to the south. The president of Oceanside's Chamber of Commerce worried about the city's beach, while several surfing advocates opposed the plan because it would remove a good part of the existing harbor beach and destroy the excellent wave conditions there. Others expressed concern about the additional pollution that another 1,200 boats might create. By far the most damaging critique, however, came from Dr. Douglas Inman, an oceanographer with Scripps Institute in La Jolla, California. He cautioned with documentation that the proposed offshore breakwaters creating sand traps would divert about 2.5 million cubic yards of sand. According to his estimates, this was approximately a twelve-year supply of littoral material, and therefore would be extremely detrimental to downcoast beaches. Rather than offshore breakwaters, Inman suggested that the Corps and Scripps Institute conduct joint experiments on the possibility of developing a sand bypassing system. The system, Inman argued, would reduce first costs greatly by eliminating the need for rock placement. It would employ what he called "crater sink-fluidizing techniques," which would allow pumps to pull the sand from the harbor and transfer it downcoast.[5] Although Inman's plan might help to solve harbor shoaling and beach erosion, it did little to eliminate the need for harbor expansion.

The Oceanside Small-Craft Harbor District Board of Directors was favorable toward the Corps plan. They had recently hired a new administrator for the District, Loren Whitney, a retired naval commander. In so doing, they abolished the old position of harbor superintendent. They had also economized space within the existing harbor limits to accommodate an additional 200 boats. By mid-1973 those spaces were full, and the waiting list was again growing. After the Corps announced its expansion proposal, the Board of Directors and the City Council began to grapple with the next funding problem. The question now was whether Oceanside voters would approve any measure for harbor expansion that carried an estimated price tag of $5 million.[6]

Many Oceanside residents were adamantly opposed to any more money being spent on harbor improvement until the beach erosion problem was solved. They considered the harbor to be a luxury used primarily by the wealthy; its condition meant little to them. Moreover, they resented the fact that the cobbles, which came from the 1962-63 excavation, remained on Oceanside beach. This kind of frustration led to some hostile journalism on the part of some of the local newspapers, much of which was directed at the Corps of Engineers. For example, a 1974 *Oceanside Blade Tribune* editorial blamed virtually all of the city's beach and harbor woes on the Corps. "The beach-harbor situation," the editorial complained, "is a typical governmental boondoggle which had its beginnings in 1942 when the Corps constructed the Del Mar boat basin at Camp Pendleton." The Corps, of course, had not built the original boat basin, and actually recommended against its construction. The editorial went on to blame the Corps for construction of breakwater improvements and the small craft harbor, and then accused the agency of continuing with each dredging to place more cobbles on the city's beach. The article closed with a recommendation that the city file a lawsuit against the Corps of

Engineers.[7] Editorials such as this served to inflame local resentment, and did little to give a clear picture of the complexity of the problems at hand.

When the time for the next scheduled maintenance dredging arrived in 1974, the Corps not only had to meet federal environmental standards, but also those imposed by the California Coastal Commission. In October, Los Angeles District Engineer Colonel John V. Foley received a letter from the executive director of the commission. To Foley's surprise it stated: "[T]he placement of spoils on public beaches, the installation of temporary onshore pipelines to transport spoil material, the construction of temporary onshore powerlines to serve dredging equipment and other similar developments all normally require a permit under the California Coastal Zone Conservation Act."[8] The commission required the Corps to appear at a public meeting to acquire such a permit. Fortunately, the Corps had been preparing environmental assessments of its dredging operations under the guidelines of NEPA. When these findings were presented to the Coastal Commission, they affirmed that the Corps' dredging practices were environmentally consistent with both federal and state standards.[9]

During this dredging episode, Corps personnel decided to try additional measures to keep the sand on the beach and out of the harbor for a longer period of time. They directed their contractor, Western Pacific Constructors of Seattle, Washington, to bring extra discharge pipes along so that the dredged material could be distributed as far south as Witherby Street, on the extreme edge of the city. As the sand was discharged, the city planned to build sand berms at low tide to keep the material onshore. In addition, the contractor was to use a slotted pipe at the point of discharge in the hope of emitting the sand-and-water mixture at a slower rate, thus allowing the sand to better settle on the beach. Steps such as these were necessary in the Corps estimation, but they were expensive. In part due to the high inflation of the period, these measures resulted in the Corps of Engineers and the Marine Corps splitting a bill of almost $1 million for the removal of about 500,000 cubic yards of sand when the operation was completed in January 1975.[10]

By the middle of the month, almost one-half of the sand placed on the beach had disappeared. The extremely fine grade again caused the sand to wash away to sea even in normal wave conditions. After a meeting with an aide of Congressman Andrew Hinshaw of Santa Ana, Oceanside Mayor Howard Richardson announced a plan for a short-term solution to beach erosion. He proposed that the city and federal lawmakers from the region push for legislation which would appropriate an estimated $900,000 for the dry-hauling of sand from the bed of the San Luis Rey River to the city's eroded beach. "What I'm proposing," Richardson declared, "would be a more immediate solution to our beach erosion problems while we are waiting for the final answer." While the Corps' preliminary report on beach erosion was in the final stages, it would take at least another year for a full project to be prepared. In the meantime, Oceanside needed the sand that this operation could bring. Since it carried a cost of less than one million, Richardson hoped that full congressional approval would not be necessary, and that the Corps could acquire the funding "speedily."

Los Angeles District personnel had been moving forward on both beach erosion and navigation studies. In December 1974, the Shore Protection Section issued a position paper which reaffirmed federal responsibility for erosion at Oceanside's beaches, and recommended the production of a detailed project report for the problem under the provisions of Section 111 of the 1968 Rivers and Harbors Act. Those provisions authorized the Corps to investigate and possibly construct projects which would mitigate shore damages resulting from federal navigation works. A project such as this could be accomplished without congressional authorization if first costs remained under one million dollars. While some in the District believed that a careful reassessment of the findings of the 1960 equity study—which charged the federal government with total responsibility for Oceanside's beach erosion control— would warrant an increase in the local share of erosion work, more argued that the results would be inconclusive. Therefore, federal responsibility remained at 100 percent.[11]

Another issue of debate in the Los Angeles District was the possible combination of the beach erosion and navigation reports. Advocates were confident that the combination would result in a cost savings and streamlining of both projects. However, they were overruled by others who argued that the two studies should remain separate, primarily because they were at different levels of completion. Meanwhile, in response to Mayor Richardson's request, the Los Angeles District requested that the South Pacific Division Engineer appropriate construction funds for "remedial restoration" of the beach at Oceanside.[12]

Corps officials in Los Angeles had submitted their position

paper on beach erosion to the Office of the Chief of Engineers in hopes of gaining quick approval to go ahead with the project report. They knew, however, that it would be 1980 at the earliest before construction of any structural solution for beach erosion could begin. Project study funding had to await OCE approval, followed by a three-year district analysis. Then Congress would have to approve the measure. Ronald Weiss gave this unpleasant message to the Oceanside Rotary Club in May 1975. During the course of these events, he recommended that the city form an advisory commission that "would help the government agency in plans for controlling erosion, and expanding and maintaining the harbor."[13] Weiss and others in the Los Angeles District were very concerned about the problems of Oceanside, and also about local hostility toward the federal government. Thus they were very anxious to find both short- and long-term solutions and to promote a better understanding of the functions of the Corps of Engineers in the federal process.

The ever-present problem of budget constraints continued to hamper the Corps' progress on the Oceanside Beach Erosion and Navigation studies. Both were scheduled for completion finalization in early 1975. However, both were delayed into 1976, simply because the Los Angeles District had insufficient funds to keep enough people working on them. Moreover, the thorough environmental analyses required additional man-hours of research at considerable expense. The structural solutions for beach erosion that had been suggested in 1971 now faced both NEPA and California Coastal Commission review. While NEPA requirements were stringent, the Coastal Commission was gaining the reputation of being generally opposed to structures built along the coast. Moreover, the commission staff often recommended against any development within commercial and well-populated sectors of the coast, thereby leaving cities like Oceanside with few options to deal with beach erosion or harbor improvement. The staff dealt with coastal problems in the aggregate rather than as specific, specialized jurisdictional units. While this may have been the proper way to deal with coastal problems under ideal conditions, human development of the world's coastlines had long ago made the aggregate approach impractical.[14]

Progress continued nonetheless on both studies. At the beginning of 1976, the Environmental Resources Branch of the Los Angeles District launched an extensive biological baseline study of the possible sites for harbor expansion which took into consideration marine biota, ichthyology, oceanography, and water quality. During that year, specialists from the Coastal Engineering Research Center joined both South Pacific Division and Los Angeles District officials in an effort to assess the historical record of littoral drift at Oceanside, and to calculate potential transportation rates. They also assessed the historical and predicted future littoral movement of each potential site. As the report neared completion, Corps personnel wanted to make sure that all things were considered adequately, including navigation safety. In the previous two years, three boating accidents had occurred within the harbor breakwaters, resulting in one death. Periodic extreme wave and tidal conditions at Oceanside made the harbor entrance channel a difficult one to navigate, giving it a dubious reputation as a port of refuge in storms.[15]

While preparations continued on these studies, the people of Oceanside grew increasingly impatient. The latest official predictions that both studies would be completed in fiscal year 1978 angered the city's newly-elected Mayor Paul Graham. A retired commandant at Camp Pendleton, Graham made his top priority as mayor the restoration of Oceanside's beaches. His initial press release upon taking office declared that "it was time to stop talking and start doing the things needed to give the people of Oceanside the recreational beach they deserve." He wrote the South Pacific Division Engineer and the Secretary of the Army complaining that the Corps' estimated 1978 completion date for the studies was "totally unacceptable." After reviewing the Corps' beach erosion measures, Graham considered—as did the Corps by then—the offshore breakwater to be the best solution. In use worldwide, the offshore breakwater had the desireable attribute of not "compartmentalizing" the beach, as a system of groins would. Along with the city manager and engineer, the mayor traveled to Washington, D.C., to lobby in Congress for the offshore breakwater.[16]

Despite the strong support of Congressman Claire Burgener of Santa Fe, California, the battle was an uphill one for the delegation. Budget cuts for such projects had become more extreme in the mid-1970s. In addition, even if Congress quickly approved the project, several years of Corps planning and design work would follow. City Engineer Alton Ruden complained of a "Catch-22 logic in Washington" concerning the Corps. "Every time we go back and testify, we seem to stumble across 'Corps capability.'

Back there they say that the Corps doesn't have the capability, but the Corps capability exists back there."[17] In August 1976, the city developed a plan to expedite the final production of the beach erosion study. Their plan included additional contact with District, Division, and Army Engineer Headquarters officials and additional congressional pressure to place the report on a faster track. The city's planning commission also developed extensive redevelopment plans for the beachfront area in 1976. City officials hoped not only to restore the eroded beach, but also to clean up a number of dilapidated structures which currently fronted the Strand. Restoring the beach and eradicating Oceanside's "skid row" were integral parts of the redevelopment plan. The planning commission therefore urged the Corps to finalize the beach erosion control report as soon as possible.[18]

The Shore Protection Section of the Los Angeles District made another step forward toward that goal in issuing a draft of the Oceanside Beach Erosion Control Study in September 1976. Contained in this report, which was being circulated throughout the Corps for review, were environmental, economic, and scientific analyses of the shoreline near Oceanside, as well as a general history of events there to date. Because it was still in draft form, the document was not yet public, and Oceanside officials were upset when they were not given copies. After an "in-house" review, however, the Corps held a public meeting in Oceanside to reveal the content of the document. Colonel Hugh Robinson, Los Angeles District Engineer, opened the 14 April 1977 meeting with a brief history of beach erosion, and then addressed eight possible alternatives to mitigate the situation. These ranged from a "no action" alternative to removal of the harbor altogether. Seawalls and sand bypassing were also mentioned, but at that time both received low priorities. Of the eight alternatives, Robinson considered that there were only three "which seemed to be in the realm of reason." They were essentially refined versions of the ones introduced in 1971 by Ronald Weiss. Of those three (groins and fill, an offshore breakwater and fill, and massive fill) only the third alternative did not carry a positive cost-benefit ratio. Robinson then announced that the Corps was attempting to acquire funding for an early start on testing alternative designs for both beach and harbor maintenance at the agency's Waterways Experiment Station in Vicksburg, Mississippi. When he told the audience that this process would take two years, sighs of discontent could be heard.[19]

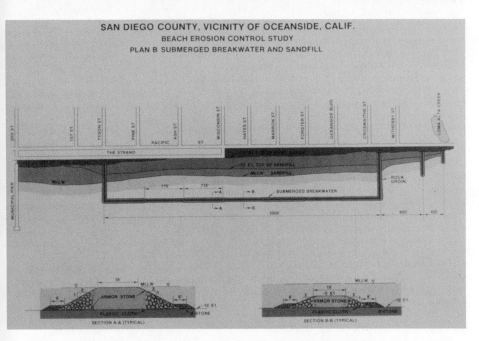

Diagram of Corps beach erosion control plans, 1976.

After Robinson finished, the seventy people present began to give their impressions to the Corps. Most apprehensions concerned the impact of an offshore breakwater on the character of the beach at Oceanside. While the structure would be submerged, it undoubtedly would have an effect on the natural wave action. One speaker feared the breakwater might "[c]hange the visual character of the project area from a panorama of rolling breakers to one of smooth water bounded on the seaside by the alternating pattern of the parallel rock barriers." Corps officials were somewhat surprised at the apparent fear of the alteration of the very waves that caused the city's erosion, but the apprehensions came from a large cross-section of the audience. Members of the Western Surfing Association lodged a formal protest against the breakwater, stating that construction of it, along with harbor expansion, "would effectively destroy surfing in Oceanside." Others expressed concern about the visual effect that a groin field would have on Oceanside. A spokesman for the California Department of Navigation and Ocean Development worried about the impact of breakwaters or particularly groins on downcoast beaches, and urged more consideration of the sand bypassing alternative. A member of the California Polytechnic Institute Sediment Study team rose finally to state that his research was revealing that Del Mar Boat Basin was not necessarily entirely responsible for beach erosion at Oceanside, and that streamflow interruption had not been considered enough. He also gave his support to the sand bypassing research. Mayor Graham spoke for the city when he said in closing that Oceanside would await the findings of the experiments at WES before endorsing one.[20] Corps officials left the meeting aware more than ever that any solution would generate an emotional response.

Funding for the work at the Waterways Experiment Station had to await congressional approval. Because of intense lobbying by Oceanside officials and the support of Congressman Burgener and Robert Badham of Newport Beach, $350,000 was earmarked in the fiscal 1978 public works appropriations bill for the experiment. This appropriation escaped the threatened veto of newly-elected President Jimmy Carter, who wanted to delete at least $168 million for funding of federal water projects for both fiscal and environmental reasons. Carter had earlier in the year drawn up a "hit-list" of water projects in an even more severe austerity program than had been implemented in the early 1970s. Only after Congress removed many of these projects from the appropriations bill did Carter sign it.[21] Carter's stance was an ominous portent for future federal water projects however.

As research began at Vicksburg on solutions for Oceanside, the harbor expansion situation became further complicated. The Corps-favored site (seaward of the southern part of the existing harbor) had come under fire by not only surfers and recreational users of the harbor beach, but also by environmental groups such as the Sierra Club, Coast Watch, and Wilderness Society. Los Angeles District officials had feared that this might happen, but had settled on this site only because the Marine Corps had already ruled out the best location. The North Beach area carried the fewest environmental impacts, was the least expensive, and required the least major modifications to the existing breakwaters. However, Camp Pendleton officials had flatly refused to allow any further consideration of that site for the small craft harbor. Mayor Graham, who knew the situation at Camp Pendleton well, did not believe that the Marines needed all of the North Beach for its new LST facility, but like the Corps, he experienced little success in convincing Camp Pendleton of that fact. Unless the Marines reconsidered, the last viable Oceanside harbor expansion alternative would be scuttled.[22]

Abruptly in October 1977, the Marines at Camp Pendleton changed their minds on civilian encroachment. They announced that they no longer needed the turning basin north of the civilian harbor entrance for training operations. This news came as such a surprise that neither the Corps nor the city was ready to take any quick action. The Corps had ruled out this possibility, and the experiments taking place at Vicksburg were conducted without considering the North Beach alternative. The Oceanside City Council spent the rest of the month developing a harbor expansion plan based on acquisition of the turning basin. They envisioned a harbor with more than twice as many slip spaces as then existed, and at only a fraction of the cost to build a new basin west of the existing complex. They also drew up plans to create a new harbor entrance further to the north which would be shared by the Marine Corps and which would "reduce or discontinue the problem of harbor entry silting and boat hazard." Winfield Collins, Chief of the Los Angeles District Shore Protection Section, agreed in concept to the Oceanside plan, but admitted that the Corps was not currently assessing this possibility in its experiment work. He promised to have it included as an option as soon as possible.[23]

For the present, it appeared that the logjam on harbor improvement might be broken. The City of Oceanside meanwhile told the Corps its preference for beach erosion measures. They expressed a desire to have a groin field at Oceanside similar to the one built at Newport Beach, about fifty miles to the north. This came as a surprise to Collins, who believed that the city favored the submerged breakwater. City officials chose the groin field after taking into consideration the views of the majority of citizens who had commented on solutions. In their opinion, people simply did not want structures to interrupt the wave activity at Oceanside, and they feared that the offshore submerged breakwater would do precisely that.[24]

Although the city's decision on groins surprised some in the Corps, it did allow the agency to move forward in establishing a milestone schedule for the beach erosion project. The sudden decision by the Marine Corps set back the Corps' schedule to complete the study by late 1979. That news also set back the schedule of experimentation at Vicksburg. Researchers there and at the Corps' Coastal Engineering Research Center at Fort Belvoir, Virginia, required additional wave data for Oceanside. Therefore, they secured funding for a one-year data collection operation beginning in the fall of 1977. Late in that year, city officials were again pressuring the Corps to accelerate the process. They recommended combining the beach erosion and navigation studies. The Corps still resisted this suggestion, however, because the two projects were becoming even more specialized and could not be considered in concert.[25]

Meanwhile, Oceanside's two familiar problems persisted. In two separate maintenance dredging operations during 1976 and 1977, the Corps and the Marines financed the removal of nearly 900,000 cubic yards of sand from the harbor entrance channel. Although every grain was placed on the beach to the south, storms soon stripped it away. The 1976 dredging followed a gale force storm which ripped the end off of what had been California's longest pier, stripped most of the sand from the beach, and hurled cobbles as though they were mortar shells into a number of structures on the Strand. During the following January, torrential rains caused more severe cliff and beach erosion at Oceanside, leaving the entire Strand vulnerable to winter waves. In the fall of 1977, another tropical storm brought several inches of rain to Oceanside, and along with it more erosion and shoaling to the beach and harbor.[26] After a period of relative calm during the early 1970s, the Pacific Ocean was again producing violent weather for the coastal regions of southern California.

As storms continued to rage during the next winter season, the need for shore protection measures was highlighted throughout California. At the same time, scientists were learning more about the causes of coastal erosion and implications for the future. According to Scripps Institute oceanographer Douglas Inman, a significant cause of erosion was the impoundment of streams. However, the phenomenon had been "camouflaged" by the building boom of small craft harbors on the California coast. As was the case with the construction of Oceanside Harbor, the excavation material from a number of such marinas was placed on beaches either upcoast or downcoast. Inman estimated in 1975 that the Corps had deposited about fifty million cubic yards of material on California beaches since 1950. Now, he believed, the deficit sand supply caused by river impoundment was beginning to reveal itself in eroded beaches throughout the southern half of the state. He predicted that some San Diego County beaches had only five to ten years of sand cover remaining. Inman had also theorized that, contrary to prevailing opinion, net littoral drift at Oceanside was upcoast.[27]

Some Corps personnel disagreed with both of Inman's contentions. They believed that river contribution to beach sand supply had been exaggerated. They also argued that although net littoral movement during certain years might be upcoast, in other years it was definitely downcoast. Corps officials had been contributing information to a study on sedimentation conducted at California Polytechnic Institute. Researchers there were arriving at the same conclusions that had prompted reassessments of the 1961 equity study which made the federal government responsible for beach erosion control at Oceanside. More important than river impoundment was the fact that no major floods had occurred in northern San Diego County since 1927. Normal rainfall, such as Oceanside had experienced since those exceptional floods, had not resulted in a flow of sufficient natural sediment to resupply eroded beaches. Moreover, the study revealed that normal sediment from the San Luis Rey and Santa Margarita rivers was exceptionally fine in grade and easily transported by wave action. Very little coarse sand

had been found in sediment sampling of the drainage areas of these
two rivers.

As evidence of such conditions, the study offered the fact that
the beaches in most of the Oceanside littoral zone sloped much
more gradually than did other sections of the coast. Many Corps
experts agreed with the Cal Tech researchers that the excellent
beach conditions that people in Oceanside recalled before construction of Del Mar Boat Basin resulted from two large floods of 1916
and 1927—as well as from other major events during the mid and
late 1800s. Only storms such as these, which sent tons of debris to
the beaches, were sufficient enough to supply significant nourishment. The absence of major storms retarded coastal bluff erosion,
the other major contributor to Oceanside's beach sands, from
supplying nourishment since the 1920s.[28]

Researchers were also discovering more about the Oceanside
littoral zone itself. The fine sand from the rivers and the powerful
ocean currents there combined to cause more sand being moved at
Oceanside than at anywhere else in southern California. At a
depth of about thirty-five feet all around the harbor, hundreds of
feet from the breakwaters, lay thousands of cubic yards of littoral
sand. The sand formed a huge alluvial fan with gently sloping,
almost flat, contours. Coastal engineers had generally thought
littoral zone regions extended to depths of eighteen to twenty-five
feet. At Oceanside, they were finding that the zone was much
larger, and consequently more difficult to engineer. The ends of
most jetty systems in southern California harbors were designed to
extend out to the seaward extreme of the littoral zone, thereby
reducing shoaling problems. The breakwaters at Oceanside fell far
short of extending beyond this littoral zone, and in fact terminated
in the middle of it. As a result, the longshore transport of the fine
sand in the area wrapped around the harbor jetties, clogged the
entrance channel, and also settled seaward thousands of feet
beyond. Upcoast and downcoast movement kept the sand in motion
far offshore.[29] The sand for Oceanside's beach was nearby, but did
not move shoreward naturally.

Beach erosion was not peculiar to Oceanside during the 1970s.
Communities all along the coast were experiencing erosion in
varying degrees. Some trouble spots had been exacerbated by
harbor construction or other structural interruption. When the
powerful storms of the mid and late 1970s occurred, the problems
were magnified with the erosive activity of the sea. The indiscrim-

inant erosion gave even more credence to theories that cited the absence of major inland floods for the paucity of beach sediment. From Ventura County, north of Los Angeles, to Newport Beach, people began to seek ways to combat erosion problems. Their searches underscored an important fact: city, county, and state governments simply did not possess the resources to deal with such a costly and difficult problem. Therefore they turned to the federal government for assistance. However, their appeals occurred as demands grew for a reduction in the scope of federal involvement in local affairs. Oceanside's example proved that federal assistance might not provide perfect solutions; but for communities battling erosion without help, any federal contribution was welcome. Unfortunately, government funds to fight erosion all over the nation were dwindling at a time when the problem was worsening.

Severe storms continued during the winter months of 1978, 1979, and 1980. As a result, Oceanside sustained damages along the Strand which totaled more than $2.5 million. City officials began an all-out effort to acquire funds for more emergency beach erosion measures. The city had also hired a special legal counsel to

Storm damage along the beachfront during 1976.

Damage to the Oceanside Strand, February 1980.

investigate the possibility of taking action against the federal
government for lack of progress in beach restoration. However,
the counsel recommended that the city first pursue legislative
solutions. Thereafter, city officials began to advocate a sand
replenishment project to supplement the deposition from the next
scheduled maintenance dredging of the harbor entrance channel.
Because no more federal funds were readily available, Oceanside
officials approached their elected state representatives. As a result
of their lobbying efforts, the city received a one-time appropriation
of $600,000 to be matched by local funds for the remedial
restoration of the eroded beach. Any replenishment plans that
used this funding were subject to the approval of the California
Coastal Conservancy, a funding agency of the state Coastal
Commission. The Conservancy rejected all onshore borrow sites
for sand on the ground of adverse environmental impacts. At this
point the city and the Corps developed plans to combine the
scheduled maintenance dredging of the harbor with excavation
from an offshore site near the harbor beach. Everyone agreed that
this was the most environmentally and economically sound plan.

When that work was completed in June 1981, 863,000 additional cubic yards of sand lay on Oceanside's beach.[30]

While this project served to protect the southern section of Oceanside beach where damage potential had been the most extreme, much of the northern part was still denuded of sand. However, the city had a second plan underway to mitigate this problem. After the severe storms of the winter of 1980, city officials invited California U.S. Senator Alan Cranston to inspect the damage. At the same time, they launched a campaign to acquire emergency federal funding for interim beach restoration. After an on-site inspection and slide presentation of the Strand, Cranston declared: "It's obvious that we have to remedy that." He vowed to those in attendance at his address that he would do everything possible to secure congressional funding for remedial restoration at Oceanside and vicinity.[31] When Cranston returned to Washington, Oceanside officials soon joined him there to lobby for the beach nourishment appropriation. Together, they secured a $3 million appropriation in a session of Congress where domestic spending was being reduced on most levels. The success of the venture in October 1980 was a testament to the continuing political acumen of the Oceanside city government, the power and efficiency of Cranston and his staff, and the support of Congressmen Claire Burgener and John Badham.[32]

Public Law 96-367, the beach nourishment legislation for Oceanside, authorized the Chief of Engineers to spend not more than $3 million for erosion control there. Los Angeles District personnel therefore began to work with the city to find the best borrow site for the operation which they estimated would place about 800,000 additional cubic yards of sand on Oceanside's beach north of the pier. They investigated several sites, on and offshore, to determine where the coarsest and most easily accessible material existed. Offshore sites were rejected because most sand there was of a fine grade, and moreover the process would contribute no new sand to the littoral zone. A problem which arose with nearby onshore sites concerned private ownership. Most potential borrow sites were not in the public domain, and owners of the properties wanted royalty payments for the sand. This placed the Corps in the difficult situation of negotiating for a maximum amount of sand in a small number of places within strict fiscal limitations.[33]

Corps and city officials were also working under additional constraints in this beach nourishment project. Environmental review of development projects, although streamlined in California by recent state legislation, still required additional planning and agency coordination. The Corps outlined several alternative sites and began environmental assessments of each before delving further into actual operational measures. By early 1981, the Corps had eliminated all offshore sites, and several onshore ones for various economic or environmental reasons. The remaining sites lay along the stream bed of the San Luis Rey River. Borrowing from this river attracted Corps personnel, for by taking sand from the stream bed of the San Luis Rey for beach erosion, the Corps widen the channel for flood control.[34]

As city and Corps officials negotiated with private owners at sites along the river they realized that paying royalties for sand could prove prohibitively expensive. Dana Whitson, special projects director for Oceanside; Donald Spencer, acting chief of the Los Angeles District Coastal Resources Branch; and Claude Wong, project manager for the work, therefore began coordinated attempts to find a borrow site that not only had the right grade of sand, but which also would minimize royalty payments. Corps geologists tested sand from a section of the river about four miles from the shore, and found that it was comparable in grain size to that taken from sites closer to the beach. One of the best aspects of this site, between Whelan Lake and Murray Road, was that the city owned all but a small portion of it. The expense of truck-hauling the sand over the added distance, they believed, would be more than offset by the fact that the material would come at no cost to the government. Since it also appeared to have few negative environmental impacts, the Corps soon designated the site as the preferred alternative.[35]

In May, the Corps issued a public notice of its intention to conduct sand excavation and beach nourishment according to this plan. The notice stressed that the proposed project was "a temporary solution" to the beach erosion problems at Oceanside, and gave a detailed account of the scope of operation. According to the notice, the plan was consistent with the Coastal Zone Management Act, and since a preliminary environmental assessment showed minimal negative impacts, a full EIS did not "seem necessary." As required by law, the Corps allowed one month for comment on the project. Among those organizations commenting was the State Resources Agency, a recently created umbrella organization for most California land use departments, including conservation, fish and game, forestry, parks and recreation, and boating and waterways. The agency also oversaw the activities of other regulatory agencies such as the State Lands Commission, Water Resources Control Board, and the Coastal Conservancy. On 1 June, the Resources Agency conditionally approved the project.[36]

The project appeared to be moving forward until Los Angeles District Engineer Colonel Gwynne Teague received a non-concurrence from the California Coastal Commission. The commission refused to issue a permit for the project until the Corps mitigated its conditions, and conducted a review to insure consistency with coastal regulations. Teague enlisted the help of Oceanside City Attorney Charles Revlett in assessing the commission's questions. Clearly dismayed over the potential delay in the beach nourishment work, Revlett informed Teague: "It is unfortunate that the Commission failed to communicate with the City before preparing their letter because, I believe, there are a number of misunderstandings which could have been easily corrected at that time." The commission questioned the Corps' "piecemeal" approach to beach restoration, the relationship of this project to flood control, and the impact of the project on the riparian environment from which the sand would be taken. Revlett responded to each of the commission's questions, first pointing out that artificial beach nourishment was a part of Oceanside's approved local coastal plan. Since the commission opposed most structural solutions to beach erosion, it had always in the past approved periodic nourishment measures. Revlett explained these facts to the commission. He also assured the commission that the flood control and beach nourishment projects, while remaining separate, were being conducted in a coordinated manner. Concerning the commission's question about environmental effects on the borrow area, Revlett pointed out the findings of the assessment, while also reminding the commission that it had no authority in this area more than two miles away from the coastal zone. Finally, he recommended that the commission approve the Corps' consistency findings without delay. One month later, the commission approved the project.[37]

As other sites proved to be unacceptable for various reasons, the Whelan Lake-Murray Road location eventually was chosen. The city worked out legal matters, while the Corps began to make final operational plans. A final environmental assessment found the site

Beach restoration, 1982, with sand dredged from the Oceanside Maintenance Project.

the best from an ecological standpoint and confirmed that no EIS need be prepared. At the same time, economic analyses revealed that the site would allow the Corps to contract the hauling of at least an additional 100,000 cubic yards of sand. When the Corps advertised the project, Dirtmaster Incorporated, a Los Angeles area trucking firm, received a contract to haul 923,000 cubic yards of sand for $2.5 million. The seven-month project began late in 1981, and was completed in May 1982.[38]

By the summer of 1982, Oceanside had a new beach, which varied from 150 to 200 feet in length. The sand was good quality, coarse, and compatible with material already there. These temporary solutions had, for the moment, allayed residents' fears of wave damage to their property and loss of recreational dollars. The summer was a good one for Oceanside, as people flocked to the wide, sandy beach. While everyone who had worked so successfully to get sand back on the beach derived great satisfaction from the results of the two projects, they also knew that these were only temporary solutions. The sea had claimed millions of yards of artificial fill over the last four decades at Oceanside, and it likely would take this sand as well. More permanent solutions to beach erosion and chronic harbor shoaling were still needed.

NOTES

[1] Memorandum for Shore Protection File from R. Weiss regarding Radioisotope Sand Tracer Field Support Requirements, 12 Jan. 1973, Oceanside Navigation file, 1971-75, LNNA RG 77/84-0018 Box 3/8; Orville Magoon to J.B. Askew, subj: Radioisotope sand tracing, 18 Oct. 1972, Oceanside Navigation file, 1971-75, or Beach Erosion file, 1972-75, LNNA RG 77/84-0018 Box 3/8; Lt. Col. James Metelios to Coastal Engineering Research Center, subj: RIST study field test, 31 Aug. 1972, Oceanside Navigation file, 1968-73, LNNA RG 77/80-0034 Box 18/20; Garth Fuquay to South Pacific Division Engineer, subj: Maintenance dredging, 30 Jan. 1973, Oceanside Operation and Maintenance file, 1971-74, LNNA RG 77/84-0018 Box 6/8; Moffatt and Nichol, *Sand Bypass Study, Phase I*, p. 1-12; *SDU* (25 Feb. 1973).

[2] U.S. Army Engineer District, Los Angeles, "Small Craft Harbor Expansion, Oceanside-Camp Pendleton, California" (pamphlet), (October 1973), located in Oceanside Public Meeting file, 1973, LNNA RG 77/79-0001 Box 1/13.

[3] *Ibid.*; Minutes of Public Meeting at Oceanside, 30 Oct. 1973, Oceanside Public Meeting file, 1973, LNNA RG 77/79-0001 Box 1/13.

[4] *Ibid.*; "Small Craft Harbor Expansion," Oceanside Public Meeting file, 1973, LNNA RG 77/79-0001 Box 1/13.

[5] Memorandum on Public Meeting at Oceanside, 30 Oct. 1973, from O. Magoon, 31 Oct. 1973, Oceanside Public Meeting file, 1973, LNNA RG 77/79-0001 Box 1/13.

[6] *OBT* (24 May 1973); *SDU* (10 Oct. 1973).

[7] *OBT* (25 July 1974); Hugh Penton to Col. John Foley, subj: Beach erosion at St. Malo, 9 July 1974, Oceanside Beach Erosion file, 1972-75, LNNA RG 77/84-0018 Box 3/8; some letters complained about the Corps on the basis that the agency had built the harbor in 1942. This was probably inspired by the *Blade-Tribune* editorial of 25 July. See Richard Jones to Sen. John Tunney, subj: Beach erosion at Oceanside, 16 Aug. 1974, Oceanside Beach Erosion file, 1972-75, LNNA RG 77/84-0018 Box 3/8.

[8] Thomas Crandall to Col. J. Foley, subj: California Coastal Commission jurisdiction over dredge deposition, 16 Oct. 1974, Oceanside Operation and Maintenance file, 1971-74, LNNA RG 77/84-0018 Box 6/8.

[9] Weiss interview; Moss, *Land use Controls*, pp. 115-116; T. Crandall to Col. J. Foley, 16 Oct. 1974; U.S. Army Engineer District, Los Angeles, "Environmental Assessment of Maintenance Dredging at Oceanside-Camp Pendleton Harbor," 14 Feb. 1975, Camp Pendleton Harbor, CA, file, 1946-74, LNNA RG 77/80-0033 Box 6/20.

[10] *OBT* (12 Sept., 11 Oct. 1974); *SDU* (24, 25 Oct. 1974).

[11] *OBT* (16 Jan. 1975); O. Magoon to Herb Humphrey, subj: Reaffirmation of federal responsibility for beach erosion at Oceanside, 12 Mar. 1975, Oceanside Beach Erosion file, 1972-75, LNNA RG 77/84-0018 Box 3/8; Memorandum from R. Weiss to Chief, Engineering Division regarding Oceanside Navigation and Beach Erosion studies, 15 July 1975, Oceanside Beach Erosion file, 1972-75, LNNA RG 77/84-0018 Box 3/8.

[12] *Ibid.*

[13] *SDU* (1 May 1975); Weiss interview.

[14] Budgetary and Completion Schedule, Oceanside Harbor, Oceanside (Camp Pendleton) California, 1 Jan. 1973, Oceanside Navigation file, 1971-75, LNNA RG 77/84-0018 Box 3/8; *OBT* (28 Apr. 1975); Memorandum for Chief of Engineering Division from Robert Joe regarding District Engineer Quarterly Letter, 6 Oct. 1975, Oceanside Operation and Maintenance file, 1975-80, LNNA RG 77/81-0005 Box 1/1; Minutes of Checkpoint II Conference at South Pacific Division, 1 July 1975, Oceanside Checkpoint II Conference, Oceanside, 1975, file, LNNA RG 77/84-0018 Box 6/8; Memorandum to South Pacific Division Engineer from Col. J. Foley regarding milestone dates for Beach Erosion study for Oceanside, 7 June 1974, Oceanside Beach Erosion file 1972-75, LNNA RG 77/84-0018 Box 3/8; Interview, author with Mayor Larry Bagley, Oceanside, CA, 28 Apr. 1986. Hereafter cited as Bagley interview.

[15]Scope of Work, Marine Biological Baseline Study of Oceanside Small Craft Harbor, Del Mar Boat Basin, and Proposed Harbor Expansion Area, 22 Jan. 1976, Del Mar Basin file, 1972-76, LNNA RG 77/84-0018 Box 7/8; Memorandum from Cyril Gavin regarding field observations at Oceanside, California, 29 Aug.-1 Sept. 1976, 3 Sept. 1976, Del Mar Basin file, 1972-76, LNNA RG 77/84-0018 Box 7/8; Memorandum for the Record from Donald Spencer regarding littoral transportation rates calculated by energy flux method, 19 Aug. 1976, Del Mar Basin file, 1972-76, LNNA RG 77/84-0018 Box 7/8; Madeline Toslund to D. Spencer and Win Collins, subj: Determination of littoral drift, 24 Aug. 1976, Del Mar Basin file, 1972-76, LNNA RG 77/84-0018 Box 7/8; Memorandum to Acting Chief, Engineering Division, from R. Joe regarding District Engineer's Quarterly Letter, 30 Sept. 1976, Oceanside Operation and Maintenance file, 1975-80, LNNA RG 77/81-0005 Box 1/1; Memorandum for Shore Protection file from R. Weiss regarding recent boating accident in Oceanside Harbor, 1 May 1974, Oceanside Navigation file, 1971-75, LNNA RG 77/84-0018 Box 3/8; Memorandum from R. Weiss regarding lawsuit against Oceanside over boating accident fatality, 25 July 1975, Oceanside Navigation file, 1971-75, LNNA RG 77/84-0018 Box 3/8; Bagley interview.

[16]City of Oceanside, Press Release regarding Mayor Paul Graham's Plan of Action, 17 Mar. 1976; P. Graham to Victor Veysey, Assistant Secretary of the Army, subj: Oceanside beach erosion, 30 Sept. 1976, Oceanside Beach Erosion Study file, 1976-77, LNNA RG 77/84-0018 Box 7/8; P. Graham to Col. R. Connell, subj: Oceanside beach erosion, 29 Mar. 1976, Oceanside Beach Erosion Study file, 1976-77, LNNA RG 77/84-0018 Box 7/8; OBT (17, 24 Mar. 1976).

[17]Ibid., (12, 19 Mar., 1 Apr. 1976).

[18]Ibid., (8 Aug. 1976); Marcia Weber Swett and Norton Hathaway to V. Veysey, subj: Oceanside beach erosion and redevelopment, 5 Apr. 1976, Oceanside Beach Erosion Study file, 1976-77, LNNA RG 77/84-0018 Box 7/8; Memorandum from Poteat regarding Oceanside beach erosion control, 2 Apr. 1976, Oceanside Beach Erosion Study file, 1976-77, LNNA RG 77/84-0018 Box 7/8.

[19]Taichi Nishihara to P. Graham, subj: In-house draft status of Sept. 1976, Beach Erosion Control Report, 21 Oct. 1976, Oceanside Beach Erosion Study file, 1976-77, LNNA RG 77/84-0018 Box 7/8; OBT (13 Sept., 11 Nov. 1976; Memorandum for the Record from O. Magoon regarding Checkpoint II Conference on Oceanside, 28 Sept. 1976, Oceanside Beach Erosion Study file, 1976-77, LNNA RG 77/84-0018 Box 7/8; Minutes, Public Meeting at Oceanside regarding Beach Erosion Control, 14 Apr. 1977, Oceanside Beach Erosion Study file, 1976-77, LNNA RG 77/84-0018 Box 7/8.

[20]Ibid. Memorandum for the Record from D.F. Eng regarding Public Meeting on Oceanside Beach Erosion Control Study, 21 Apr. 1977, Oceanside Beach Erosion Study file, 1976-77, LNNA RG77/84-0018 Box 7/8; Tony Gershler to Los Angeles District, subj: Surfers' opposition to offshore breakwaters at Oceanside, 15 Apr. 1977, Oceanside Beach Erosion Study file, 1976-77, LNNA RG 77/84-0018 Box 7/8.

[21]OBT (15 June 1977).

[22]Col. Hugh Robinson to South Pacific Division Engineer, subj: Request for model study of Oceanside, CA, 7 June 1977, Oceanside Operation and Maintenance file, 1975-80, LNNA RG 77/81-0005 Box 1/1; T. Nishihara to Director, Waterways Experiment Station, subj: Proposed model study of Oceanside Beach, 26 Apr. 1977, Oceanside Operation and Maintenance file, LNNA RG 77/81-0005 Box 1/1; Maj. Gen. C.W. Hoffman to Los Angeles District Engineer, subj: Opposition to further sharing of military property for small craft harbor, 23 July 1976, Oceanside Shore Protection file, 1970s, LNNA RG 77/84-0018 Box 7/8; San Diego Reader (9 Mar. 1977).

[23]SDU (30 Nov. 1977); OBT (29 Nov. 1977).

[24]Ibid.; Draft Environmental Impact Statement, Oceanside Harbor, CA, 1978, Oceanside file, 1978, LNNA RG 77/82-0005 Box 3/3.

[25] Norman Arno to South Pacific Division Engineer, subj: Milestone dates for Oceanside Beach Erosion and Navigation studies, 14 June 1977, Oceanside Operation and Maintenance

file, 1975-80, LNNA RG 77/81-0005 Box 1/1; Col. H. Robinson to South Pacific Division Engineer, subj: Oceanside beach erosion milestones, 16 Sept. 1977, Oceanside Operation and Maintenance file, 1975-80, LNNA RG 77/81-0005 Box 1/1; Col. H. Robinson to Gen. R. Connell, subj: Quarterly Report, 8 Aug. 1977, Oceanside Operation and Maintenance file, 1975-80, LNNA RG 77/81-0005 Box 1/1; Col. H. Robinson to Director, Coastal Engineering Research Center, subj: Littoral environment observations at Oceanside, 15 Aug 1977, Oceanside Operation and Maintenance file, 1975-80, LNNA RG 77/81-0005 Box 1/1.

[26]*OBT* (7 Jan., 18 Apr. 1976, 18 Oct. 1977).

[27]Herron interview; *LAT* (14 Apr., 11 Aug. 1975).

[28]*Ibid.*; Herron interview; Weiss interview; California Institute of Technology, *Sedementation Study of Inland California* (Los Angeles, 1978), *passim*.

[29]Herron interview.

[30]*OBT* (12 Feb. 1978, 8, 13 July, 2 Sept. 1980); Interview, author with Dana Whitson. Oceanside, CA, 28 Mar. 1986. Hereafter cited as Whitson interview; Interview, author with Charles R. Revlett, Oceanside, CA, 27 Mar. 1986. Hereafter cited as Revlett interview; Whitson and Bagley, "Putting the Beach Back," p. 26; A split hull dredge was employed in the beach restoration project, O. Magoon to Chief, Planning Division, subj: Use of hopper dredges, 12 Jan. 1981, Oceanside Maintenance Dredging file, 1977-80, LNNA RG 77/84-0018 Box 6/8; Moffat and Nichol, *Sand Bypass Report, Phase I*, p. 1-12; N. Arno to Thomas Tobin, subj: Coastal Commission approval of private revetment work at Oceanside, 6 Nov. 1979, Oceanside Operation and Maintenance file, 1975-80, LNNA RG 77/81-0005 Box 1/1; See California Assembly Bill 1143, General Session, 1979-80, for reference to this appropriation, Oceanside Planning Department to Beach Restoration Task Force, subj: Actions taken at 15 July Task Force Meeting, 16 July 1980, Oceanside City files.

[31]*OBT* (16 July 1980).

[32]Whitson interview; Revlett interview; Bagley interview; *OBT* (9 Oct. 1980).

[33]*Water Resources Development Act*, 90 Stat. 2917, 1976; *Beach Erosion Control Project, Vicinity of Oceanside, CA*, 94 Stat. 1337, 1980; Whitson and Bagley, "Putting the Beach Back," p. 26; Whitson interview; Revlett interview; Whitson interview; Interview, author with Claude Wong, Los Angeles, CA, 2 Apr. 1986. Hereinafter cited as Wong interview; U.S. Army, Corps of Engineers, *Annual Report of the Chief of Engineers on Civil Works Activities* (Washington, DC: G.P.O., 1981), p. 33-31.

[34]See California Assembly bill 884, General Session, 1977-78; Interview, author with Donald Spencer, Los Angeles, CA, 29 Apr. 1986. Hereinafter cited as Spencer interview; Whitson and Bagley, "Putting the Beach Back," p. 26; R. Kahler Martinson to Col. G. Teague, subj: Endangered species in beach erosion control project area, 7 Dec. 1979, Oceanside Beach Erosion, Shore Protection file, LNNA RG 77/81-0005 Box 1/1.

[35]Donald Spencer to South Pacific Division Engineer, subj: Site locations for Oceanside Beach Erosion borrow area, 26 June 1981, Oceanside Beach Nourishment Project file, LNNA RG 77/84-0018 Box 3/8; City of Oceanside Resolution 81-2, 10 June 1981; Contract for beach erosion work, Jaykim Engineers, Inc., 3 June 1981, Oceanside Beach Nourishment Project file, 1972-75, LNNA RG 77/84-0018 Box 3/8; Whitson interview; Public Notice: Oceanside Beach Nourishment, 5 May 1981, Oceanside Beach Nourishment Project file, LNNA RG 77/84-0018 Box 3/8.

[36]*Ibid.*; James Burns to Col Gwynne Teague, subj: Beach Nourishment comments, 1 June 1981, Oceanside Beach Nourishment Project file, LNNA RG 77/84-0018 Box 3/8.

[37]Charles Revlett to Col. G. Teague, subj: California Coastal Commission questions on Beach Nourishment Project, 16 June 1981, Oceanside Beach Nourishment Project file, LNNA RG 77/84-0018 Box 3/8; California Coastal Commission Staff Report and Recommendation of Consistency Determination, 7 July 1981, Oceanside Beach Nourishment Project file, LNNA RG 77/84-0018 Box 3/8; the alternative borrow site closer to shore proved infeasible because of potential damage to archaeology and endangered species, South Pacific Division to Los Angeles District, subj: Alternative borrow site, 17 July 1981,

Oceanside Beach Nourishment Project file, LNNA RG 77/84-0018 Box 3/8; Michael Fisher to Col. Roger Higbee, subj: Coastal Commission consistency determination, 20 July 1981, Oceanside Beach Nourishment Project file, LNNA RG 77/84-0018 Box 3/8; In 1976, in an effort to bring more local control into the review process, each coastal city was to prepare a plan which would be reviewed and certified by the California Coastal Commission.

[38]D. Spencer to Gary Hunt, subj: Alternative borrow site, 20 Aug. 1981, Oceanside Beach Nourishment Project file, LNNA RG 77/84-0018 Box 3/8; Danal Whitson to C. Revlett, subj: Legal matters pertaining to sandfill project, 6 July 1981, Oceanside Beach Nourishment Project file, LNNA RG 77/84-0018 Box 3/8; W.N. Sauer to D. Spencer, subj: Beach Nourishment borrow sites, 1 Oct. 1981, Oceanside Beach Nourishment Project file, LNNA RG 77/84-0018 Box 3/8; Memorandum for the Record from South Pacific Division to Los Angeles District, subj: Alternative borrow site, 29 July 1981, Oceanside Beach Nourishment Project file, LNNA RG 77/84-0018 Box 3/8; Theodore Stroup to Sen. Alan Cranston, subj: Status of Beach Nourishment Project, Sept. 1981, Oceanside Beach Nourishment Project file, LNNA RG 77/84-0018 Box 3/8; J.R. Aichele to Los Angeles District Engineer, subj: Borrow site on Santa Margarita River, 16 Aug. 1981, Oceanside Beach Nourishment Project file, LNNA RG 77/84-0018 Box 3/8; Environmental Assessment for Beach Nourishment Project, c. Nov. 1981, Oceanside Beach Nourishment Project file, LNNA RG 77/84-0018 Box 3/8; Memorandum for the Record from Col. Paul Taylor regarding findings of Environmental Assessment, Oceanside Beach Nourishment Project, 14 Oct. 1981, Oceanside Beach Nourishment Project file, LNNA RG 77/84-0018 Box 3/8; Felix Fredieu to U.S.A.R. Center, subj: Street sweeping along haul route, 29 Apr. 1982, Oceanside Beach Nourishment Project file, LNNA RG 77/84-0018 Box 3/8; Whitson and Bagley, "Putting the Beach Back," p. 26.

CHAPTER V

Experiment in Coastal Engineering

During the planning phases of the two remedial sandfill projects at Oceanside in 1980 and 1981, both city officials and Los Angeles District personnel remained hopeful that they could achieve permanent solutions to beach erosion and harbor shoaling. By 1980, modeling research neared completion at the Corps of Engineers Waterways Experiment Station in Vicksburg, Mississippi, on a variety of possible structural solutions to both of these problems. Meanwhile, Los Angeles District personnel were preparing a survey report based on this information. Although progress had been made on solutions to beach erosion and remedial measures were under way, harbor expansion plans appeared to be thoroughly impeded by a number of environmental and jurisdictional constraints. With each new alternative reached in the Corps' navigation study for Oceanside Harbor improvement and expansion, another set of adverse environmental impacts arose to thwart the plan. Both city and Corps officials knew that the harbor would continue to operate in a deficit situation without expansion. However a suitable plan remained elusive. The only viable plan was expansion within the existing Marine Corps turning basin. Yet that idea was also threatened by budget constraints. As a result, Oceanside residents were left with a harbor too small to operate profitably, an entrance channel to the facility which was sometimes dangerous and regularly required dredging, and a beach that often consisted only of cobbles.

Before Corps officials could suggest solutions for either problem, they had to receive the results of the modeling work being done at Vicksburg, Mississippi. The $350,000 congressional appropriation in 1977 for the Oceanside experiment at WES had given researchers there the funding to deal with an extremely difficult modeling task. The powerful ocean surges and uncertain direction of waves at Oceanside proved challenging to those attempting to simulate conditions there. Because expansion of the harbor seemed unlikely, Corps researchers had narrowed the parameters of their testing to include only the present harbor configuration. Modeling the harbor and constructing various offshore breakwater systems proved difficult enough. The uncertainty and conflicting theories of littoral drift at Oceanside further complicated the task. Radioisotope sand tracing in the early 1970s had proven inconclusive, and there was disagreement among experts whether the transport was north, south, or in relative equilibrium. Between 1977 and 1979, WES researchers conducted experiments on over eighty different groin, breakwater, and sandfill models. During the process, the Corps personnel kept the public apprised of progress. They also brought Oceanside officials to Vicksburg for a tour of the work being conducted.[1]

The results of these experiments first appeared in a draft survey report on beach erosion control for Oceanside and vicinity, prepared by the Los Angeles District in April 1980. The report listed nine plans of action. The first five included: no action at all, construction of a rubble-mound seawall, construction of a concrete seawall, removal of the harbor complex, and land and improvements acquisition. None of these was considered feasible.

The Corps considered the remaining four alternatives in more detail. At Vicksburg, the Corps tested eight different groin and sandfill plans. The plan which proved most promising was a system of eleven groins averaging 724 feet in length, built perpendicular to the beach and spaced 1,000 feet apart. Three other groins tapering down to 200 feet in length would be built on the downcoast end of the system to allow for a smooth transition from the groins to the shore. Researchers also tested five submerged breakwater designs. The best consisted of a continuous 10,800-foot system composed of alternating segments of five- and ten-foot heights. The breakwater would be constructed at the minus ten-foot contour, ten feet below the mean lower low water level. At each end of the breakwater, groins would be built to stop sand movement north or south. In each of these plans, about 1.2 million cubic yards of sand would be placed onshore initially, with an estimated annual replenishment requirement of about 20,000 cubic yards. The sandfill experiments described in the report involved the placement

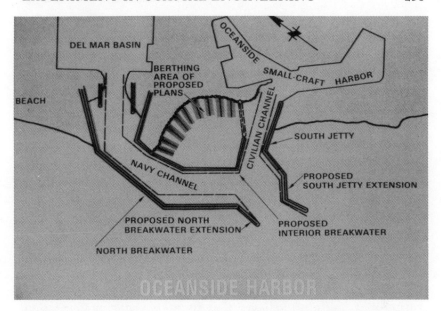

Plan of improvements by the Waterways Experiment Station, 1979.

of about 2.75 million cubic yards of sand on Oceanside's beaches in operations similar to past projects.[2]

Another alternative appearing in the draft report had not been tested at Vicksburg for Oceanside conditions. However, researchers there had in the past constructed models for other settings. In 1979, Los Angeles District personnel requested that WES researchers send all available information on mechanical sand bypassing. Because of support from a number of oceanographers who preferred nonstructural solutions for beach erosion control, the Corps included testing for a sand bypassing system as one of the four reasonable alternatives. Prototypes of such systems were in operation in several locations in the United States, and had proven successful. The basic concept employed fixed pumps which pulled sand from upcoast accretion points through pipes which would discharge the material on eroded areas downcoast. Proponents of the system for Oceanside hoped that it would solve, or at least ease, both beach erosion and harbor shoaling. By pulling sand from the harbor entrance channel and placing it on the beach downcoast, the system might prove to be a substantial part of a permanent solution. The system described in the report included one primary jet pump which would be housed on the north breakwater of the harbor. Three groups of three pumps each would be attached to the primary pump and to a booster station on the south jetty. The report estimated that the system could pump 500,000 cubic yards of sand from the entrance channel annually. All material would be pumped through discharge pipes which would extend to the south end of Oceanside beach.[3]

Of the four alternatives given full consideration in the report, the Corps favored the groin and sandfill plan. Having an estimated benefit/cost ratio of 1.3 to one, this plan most closely met with the requirements of national economic development (NED), and environmental quality (EQ). The Federal Water Resources Council had set these requirements for federally-assisted water development projects in 1973. All of the other plans had a zero or negative benefit/cost ratio. Moreover, the report noted, the submerged breakwater, sand bypassing, and sandfill were "unacceptable" to local interests. Opposition to the breakwater was substantial, and most believed that another sandfill project would bring only temporary relief. Sand bypassing did not ensure that the beach would be restored sufficiently. The Corps estimated that sand pumped by the bypass system annually would not keep up with erosion losses. Although the groin system had some negative aspects, most of those were temporary, and the draft report endorsed it as the one plan in which the "NED objective [was] maximized."[4]

The Corps' groin plan soon became the focus of intense criticism. The most influential critics were scientists at the Scripps Institute of Oceanography in La Jolla. Jeffrey Frautschy and Douglas Inman both questioned the validity of the Vicksburg testing of the groin system on the grounds that all realistic factors could not be simulated, and that the large number of tests run demonstrated that researchers there had a "lack of direction" toward solving the problem. In late April 1980, Inman presented his opinions to the San Diego Regional Coastal Commission. He argued that it was wrong to consider Oceanside's erosion problems singularly. Groin construction at Oceanside, he warned, might start a "chain reaction" of erosion problems downcoast. "It's quite inappropriate," he stated, "to look at Oceanside and Oceanside Beach problems without giving careful attention to the fact that if you start placing groins in Oceanside you'll have to place them all the way to La Jolla."[5]

The Scripps critique spread panic to residents and elected officials of coastal communities directly south of Oceanside during the spring and summer of 1980. Their fears were magnified by a series of severe storms during the previous winter, which had damaged numerous coastal structures in the Del Mar area just north of San Diego. Several towns south of Oceanside organized committees to study the impact of groin construction, and also to examine beach erosion on a regional basis. On these committees were representatives from the towns of Carlsbad, Del Mar, Leucadia, Cardiff, and Encinitas. By mid-summer, representatives from all of these towns had made formal protests to both Oceanside and the Corps over the groin construction plan. They argued that Oceanside should join their efforts to solve long-term erosion on a county-wide basis. When Oceanside Mayor Larry Bagley refused to withdraw the city's support for the groin proposal, it was clear that the northern San Diego coastal communities were at odds over the issue.[6]

City officials at Oceanside were strongly in favor of having the groin system built. Two major sandfill projects were already planned to restore the beach, and protective groins, if built in time, could serve to protect the new fill. The city again had the support of Senator Alan Cranston on the groin issue, and his assurances that downcoast beaches would be preserved helped the Oceanside campaign. Heartened also by the Corps' early endorsement of the groin plan, the City Council was chagrined over the agency's announcement that, even if no objections were raised, groin construction could not begin before 1984. By mid-1980, members were reluctantly becoming convinced that Scripps' and downcoast community opposition virtually assured that there would be strong objections to groins. The exasperated Council members knew that if they missed this opportunity, the next chance for a lasting solution to beach erosion might not come for a decade. As one observer noted, "Everyone has said, 'Don't do anything. You might hurt something.' For thirty years we've done nothing. Now our backs are against the wall."[7]

As the groin proposal drew more criticism during the summer of 1980, Los Angeles District personnel viewed the plan more apprehensively. They recalled the environmental objections which had logjammed Oceanside Harbor expansion plans and feared a singular situation. As Inman continued his assault on the plan, calling it "ill-conceived" and a "risky venture," Corps support for groins wavered even more.[8] Most in the Corps disagreed with the argument that groins would have to be built all the way to La Jolla. Although they still believed that the system was well tested, environmentally sound, and cost effective, they knew that this solution was likely to become embroiled in regulatory prohibitions. The California Coastal Commission, now well known for its opposition to structural solutions for beach erosion control, would undoubtedly place many conditions on any permit; or it might reject the plan altogether. Top officials in the South Pacific Division recognized that this plan would probably not have an easy review, and thus recommended that the Los Angeles District give more consideration to alternative plans.

Other factors began to undermine the groin solution. The uncertainty of littoral drift near Oceanside continued to perplex Corps research on groin models. While groins would successfully prevent losses from longshore transport with sufficient sand nourishment, they could not stop offshore loss. Direct wave action, often powerful and unpredictable at Oceanside, might pull the sand between the groins offshore resulting again in denuded beaches. If longshore transport was in relative equilibrium at Oceanside, then offshore losses would not necessarily be countered by upcoast or downcoast movement. An offshore breakwater with enclosed ends, on the other hand, would essentially stop all longshore and offshore losses, thus compartmentalizing the beach and trapping the sand. Referred to as a "sand box," the system employed a phenomenon known as the "tombolo effect," whereby sand accumulates shoreward of a submerged structure such as breakwater system, forming a sand trap. Corps officials were certain the breakwater system would work well as a beach erosion control measure. However, they were also aware of its unpopularity among residents.[9]

With these considerations in mind, Los Angeles District personnel revised the April 1980 draft to favor an offshore breakwater, despite the fact that groins and sandfill still had the highest benefit/cost ratio. City officials were upset when Corps personnel told them informally in August that the breakwater had become the preferred alternative. Cost estimates of groins, an offshore breakwater, and sand by-passing were $9.2 million, $12.85 million, and $11.5 million, respectively, according to the survey report issued in September 1980.[10] The Corps announced that a public meeting would be held in Oceanside in November to present the findings and allow for comment.

While Corps officials expected opposition from surfers and from groin proponents in the city council, they did not expect an almost universal condemnation of the breakwater concept. More than 300 people gathered at Oceanside's city council chambers on the night of 13 November. The size of the crowd forced the meeting to be moved to a nearby senior citizens' center. During the four-hour session, only one individual rose to support the breakwater. All of the other speakers condemned the idea for various reasons. Surfers, wearing shirts bearing a "STOP OCEANSIDE BREAK-WATER" logo, stood one after another to attest that such a system would destroy wave activity, thus ending all surf recreation and harming the local economy. Surfing was an important part of Oceanside's economy. Known throughout southern California as one of the finest wave areas, the city hosted annual international surfing competitions and several other major water-related events.[11] Keeping a close watch on the diminishing number of good wave sites in California, surfers had developed a powerful lobby for their interests.

As the meeting progressed, it became obvious to Corps and Oceanside officials that surfers were not the only opponents of the breakwater concept. Among other speakers in the sometimes heated session were beach-front property owners, people concerned over the environmental impact of breakwaters, and beach users. All condemned the breakwater. While many of them voiced support for the groin system, far more favored another alternative: sand bypassing. Los Angeles District Engineer Colonel Gwynne Teague, who fielded questions and criticisms for the Corps of Engineers, explained carefully why he favored the breakwater at that time, and why the groin system might prove inadequate to prevent offshore sand losses. After listening to a litany of complaints and demands for another alternative, Teague cautioned that a rejection of the Corps' breakwater proposal would result in further delays in implementation of a beach erosion solution for Oceanside. With no further complications, construction of the breakwater would not begin until 1984. However, if the city council rejected this idea, it would mean a delay of about one year to restudy the groin proposal; and if the council voted for sand bypassing, there would be at least a two-year delay in implementation.[12]

Following the meeting, the council pondered its present options in the long battle with beach erosion. The beach fill projects planned and under way could be jeopardized without a structural solution. Yet if groins did not work well, as Corps officials were now suggesting, that option could become a very expensive mistake. However, it was clear that construction of a breakwater would result in the enmity of a number of social and economic groups toward the current city council. While this system might work best to hold sand on the beach, residents and beach users had firmly established the fact that they wanted both sand and surf—and not one without the other. People were convinced that the breakwater would transform the dynamic sea at Oceanside to something resembling a pond. Thus it was apparent at this time that neither a breakwater nor groins were feasible alternatives for the city. Since the sand fill alternative was only a temporary one, the council began to review the prospects of sand bypassing. In December the council voted to reject the breakwater concept, and at the same time urged the Corps to pursue sand bypassing as a solution.[13] Despite the fact that the decision meant a long delay in construction of a beach erosion solution, and that the city's beach would be left vulnerable for a number of years to come, the council believed that there was no other option in the winter of 1980.

In order to expedite the implementation of the sand bypass system, Oceanside officials again traveled to the nation's capital to lobby for their cause. The city hired several engineering and oceanographic consultants who prepared reports on the economic and environmental efficacy of such a system. One of those consultants was Douglas Inman of the Scripps Institute. The design which he prepared for the city resembled closely the one that the Corps had presented in the draft survey study on beach erosion control. City officials had little trouble in gaining the support of downcoast communities for a system that would add a constant supply of sand which would likely move south. The California Coastal Commission initially supported sand bypassing as well, because it represented something other than a structural beach erosion solution—and in fact most closely simulated the natural littoral processes of the shoreline. Regional organizations such as the San Diego Association of Governments (SANDAG) also endorsed the city's efforts.[14]

Such endorsements and favorable assessments gave Oceanside officials a powerful bargaining position in Washington. They enlisted support from elected officials from the northern San Diego County area. Most influential of those was Congressman Claire Burgener, who used his seat on the House Energy and Water

Development Subcommittee to argue for the sand bypass concept. Also instrumental in the quest were Senators Alan Cranston and S.I. Hayakawa, and Congressman Robert Badham. The effort was complicated by the fact that this was not the Corps' recommended project, and thus was not authorized. City officials such as Mayor Larry Bagley and City Attorney Charles Revlett nonetheless argued forcefully that their community had suffered severe economic dislocations as a result of beach erosion, and that the current sandfill operations costing an estimated $6 million would be jeopardized without additional and consistent replenishment. They also contended that because of rising energy costs, sand bypassing in the joint military-civilian harbor entrance channel might prove more cost-effective than maintenance dredging.[15]

While lobbying in Congress, Oceanside officials also approached the Office of the Chief of Engineers with their cause. Now fully aware that neither of the structural solutions would be implemented in the near future, Corps officials in Washington, San Francisco, and Los Angeles had decided not to finalize the beach erosion study. Furthermore, the Corps had no funding to pursue the sand bypassing alternative that the city had requested. While Corps officials were interested in investigating sand bypassing at length, they also knew that this alternative presented some drawbacks that had been outlined in the draft survey report of September 1980. Most problematical of those drawbacks was the fact that no system had ever been tested in an open-ocean setting like Oceanside.

Because of the degree of uncertainty that it posed to engineering and design, the Corps had not made sand bypassing its preferred alternative in the draft report. Their apprehensions about the effectiveness of groins had led them to support a breakwater which they believed would work. Yet the groundswell of opposition to that measure led them to reconsider sand bypassing. The Corps was clearly taking a conservative approach toward sand bypassing at Oceanside, not only because of the acute shoaling and erosion problems there, but also because of the experimental nature of the system.

The draft report had concluded that sand bypassing was the most environmentally sound option, and many in the Corps agreed that the system might actually reduce the expense devoted to maintenance dredging. Moreover, the system also had the added attraction of possibly serving two purposes: harbor maintenance and beach erosion control. None of the other options had even the possibility of accomplishing two objectives. Yet without a congressional directive, the Corps could not expand its study of sand bypassing for Oceanside. As a result of the city council's resolution in December 1980, and the current lobbying in Washington, Corps personnel had been further reconsidering their position on sand bypassing. City officials were convinced that with Corps backing they could obtain congressional authorization for sand bypassing. In March 1981, Corps officials complied, giving their willingness to "publicly support" sand bypassing.[16]

With Corps of Engineers interest in pursuing a sand bypassing solution for Oceanside and strong arguments for testing such a system somewhere in southern California, Congressman Burgener was able to earmark—as a part of the Energy and Water Appropriation bill of 1982—$700,000 for the study of the system. When the bill later went through the Senate, Cranston and Hayakawa made certain that the appropriation remained in that version. Congress thereby directed the Corps to study further, and "to underake procurement and installation of a sand bypass system at Oceanside Harbor, California." The Corps was to proceed with engineering and design of the system "in consultation with representatives of the local and State governments and report to the Committee not later than 31 March 1982."[17]

Los Angeles District personnel had actually resumed research on sand bypassing before the congressional authority came through. Since it now appeared, after opposition arose to the offshore breakwater, that sand bypassing was the only viable alternative, they had begun to examine it in more detail. The plan developed in the draft survey report had only been a conceptual model of a system which would pump sand from both the north breakwater and the south jetty. While this was the general plan that the Corps continued to explore, much more detailed research and design remained. In June 1981, Los Angeles District officials secured $11,000 from the Corps budget so that the Waterways Experiment Station could identify existing systems, and work on conceptual designs for a sand bypassing system at Oceanside.

The Waterways Experiment Station had been testing sand bypassing in varying wave environments since the early 1970s. At Mexico Beach, Florida, researchers had installed a jet pump system to pass sand under the harbor breakwaters in 1973. After reasonable success in this harbor on the Gulf of Mexico, they

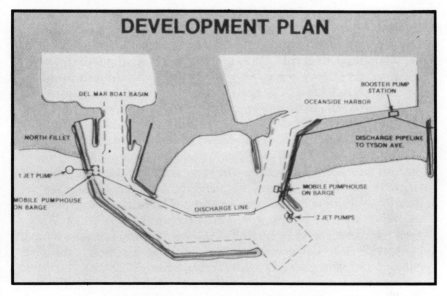

Sand bypass system schematic, 1982.

installed a similar system for testing on the harsher wave environment of the eastern seaboard at Rudee Inlet, Virginia. From 1976 to 1978, they tested a sand bypass system in a protected part of the harbor at Santa Cruz, California. In approximately one year, the system bypassed 200,000 cubic yards of sand which was discharged about 2,000 feet downcoast. The Waterways Experiment Station was also testing a system on Lake Huron at Port Sanilac, Michigan. Another system in use was built by the Canadian Public Works Department at Naufrage, Prince Edward Island, Canada. Three other systems had been tested and dismantled: the University of Hawaii had installed an experimental system in Keohou Bay, Hawaii, and the Scripps Institute of Oceanography had tested two small systems at Agua Hedionda Lagoon in northern San Diego County, and at the sand spit in the entrance of Del Mar Boat Basin, inside the breakwaters of Oceanside Harbor. The Del Mar Boat Basin experiment, taking place in just five days during 1974, demonstrated that a system could work there, but that cobbles often clogged the jet pump intakes.[18]

When the $700,000 congressional appropriation came, Los Angeles District Engineer Colonel Gwynne Teague appointed a technical panel consisting of four coastal experts: Robert Wiegel of the University of California at Berkeley, Robert Dean of the University of Delaware, Richard Seymore of the California Department of Boating and Waterways, and Douglas Inman of the Scripps Institute of Oceanography. Each member of the panel began preparing individual reports outlining their optimum plan for sand bypassing at Oceanside. Corps officials in Los Angeles coordinated the entire report process, and continued to gather data on existing systems while awaiting sand bypass testing results from Vicksburg. Between July 1981 and January 1982, Thomas Richardson and Clark McNair of the Waterways Experiment Station wrote two extensive reports on sand bypassing for Ocean-side—the first concerning planning a hydraulic design of jet pumps, and the second outlining three specific configurations for such a system. The congressional authorization for the study mandated close contact with local interests. Therefore, the City of Oceanside formed a seven-member group consisting of city, county, and Camp Pendleton representatives.[19]

The efficient production of this report underscored a high level of cooperation among federal, state, and local agencies, private consultants, and the interested public. The short timespan which Congress allowed for the report's completion required everyone to cooperate and to work quickly. The Corps planned four technical meetings between November 1981 and February 1982. Each of the meetings had a detailed agenda, and all present participated in the proceedings. Through each phase of the report, both the technical panel and the Oceanside working group informed Corps personnel of their opinions. Meanwhile, the city working group gathered additional information about residents' concerns and expectations for a sand bypass system. The group found enthusiastic support and optimism over the prospect of sand bypassing among the people, and the Marine Corps supported the idea as long as it did not interfere with operations or encroach on Camp Pendleton property.[20]

A high level of involvement was the key ingredient in the smooth progress of this report. Since the passage of strict environmental laws had mandated full public disclosure of federal development projects, a more thorough and efficient review process had been evolving. More disclosure had piqued additional public interest, and allowed the legal framework of the review process to develop fully. All people involved at Oceanside were interested in developing solutions quickly and adequately. The review process established for Corps projects facilitated such an outcome.

After the initial meeting in November 1981, the technical group members completed their individual reports. These reports, prepared by Inman, Dean, Seymore, and Wiegel, included two designs. The first one incorporated fixed jet pumps and fluidizers at the entrance to the harbor channel, and the second called for a modification of the north breakwater to create a littoral deposition basin from which a portable dredge would collect material and then place it on the beach to the south. The Los Angeles District staff used these design concepts to formulate what they believed was the most efficient system. On 16 February 1982, the technical group met again with the Corps at the Scripps Institute in La Jolla. At this meeting the staff of Corps researchers presented nine alternatives which employed the findings of each of the individual reports. The first employed a split hopper dredge which would operate during daylight hours in the entrance channel, and then be moved near Oceanside beach where its contents would be dropped near the shore. Although the plan was technically feasible, the manner of deposition would severely affect recreational use of the beach. The second plan employed a crane, trestle, and truck haul system wherein the first two components would excavate sand from beaches north and south of the harbor to be trucked to Oceanside beach. The engineers projected that this system would also interfere with recreational use of the beach, require permanent fixtures, and have little effect on harbor shoaling. Moreover, the Marine Corps currently would not allow this or any other alternatives which called for permanent structures on beaches north of the harbor. Two other alternatives required the use of a floating breakwater system which would house portable jet pumps or a dredge, but the researchers feared that the breakwater would provide inadequate protection "in the Pacific Ocean wave climate." The two remaining alternatives called for fluidizers and a jet pump system in a fixed arrangement.[21]

The Los Angeles District staff also presented these alternatives to the Waterways Experiment Station, the Office of the Chief of Engineers, the Coastal Engineering Research Center, the South Pacific Division, and the city working group. Members of the working group quickly rejected each of the nine alternatives either because of the reasons stated above, or that individually, none provided adequate solutions for beach erosion and harbor shoaling. Therefore, with less than two months remaining before the congressional deadline for the report, the staff went to work on formulating an alternative that would be acceptable to all parties concerned. Combining the best features of several of the original plans, they developed—after refinement in consultation with the technical panel and the city—a new alternative by mid-February 1982.[22]

The plan resulting from this compromise called for bypassing equipment in two major parts of the harbor: the north fillet and the entrance channel. The north fillet was a large sand accretion upcoast of the north breakwater. Sand had been accumulating there since the original jetty construction in 1942. Moreover, sand accreting in the north fillet made its way through voids in the north breakwater and into the harbor. Jet pumps, which used high-velocity water for suction, would pull sand into discharge pipes running under the harbor. The discharge pipes would extend to Oceanside beach, where the sand and water could be released in desired spots. In order to place the sand in the north fillet into suspension, fluidizers—slotted pipes buried in underwater craters—would be used. Centrifugal pumps housed on the south jetty of the harbor would force water through these pipes, thus placing sand in the craters into suspension. The jet pumps in this crater (two were then planned) would then have an ample supply of sand to remove.

The plan also called for a system of eight fixed jet pumps arranged in a line at the south edge of the harbor entrance channel. The staff hoped this system would help to reduce shoaling by trapping sand as it entered the channel. All the sand pumped would be transported to pipelines beginning at the south jetty. These pipes would discharge sand on the south side of the jetty in a trap, and two fixed jet pumps would transfer it into the beach discharge line. The discharge system would be powered from the main pumphouse on the south jetty. The pipeline would run along the jetty, and then be buried for a distance of 1.9 miles along Oceanside beach to Wisconsin Avenue.[23] This was essentially the Corps' alternative for accomplishing beach erosion control and reducing the need for harbor maintenance dredging.

With the endorsement of the technical panel and the city working group, the Corps staff at the Los Angeles District composed the report that was sent to Congress on 12 March 1982. Estimated cost of construction at that time was $4.5 million. With

the report in Washington, Oceanside officials again traveled there
to lobby for the appropriation. Mayor Larry Bagley, City Attorney
Charles Revlett, and Special Projects Director Dana Whitson
were among those who went to Washington to insure, first of all,
that the report was forwarded to Congress from the Office of
Management and Budget. Many federal appropriations bills, as
Oceanside officials well knew, were terminated before they ever
reached Congress in this federal clearinghouse. Armed with
support of the San Diego area House delegation, both California
Senators, and a memo from the White House stating that the
Reagan Administration "would rather not see the project in OMB,"
city officials descended on that office. As Whitson assessed the
results of the meeting: "OMB got a clear picture of the political
interest in the project." The delegation was confident that if the
report was forwarded to the committee, Congressman Burgener
and other supporters would insist on the appropriation for
Oceanside.[24]

Because of such pressure, the Corps of Engineers report on the
sand bypass system cleared the Office of Management and Budget
during the summer of 1982. The report made a strong bid for
implementation of the sand bypass, but the Corps still cautioned
that such a system had never been operated in an open-ocean
setting, and insisted that its status remain experimental for that
reason. Political pressure to find solutions had been significant in
the Corps' endorsement of this project. Because of the uncertainty,
the report recommended that the system be evaluated for five
years, and that an extensive monitoring program also be installed
"for gathering baseline data during the pre-operation period,
monitoring during the five-year period of the experiment, and
system evaluation." The total cost projection for installation,
operation, and monitoring of the sand bypass system over eight
fiscal years came to $11.447 million. The experimental nature of
the project actually helped in gaining the appropriation because it
represented a full-scale model tested in a difficult coastal setting.
The report argued strongly for close monitoring in that regard,
"because the system being installed is experimental, and because
measurements of the system effectiveness must be precise to be
useful in determining if the system is meeting its goals (and thus is
a good model for other sand bypass systems)."[25]

Another principal selling feature about the sand bypass system,
which the report specified as the primary reason for its construc-

244   OCEANSIDE HARBOR

tion, was that it would reduce maintenance dredging of the harbor entrance channel. In purely economic terms the system might prove considerably less expensive than periodic maintenance dredging over several decades of operation. By simply lengthening the periods between dredging operations, sand bypassing might eventually pay for itself. Such arguments proved influential to lawmakers attempting to reduce federal deficit spending. Despite congressional inability to reach a budget accord with the executive branch, the political forces which brought Oceanside's sand bypass proposal this far were sufficient to secure funding in February 1983.

Probably no structure or artificial system of any kind would have saved Oceanside from the damage that came that winter. During the congressional deliberations on funding, a series of violent Pacific storms battered the entire coast of southern California, and continued to arrive on a regular basis until May 1983. Some observers contended that the planet had experienced a thirty-year period of mild weather which was now over. Another theory on the cause of the storms maintained that a volcanic eruption in southern Mexico in 1982 had placed sufficient ash into the atmosphere to cause abnormal cooling of the waters of the South Pacific. As a result, an effect known as "El Niño" sent powerful cyclonic storms directly to the southern California coast throughout the winter of 1982-83. Compounding the impact of these powerful storms were some of the highest tides of the century. Damage to California coastal areas numbered in the tens of millions of dollars. An intense storm on 1 March even spawned a rare and destructive tornado which touched down in downtown Los Angeles.[26]

Oceanside was among the communities sustaining the most damage during the siege. Only six months after the last truckload of sand from the second of two major sandfill projects was dumped on Oceanside's beach, the first of the storms washed much of it away. January storms removed most of the remaining sand, forcing the city to dump 1,700 tons of riprap along the beach to save the Strand. Another series in the beginning of February did an estimated $8.5 million in damage to the harbor and beach. Later that month President Ronald Reagan declared San Diego and sixteen other California counties disaster areas. Storms in March caused further damage to Oceanside and other communities,

1983 storm damage on the Oceanside Strand.

leaving many coastal residents in doubt about continuing to live
and build on the shores of the Pacific Ocean. By the end of the
winter, Oceanside's pier teetered precariously on its westernmost
end, as huge breakers threatened to sweep that section out to sea.[27]

Shortly after the first major storm in December 1982, the
Oceanside City Council held a beach-erosion workshop. The
session was called by those members who demanded federal action
to deal with beach erosion. In the five-hour meeting, suggestions
ranged from removing the harbor and building groins with city
funds, to filing a lawsuit against the Corps of Engineers for inaction
on beach erosion control. Mayor Bagley and a special legal counsel,
Kathy Stone of the firm of Burke, Williams, and Sorenson of Los
Angeles, warned against legal action. Echoing the findings of the
report that the law firm had completed for the city in 1980, Stone
and Bagley argued that such action might remain in litigation for
five years, cost the city up to $1 million, and yield no tangible
results. Moreover, the action might cause the Corps to once again
reconsider the evidence that led to federal acceptance of one
hundred percent responsibility for beach erosion control. With
additional studies and opinions questioning these findings since

the last reassessment, the amount of federal responsibility could only be revised downward. Cooler heads prevailed at the workshop, and the council decided to forego any legal action. One month later, the council agreed to allow the Corps to study the effectiveness of sand bypassing for five years before taking any structural steps toward beach erosion control.[38]

Meanwhile, in anticipation of congressional funding for construction of the project, the Los Angeles District staff continued to coordinate with the technical panel and the city on hiring a consulting firm to prepare a final concept for the system. Shortly after completion of the preliminary design report, the Corps awarded the contract for that work to Moffatt and Nichol, Engineers, of Long Beach, California. The contract specified that Moffatt and Nichol conduct the research in four main phases. The first, data collection and analysis, included site investigations, preliminary hydraulic calculations, and conceptual presentations of the alternative systems. The second phase consisted of specific hydraulic calculations and drive system selection. The third phase, the final concept, included specific layouts for the pumphouse, cost estimates, and construction schedules, while the fourth called for a report of all plans and specifications for the sand bypass system. During all phases of the detailed engineering and design Moffatt and Nichol engineers coordinated closely with Los Angeles District Corps liaisons Charles Fisher, Donald Spencer, and Claude Wong. Through these connections, Moffatt and Nichol received analysis and advice from the technical panel and city working group.[29]

Work on the first phase of the analysis, which was completed in January 1983, took the Moffatt and Nichol research staff to several locations across North America in order to inspect operational sand bypass systems. Those field trips included Rudee Inlet, Virginia; Detroit, Michigan; and Naufrage, Prince Edward Island, Canada. They also visited the Waterways Experiment Station to inspect modelling work being conducted there on sand bypassing. Several field investigations at Oceanside highlighted the need to employ jet pumps that would be easily accessible for maintenance. Jet pumps there, the researchers believed, would be prone to debris clogging and have extensive "downtime" if they were not readily accessible. The north fillet system was to use a jet pump on a trailer mounted on a floating vessel. If self-propelled, the vessel could both serve the north fillet jet pump system and serve as a repair platform for the entrance channel system. The Moffat and Nichol report also explored the effect of sand grain size on pumping ability, the best type of pipe to use, alternative discharge line routes, fluidizer design, crater-slope effects, and extra equipment that might be required. The report concluded that "the system can be installed and would have a reasonable chance of success. The key to success lies in the ability to recover and repair clogged jet pumps and to clean craters of debris. Success. . . does not infer that all material entering the harbor will be bypassed, but that maintenance dredging frequency can be decreased."[30]

The second and third phases of the Moffatt and Nichol study were completed in June 1983 and August 1984 respectively. Phase II was an elaborate technical compendium of hydraulic calculations and comparisons of various drive systems. Researchers investigated many sizes and configurations of jet pumps and fluidizers, and recommended equipment based on performance comparisons and adaptability to Oceanside. They also determined that diesel engines were more appropriate and less expensive overall in comparison to natural gas and electric motors. The report concluded that "the system is hydraulically feasible and it is recommended that the Phase III study proceed."[31]

During the interim between production of the second and third phases, events occurred which changed the overall system plan considerably. Cost estimates for the completed system as outlined in Phase II had soared to $10.5 million—more than double the amount budgeted for the project. A cost reduction meeting with representatives from the Los Angeles District, South Pacific Division, Coastal Engineering Research Center, Waterways Experiment Station, Office of the Chief of Engineers, and Moffatt and Nichol, convened during June 1983. Subsea pipelines for the jet pumps and fluidizers proved to be the most expensive part of the project, and those present at the meeting found a way to reduce the amount of undersea pipe needed by employing remote control pinch valves. They eliminated a fixed pump house at the end of the south jetty in favor of a mobile one, and also one drive set of engines because the jet pumps and fluidizers would not need to be operated simultaneously. The most significant result of the cost reduction meeting, however, was the decision to build the system in phases. When the Phase III report was issued, it contained those modifications, and a plan for development of the sand bypass system in six separate construction segments.[32]

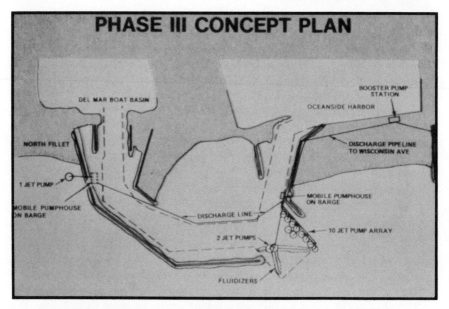

Oceanside Harbor Complex, Sand Bypass System, Phase III.

The decision to build the system in phases was logical and necessary. Costs could not exceed $5 million, and the first phase, known as the development phase, would total almost exactly that amount according to estimates. In preparing plans for that phase, Corps researchers met with the technical panel to work out details. Both groups agreed that the initial phase must be extensive enough to test all of the project objectives, including the debris problems, jet-pump and fluidizer efficiency, and the impact of the remote control pinch valves. One of the major cost savings of this plan was the use of temporary pipelines instead of more costly, permanent subsea lines. Also, the discharge line would extend only as far south as Tyson Avenue in this part of the experiment.[33] The philosophy was to test all performance variables in the first phase before proceeding to the next.

Specific features of the development phase included complete construction of the north fillet system, but only a partial building of the entrance channel array. In the final concept, everyone agreed to the employment of a stiff-leg crane fixed on the north breakwater rather than a floating system. The crane would be able to lower the jet pump and fluidizer to various spots on the fillet where sand was the most plentiful. A single six-inch jet pump capable of pumping up to 200 cubic yards of sand per hour would be used there, and it would be powered by a 1,000 horsepower diesel engine mounted on a mobile barge. Two four-inch jet pumps would be installed on the south jetty capable of pumping one hundred cubic yards of sand per hour. They too, would be powered by the diesel engine on the mobile barge. Sand slurry from both pumping locations would pass into a main discharge line. Along the discharge line, at the edge of the harbor beach, a booster pumping station would be built in order to send material to the end of the fourteen-inch pipeline to be buried under the beach. Estimated first costs of the development phase, the final concept reported, were $4.3 million. The report recommended that the north fillet system should be operated first during the winter, when downcoast littoral movement was greatest. Conversely, the south jetty array should be tested in the first summer after operation of the north fillet system.[34]

With completion of plans and specifications for the beach discharge pipeline later that year, the complex engineering and design portion of the sand bypass project was complete. The Los Angeles District shortly thereafter awarded contracts for construction of the discharge line and for the development phase of the project. By early 1985, the discharge line was completed to Tyson Avenue. The line was designed to allow for spot nourishment at two points along its span. The Corps awarded the contract for construction of the development phase to Macon Construction Company. On 30 September 1985, the Corps held a ground-breaking ceremony at Oceanside Harbor, marking the beginning of construction on a project that all interested people hoped would not only reduce the costs of maintenance dredging, but also ameliorate to some degree Oceanside's chronic beach erosion problems.[35]

Since construction began in 1985, a number of design changes in the development phase have occurred. Among those has been the addition of a booster pump on a hoist barge at the north breakwater, to assist the flow of slurry under the harbor to the south jetty. Engineers working on the sand bypass system also decided to use a truck-mounted crane, instead of a fixed one, for moving the jet pump and fluidizer system of the north fillet system. The jet-pump fluidizer design has changed as well. Now the system uses deployment fluidizers which will operate simultaneously with the jet pumps, providing not only sand slurry, but also freeing the jet pumps when they are embedded in sand. In future construction phases of the system, the Corps hopes to use crater-fill fluidizers in addition to the deployment fluidizers of the early phases. While deployment fluidizers operate with the jet pumps, crater-fill fluidizers will function independently. They are pipes up to 400 feet long drilled horizontally into the shore bottom at a one percent slope. Placed near existing jet-pump craters, the fluidizers force more sand to the pumps, into the system, and out of the harbor.[36]

Corps officials have installed a sophisticated and complex monitoring system called the Supervisory Control and Data Acquisition System. With this system in operation, Corps personnel are able to determine the performance of sand bypassing at Oceanside, as it keeps track of virtually all of the mechanical functions. From these data, from depth soundings in the harbor entrance, and from intensive physical and biological monitoring, they will determine when the next phases will be built.[37]

The true determinant of the efficacy of sand bypassing at Oceanside is its value as a cost-cutting measure for maintenance dredging. However, a crucial by-product of the operation to the people of Oceanside is the consistent nourishment of the city's beach. Experts hope that constant nourishment will be more successful than periodic placement of large quantities of sand resulting from maintenance dredging or fill projects. Both beach erosion control and harbor improvement are crucial to Oceanside's prosperity and have been the focus of much of the city's political action for the past four decades. If the system works well, both problems, while perhaps not being entirely solved, will be eased. Sand bypassing more closely simulates natural longshore movement than any other solution considered. The system remains a bold experiment, especially in the harsh open-ocean setting of Oceanside. A variety of factors can affect its performance adversely. Yet if sand bypassing proves to be an efficient and effective system at Oceanside, then the experiment will be worthwhile not only for the sake of the city, but also for its value in a number of other locations. Should this prove to be the case, then sand bypassing is truly a coastal engineering system for the future.

NOTES

[1]U.S. Army Engineer District, *San Diego County, Vicinity of Oceanside, California, Draft Survey Report for Beach Erosion Control, Main Report, Environmental Impact Statement, and Appendixes* (Los Angeles: April 1980), p. A-1. Hereafter referred to as *Draft Beach Erosion Control Report, April 1980;* Weiss interview; Memorandum for Shore Protection file from Win Collins, 14 Nov. 1977, Oceanside Beach Erosion Study, 1976-77, LNNA RG 77/84-0018 Box 7/8.

[2]*Ibid.; Draft Beach Erosion Control Report, April 1980,* pp. 48-65, D7-D15; U.S. Army Engineers Waterways Experiment Station, Technical Report HL-80-10, *Oceanside Harbor and Beach, California, Design of Structures for Harbor Improvement and Beach Erosion Control: Hydraulic Model Investigation: Final Report* (Vicksburg, MS: June 1980). Hereafter referred to as *Oceanside Model Investigation.*

[3]Moffatt and Nichol, Engineers, *Experimental Sand Bypass System at Oceanside Harbor, California, Phase I Report: Data Collection and Analysis* (Los Angeles: January 1983), pp. 3, i; Charles Fisher to Richard Sager, subj: Request for WES report preparation on sand bypassing, 20 Dec. 1979, Oceanside Beach Erosion, Shore Protection file, LNNA RG 77/81-0015 Box 1/1; *Draft Beach Erosion Control Report, April 1980,* pp. 52-54, plate 2; *Oceanside Model Investigation.*

[4]*Ibid.,* pp. 7, C5-C15; *Oceanside Model Investigation.*

[5]*OBT* (2 Apr. 1980); *LAT* (29 Apr. 1980).

[6]*OBT* (19 May, 15 July 1980); *SDU* (6 July 1980).

[7]*Ibid.; LAT* (17 July 1980).

[8]*SDU* (6 July 1980).

[9]Interview, author with Claude Wong, Los Angeles, CA, 2 Apr. 1986. Hereinafter referred to as Wong interview; *OBT* (6 Oct. 1980).

[10]*Ibid.,* (13 Aug. 1980).

[11]Revlett interview; *OBT* (14 Nov. 1980).

[12]*Ibid.*

[13]*Ibid.;* Bagley interview; Whitson and Bagley, "Putting the Beach Back," pp. 27-28.

[14]*Ibid.,* p. 27; Whitson interview; Revlett interview; Bagley interview.

[15]Whitson and Bagley, "Putting the Beach Back," p. 28; Whitson interview; Revlett interview.

[16]Wong interview; Revlett interview; Whitson interview; *OBT* (23 Mar. 1981).

[17]U.S. Congress, House, *Energy and Water Development Appropriation Bill,* 97th Cong. 1st sess. 1981, H.R. 177; Whitson interview; U.S. Army Engineer District, *Report on a Program for Installing, Monitoring, and Evaluating the Effectiveness of a Sand Bypass System as a Means of Maintenance of the Harbor Channels: Oceanside Harbor, California* (Los Angeles: Mar. 1982). Hereinafter referred to as *Sand Bypass Program Report, 1982.*

[18]Purchase Order: From Los Angeles District to Waterways Experiment Station for the Evaluation of littoral parameters as they relate to the conceptual design of possible sand bypassing schemes, 22 June 1981, Oceanside Beach Nourishment file, LNNA RG 77/84-0018 Box 6/8; Wong interview; Moffatt and Nichol, *Sand Bypass Report, Phase I,* pp. 3-1-3-17.

[19]See Moffatt and Nichol, *Sand Bypass Report, Phase I,* pp. 1-7-1-9, see reference to those reports; *Sand Bypass Program Report, 1982.*

[20]*Ibid.; LAT* (20 Mar. 1983).

[21]*Sand Bypass Report, 1982,* pp. 6-12.

[22]Congress set a deadline for this report to come to the House Energy and Water Development Committee at 31 Mar. 1982. See *ibid.*

[23]*Ibid.; OBT* (18 Feb. 1982).

[24]*Ibid.,* (27 Apr, 27 May 1982); Whitson interview; Revlett interview; Bagley interview.

[25]*Sand Bypass Program Report, 1982; OBT* (13 Jan., 2 Feb. 1983); *Energy and Water Appropriations Act of 1983,* 97 Stat. 247, 98th Cong., 1st sess., 1983.

[26]*SDU* (6 Feb. 1983); U.S. Army Engineer District, *Coastal Storm Damage, 1983* (Los Angeles: 1984). Hereafter cited as *Coastal Storm Damage.*

[27]*Ibid.; OBT* (1 Dec. 1982, 30 Jan., 1, 2, 10, 11 Feb. 1983); *LAT* (3 Feb., 6 Mar. 1983); *SDU* (23 Dec. 1982).

[28]*Ibid.;* Revlett interview.

[29]Moffatt and Nichol, *Sand Bypass Report, Phase I*, pp. i, iii; *Sand Bypass Program Report, 1982;* Wong interview; Interview, author with Robert Joe, Los Angeles, CA, 29 Apr. 1986. Hereinafter cited as Joe interview.

[30]Moffatt and Nichol, *Sand Bypass Report, Phase I*, pp. iii-v.

[31]Moffatt and Nichol, *Experimental Sand Bypass System at Oceanside Harbor, California, Phase 2: Hydraulic Calculations and Drive System Selection* (Los Angeles: June 1983), pp. 69-70.

[32]*Ibid.*, Phase 3: Final Concept (Los Angeles: August 1984), pp. 4-1-4-8; Wong interview.

[33]Moffatt and Nichol, *Sand Bypass Report, Phase III*, pp. 4-8-4-9.

[34]*Ibid.*, pp. 8-1-8-2, 5-1-5-2; Interview, author with Doug Diemer, Los Angeles, CA, 2 Apr. 1986, hereinafter referred to as Diemer interview; U.S. Army Corps of Engineers, *Specifications for Pump System and Facilities, Experimental Sand Bypass System at Oceanside, California,* (Los Angeles: U.S. Army Engineer District, 1985), pp. SC1-SC9; U.S. Army Corps of Engineers, Los Angeles District, *The Experimental Jet-Pump Sand Bypass System at Oceanside: An Operation and Maintenance Program Under Test by the U.S. Army Corps of Engineers to Solve Some Recurring Problems: Harbor Shoaling, Beach Erosion* (Los Angeles, U.S. Army Engineer District, July 1987), pp. 6-13.

[35]Spencer interview; Diemer interview.

[36]Los Angeles District, *The Experimental Jet-Pump Sand Bypass System at Oceanside, 1987*, pp. 9-12.

[37]Spencer interview; Diemer interview.

CHAPTER VI

Sand Bypassing and the Future

Hopes and expectations run high for sand bypassing at Ocean-side, California. Public officials of the city of Oceanside place great faith in the experimental sand bypass system as an effective means of ameliorating beach erosion. Corps of Engineers personnel hope the system will perform that task, as well as its primary function of reducing the costs of maintaining the Oceanside-Camp Pendleton Harbor entrance channel. The success of sand bypassing could possibly bring the chronic problems that have perplexed everyone associated with beach erosion and harbor navigation for the past forty-five years to a manageable conclusion. Most experts believe that the sand bypass system will at least lengthen the time intervals between maintenance dredging, and all of the sand removed will be placed on Oceanside beach at a consistent rate.

The success of the system at Oceanside Harbor rests on a number of variables. With no natural sand trap there, experts are concerned that there might be an insufficient sand supply within the reach of the jet pump and fluidizer assemblies. Moreover, coastal scientists now believe that diminishing sand supply may be a reality in varying degrees throughout the earth's coastal zones. Only if the system can pump large quantities of sand from both the north fillet and the entrance channel will it reduce the need for maintenance dredging sufficiently to justify expansion or continued operation. The system the Corps is currently constructing also will operate in one of the harshest wave environments of the Pacific coast. Wave conditions are an uncertain factor which could greatly reduce the amount of time in which the system can operate. However, powerful ocean currents also can prove to be a problem for the system's performance, as they will undoubtedly carry all kinds of debris which can clog the jet pumps. Storms coupled with high tides will likely test the design and construction quality of the sand bypass system with waves that can break over the tops of the jetties. Just as any other machine, the complex sand bypass system is subject to any number of equipment breakdowns caused by a variety of factors. This leads engineers to be very concerned with the amount of downtime the system will experience.[1]

Building such a complex system in a harsh environment prompted the Corps to prepare designs requiring rigorous construction measures. This created another variable in the sand bypass system's overall feasibility. Such measures have resulted in large cost increases over the initial congressional appropriations for the development phase. However, Corps officials believe the high standards set for construction are necessary to insure that sand bypassing at Oceanside will be efficient and cost-effective over its years of operation. While funding is assured for the development phase, each of the five following phases will require additional congressional approval. Moreover, the Corps and the city will have to secure congressional appropriations each year for funding to operate and maintain the existing system. In regard to future funding, one Corps official conceded: "It's going to be tough."[2]

The most important by-product of the successful operation of the system will be the arrival of desperately-needed sand on Oceanside's beaches. As events of the past half-century have revealed, the causes of beach erosion at Oceanside are complex and still not fully understood. The combination of jetty construction to the north, fine grade sand, powerful and multi-directional wave motion, an absence of inland sediment supply, violent storms, and high tides have all contributed to erosion and the disappearance of millions of cubic yards of artificial sandfill. Regardless of causes or responsibilities, Oceanside's beaches often require extensive re-nourishment. A virtue of sand bypassing will be its ability to provide constant replenishment. In the development phase either the south jetty or north fillet systems are designed to operate sixteen hours per day, with the ability to pump 150 to 200 cubic yards of sand per hour under the best of conditions. In the event of an erosive storm or wave episode, operators will be able to begin replenishment as soon as weather conditions permit. They will also be able to discharge the sand at two different points along the discharge line; ultimately the project will include three discharge points. However, during the development stage operators will be limited to the amount of sand which falls into the fluidizer craters. The complete system will afford many more options with additional craters, fluidizers, and jet pumps. This constant sand replenishment will most closely simulate the natural sedimentation processes that have historically nourished beaches. Oceanside officials have agreed to allow the Corps to assess the value of sand bypassing as a beach erosion control measure for a period of five years before reexamining structural solutions to the problem.[3]

A crucial component of that assessment, and a contributing factor to the increased cost of sand bypassing, is the sophisticated Supervisory Control Data Acquisition System which regulates all of the mechanical functions of the complex system, including engine operations, valve status, pressure levels within the miles of pipes and lines, and flow level rates of the sand-water mixtures. Analysts monitor carefully the amount of sand that the system pumps during the development phase. Coupled with harbor-depth soundings, the data show the overall performance of sand bypassing at Oceanside.[4]

This history of the Corps of Engineers' activities in the vicinity of Oceanside, California, began with the Navy's construction of Del Mar Boat Basin for the use of the Marine Corps at Camp Pendleton. The choice of that site had a dramatic impact upon Oceanside in contributing to the city's beach erosion problems. Yet it also afforded Oceanside officials a principal bargaining factor in efforts to build a small craft harbor sharing the same entrance channel as the military facility. While they achieved that goal in 1963, questions about harbor improvement and expansion still remain unanswered. Oceanside Small Craft Harbor is, as one city official appraised it, "the crown jewel of the city" and remains a substantial revenue-producing facility. However, Oceanside officials have wanted to expand the harbor and improve the entrance channel since the mid-1960s. In order to operate profitably, the harbor needs additional slips. Since 1977, there has been a potential site for expansion on the North Beach area of Camp Pendleton, but plans have been thwarted by severe federal budget constraints which place recreational boating—as well as other recreational expenditures—on an extremely low priority.

Unless the city can again produce its own funding, it is unlikely the federal government will undertake such a project in the near future. However, the methods which Oceanside employed in the early 1960s to acquire harbor construction funds are now much more difficult to use successfully. Not only has recreational boating lost much of its investment appeal, losses in revenues through tax-cutting measures have exhausted the state's ability to loan money for such projects.[5] Moreover, expansion plans also have come under the meticulous scrutiny of both federal and state environmental laws. Both the regulations of NEPA and those of the California Coastal Commission, while not ruling out expansion altogether, have placed extreme restrictions on coastal development of this scale.

Currently, Oceanside officials are more interested in harbor improvements than harbor expansion. Historically, the open-ocean setting has at times made both the entrance channel and the turning basin a treacherous navigation endeavor. As a harbor of refuge, Oceanside officials are most anxious to improve the navigation features. During the last eight years, ten boating-accident deaths have occurred inside the harbor breakwaters. Moreover, the powerful surges that can occur throughout the harbor have caused millions of dollars in damages to the facilities. The Corps' navigation study of Oceanside, which included both harbor improvement and expansion, was discontinued in 1983 because funding expired. Now the city hopes to supply the remaining funding needed to complete the study, and then extract the sections dealing with harbor navigation improvement. At that time, Oceanside officials will, as they have done so many times in the past, attempt to pressure Congress to fund these crucial improvements which will make the harbor safer and less expensive to maintain.[6]

The city's ability to solve this problem will mark a continuation of successes in working within the federal system. As with beach erosion and harbor construction, Oceanside has been fortunate to have had a succession of aggressive, politically-aware officials who have worked the governmental system to their advantage in order to resolve past and future problems. In their dealings with the federal government, Oceanside officials have been very successful in the past. However, new cost sharing legislation passed during the mid-1980s will make it more difficult for cities like Oceanside to acquire federal funding for beach erosion projects or the expansion of the sand bypass system. As a result of cost sharing, local governments will be required to provide a greater percentage of the funding for civil works studies, projects, and construction taking place in their jurisdiction. With requirements of as much as fifty percent of the overall cost, localities like Oceanside will be hard-pressed to produce the funds required for relatively inexpensive studies, and even harder-pressed to help fund large civil works projects like the expansion of the sand bypass system. Cost sharing, moreover, will probably have a significant negative impact on the Corps' undertaking of new studies which lead to new projects.[7]

Oceanside officials will nonetheless be lobbying hard for continued sand bypass funding. Only if the system is expanded to completion can its overall effectiveness be evaluated. The maintenance of the harbor is important, but their primary concern is the by-product of a sandy beach. They hope that such a beach, combined with an ambitious and extensive community redevelopment plan, will improve the city's ability to attract resort tourism. Contained in redevelopment plans is a renovation of the Strand, the pier, and nearby sections of the downtown area, and also the construction of at least one large luxury resort hotel.[8] The success of this plan is tied inextricably, however, to the maintenance of a good beach. Sand bypassing, everyone hopes, will make a significant contribution to the economic revitalization of the city.

The Corps of Engineers' role at Oceanside since the 1940s has been in constant transition. Those changes underscore what was occurring nationally as well, as the Corps expanded its post-World War II public works program. The Oceanside example represents a situation in which non-Corps elements became involved not only in solutions, but also in project development. Corps personnel became the liaisons between city government, the military, and state resource agencies. In response to concerns for the environment, the Corps fortified its ecological-investigation capabilities, and the Corps works with all concerned agencies and individuals to minimize the environmental impacts of its projects. As a result, the Corps now faces problems with heightened public awareness of the issues involved, and an increased sensitivity for environmental concerns.

The coastal engineering which has taken place at Oceanside over the past 45 years demonstrates both the technological advances made since then, and the vulnerability of the shoreline there. The original construction features quickly resulted in a shoaled-in harbor and an eroded downcoast beach. While breakwater improvements have helped, shoaling remains a problem. The site of the harbor, between two major rivers, may yet prove to be ill-conceived in the event of a major flood. However, the construction of a civilian marina at the same site has proven thus far to have been a valuable addition to California's chain of harbors. Beach erosion control measures at Oceanside have provided only temporary relief; but structural solutions, still untested there, may also prove ineffective.

Sand bypassing, while designed primarily to reduce maintenance dredging costs, may prove to be an efficient beach erosion control measure. The system is the state of the art in coastal engineering technology and could be operated properly only with modern computerized controls. At the same time, the system is the most environmentally-acceptable of all navigation and beach erosion plans. With harbor shoaling and beach erosion occurring world-wide, sand bypassing may prove a viable solution for many coastal communities, and an economically-feasible Oceanside experiment will further that possibility. The successful performance of sand bypassing in this harsh environment will be a triumph for the art of coastal engineering, and on the local level provide Oceanside residents with solutions to the long-standing problems associated with their harbor and beach.

NOTES

[1]Diemer interview; Spencer interview; *SDU* (6 May 1983).

[2]Interview, author with Carl Enson. Los Angeles, CA, 23 May 1986; Diemer interview. Current cost estimates run as high as $8 million for the development phase, and $20 million for the entire system.

[3]Commercial sand mining operations on privately-owned stretches of the San Luis Rey River also diminish inland sediment supply, see *OBT* (1 Apr. 1983); Moffatt and Nichol, *Sand Bypass Report, Phase 3*, pp. 1-1-1-5; Diemer interview; Spencer interview; Enson interview.

[4]Diemer interview.

[5]Enson interview; Joe interview; Bagley interview; Maj. Gen. E.R. Heiberg, III, "Coastal Engineering in the Eighties," *Shore and Beach* (July 1982), p. 3.

[6]Bagley interview; Enson interview; Joe interview; William Herron, Jr., "The Influence of Man Upon the Shoreline of Southern California," *Shore and Beach* (July 1983), pp. 17, 26.

[7]Joe interview; Enson interview.

[8]Whitson interview; Revlett interview.

Bibliography:
Humboldt Bay

Published Primary Sources

Democratic Standard. Eureka, Cal. Same as *Humboldt Standard.*

Humboldt Standard. Eureka, Cal. Also known as *Humboldt Daily Standard.*

Humboldt Times. Eureka, Cal. Also known as *Humboldt Daily Times.*

Times-Standard. Eureka, Cal.

McKenny, L.M. *Business Directory of San Francisco and Principal Towns of California and Nevada, 1877.* San Francisco: L.M. McKenny, 1877.

Pacific Coast Publishing Co., compiler. *Directory of Humboldt County, 1898-1899.* San Francisco: Pacific Coast Pub. Co., 1898.

U.S. Army. Corps of Engineers. *Annual Report of the Chief of Engineers, 1871, 1877, 1881-1972.* Washington, DC: G.P.O., 1871, 1877, 1881-1972.

U.S. Army. Corps of Engineers. *Brief Design Memorandum, Repairs to Humboldt Harbor and Bay Jetties.* San Francisco: U.S. Army Engineer District, 1970.

U.S. Army. Corps of Engineers. *Humboldt Harbor and Bay, Repair of Jetties, Humboldt County, California.* San Francisco: U.S. Army Engineer District, 1978.

U.S. Army. Corps of Engineers. *Review of Reports on Humboldt Harbor and Bay, California for Navigation.* San Francisco: U.S. Army Engineer District, 1966.

U.S. Army. Corps of Engineers. *Survey Report, Humboldt Bay, California, February 1950.* San Francisco: U.S. Army Engineer District, 1950.

U.S. Coast and Geodetic Survey. *Maps of Humboldt Bay, 1851-1929.* Washington, DC: G.P.O., 1851-1929.

U.S. Congress. Senate. *Letter from the Secretary of War, Submitting a Statement from James B. Eads Relative to Work Executed at the South Pass of the Mississippi River.* Ex. Doc. 78, 45th Cong., 2d sess., 1878.

U.S. Congress. House. *Certain Harbors in California.* House Ex. Doc. 22, 45th Cong., 3d Sess., 1879.

U.S. Congress. House. *Letter from the Secretary of War, Transmitting Report upon Improvement of Humboldt Bay, made by Lt. Col. G.H. Mendell, Corps of Engineers.* House Ex. Doc. 59, 46th Cong., 3d sess., 1881.

U.S. Congress. House. *Improvement of the Entrance to Humboldt Bay, California.* House Ex. Doc. 102, 47th Cong., 2d sess., 1883.

U.S. Congress. House. *Removal of Lighthouse at Humboldt Harbor California.* House Ex. Doc. 91, 49th Cong., 1st sess., 1886.

Archival Primary Sources

Arcata, California. Humboldt State Univ. Humboldt Room Collection.

Arcata, California. Humboldt State Univ. Susie Baker Fountain Papers.

Eureka, California. Humboldt County Library. Steenfott Photographs.

Eureka, California. Humboldt County Public Works. Natural Resources Division, Historical File.

Eureka, California. Humboldt County Recorders Office, Deed Books.

Eureka, California. Humboldt County Supervisors Office, Minute Books.

San Bruno, California. National Archives and Records Administration, Record Group 77.

Secondary Published Sources: Books

Bogue, Donald J., and Beale, Calvin L. *Economic Areas of the United States.* New York: The Free Press of Glencoe, Inc., 1961.

Carranco, Lynwood. *Redwood Country.* Belmont, CA: Star Pub. Co., 1986.

Carranco, Lynwood, *et al. Logging the Redwoods.* Caldwell, ID: the Caxton Printers, Ltd., 1975.

Cowdrey, Albert E. *Lands End.* New Orleans, LA: U.S. Army Engineer District, 1977.

Coy, Owen C. *The Humboldt Bay Region, 1850-1875.* Los Angeles: Calif. State Hist. Assoc., 1929. Reprinted: Eureka, CA: Humboldt County Hist. Soc., 1984.

Crook, George. *General George Crook, His Autobiography.* Norman, OK: Univ. of Oklahoma Press, 1946.

Dean, Gerald W., *et al. Structure and Projections of the Humboldt County Economy: Economic Growth versus Environmental Quality.* Davis: Univ. of Calif., Dept. of Agricultural Economics, 1973.

Doyle, Don H. *The Social Order of a Frontier Community.* Chicago: Univ. of Illinois Press, 1983.

Eddy, J.M., compiler. *In the Redwoods Realm, Humboldt County California.* San Francisco: D.S. Stanley & Co., 1893.

Hagwood, Joseph Jeremiah. *Engineers at the Golden Gate.* San Francisco: U.S. Army Engineer District, 1980.

Heizer, Robert, ed. *An Anthropological Expedition in 1913.* Berkeley: Univ. of California Press, 1970.

Hoopes, Chad L. *Lure of the Humboldt Bay Region.* Dubuque, IA: Wm. C. Brown Book Co., 1966.

Humboldt County Board of Supervisors. *Humboldt County Atlas.* Eureka, CA: Humboldt County Board of Supervisors, 1974.

Irvine, Leigh H. *History of Humboldt County, California, with Biographical Sketches.* Los Angeles: Historic Record Co., 1915.

Johnson, A.J. *Johnson's New Universal Cyclopaedia. A Scientific and Popular Treasury of Useful Knowledge.* New York: A.J. Johnson & Co., 1881.

Kortum, Karl, and Olmstead, Roger. *"...it is a dangerous looking place": Sailing Days on the Redwood Coast.* San Francisco: California Hist. Soc., c. 1980.

Noble, R.M. *Shoreline changes, Humboldt Bay, California.* Berkeley: Univ. of California Hydraulic Engineering Laboratory, 1971.

Paquin, Cyril E., State Supervisor, Survey of Federal Archives Project. *Ship Registries and Enrollments, Port of Eureka, California, 1859-1920.* San Francisco: National Archives, 1941.

Pearsall, Clarence E., *et al. The Quest for Qual-a-Wa-Loo.* Oakland, CA: Holmes Book Co., 1966.

Shanks, Ralph C., Jr. *Lighthouses and Lifeboats on the Redwood Coast.* San Anselmo, CA: Costano Books, 1978.

Stevenson, Thomas. *The Design and Construction of Harbours.* Edinburgh: Adam & Charles Black, 1864.

Thornbury, D.L. *California's Redwood Wonderland: Humboldt County.* San Francisco: Sunset Press, 1923.

U.S. Army Corps of Engineers. *Shore Protection Manual.* Washington, DC: G.P.O., 1984.

Willingham, William F. *Army Engineers and the Development of Oregon, A History of the Portland District U.S. Army Corps of Engineers.* Portland, OR: U.S. Army Engineer District, 1983.

Secondary Published Sources: Articles

Allardt, G.F., *et al.* "Discussion of Symons Single Jetty Harbor Improvement." *Transactions, Amer. Soc. of Civil Engineers,* 36 (Dec. 1896): 125-38.

Anderson, John W. "Offshore Technology." *Military Engineering,* #67 (May-June 1975): 158-60.

Barsness, Richard W. "Maritime Activity and Port Development in the United States since 1900: A Survey." *Journal of Transport History,* #2 (Feb. 1974): 167-84.

Bethel, Edwin A. "Making Concrete Blocks for Jetties." *The Military Engineer,* 16 (May-June 1924): 218.

Bixby, William H. "River and Harbor Improvements: Progress and Needs in the United States, 1911." *Professional Memoirs,* 4 (Jan.-Feb. 1912): 114-28.

Black, W.M., "Formation of Channels Across Ocean Bars." *The Military Engineer,* 14 (Nov.-Dec. 1922): 373-75.

Bond, Aubrey H. "Meteorological Studies at Humboldt Bay." *The Military Engineer,* 19 (Nov.-Dec. 1927): 507-09.

Carey, Walter C. "Hot Asphalt Mix — A Jetty Construction Material?" *The Military Engineer,* 59 (July-Aug. 1967): 263-66.

Carr, Housley F. "Return of the Jetties." *Sierra,* 70 (March-April 1985): 23-26.

Carranco, Lynwood. "Maritime Fiasco on the Northern California Coast." *California History,* 60 (Fall 1981): 206-20.

Carranco, Lynwood. "When Crossing Humboldt Bar Cost 18 Lives." *Humboldt Historian,* 36 (Sept.-Oct. 1985): 16-19.

Chittenden, H.M. "Ports of the Pacific, with Discussion." *Transactions, Amer. Soc. of Civil Engineers,* 76 (Dec. 1913): 155-240.

Coursey, Greer E. "New Shape in Shore Protection." *Civil Engineering,* 43 (Dec. 1973): 68-71.

Cowdrey, Albert E. "Pioneering Environmental Law: The Army Corps of Engineers and the Refuse Act." *Pacific Hist. Rev.,* 44 (Aug. 1975): 331-49.

Crichton, R. Chalmers. "Tug Ranger's Colorful Role in Shipping." *The Humboldt Historian,* 35 (July-Aug. 1985): 10-11.

Defontaine, A.J. Ch. "Extracts from Des Travaux de Fleuve de Rhin." *Professional Memoirs*, 9 (Oct.-Dec. 1917): 508-27.

DeLong, Harriet Tracy. "Humboldt Memories — as told by Will Simpson." *The Humboldt Historian*, 27 (July-Aug. 1979): 1, 9-10.

Dennison, W.E. "Humboldt Bay and its Jetty System." *Overland Monthly* (Sept. 1896): 381-90.

Finch, Henry A. "The Humboldt Bay Jetties." *The Dock and Harbor Authority* (June 1934): 215-53 and (July 1934): 266-72.

Genzoli, Andrew. "Humboldt Bay and Harbor." *The Humboldt Historian*, 29 (Nov.-Dec. 1981): 16-17.

Genzoli, Andrew. "Remembering a Daring Transition — from Sail to Steam." *The Humboldt Historian*, 31 (Jan.-Feb. 1983): 18-19.

Genzoli, Andrew. "The Seas were too Heavy for the Little Chilkat." *The Humboldt Historian*, 31 (March-April 1983): 8-9.

Harts, William Wright. "Harbor Improvement on the Pacific Coast of the United States." *Professional Memoirs*, 3 (Oct.-Dec. 1911): 618-41.

Harts, William Wright. "Description of Coos Bay, Oregon, and the Improvement of its Entrance by the Government, With Discussion." *Transactions, Amer. Soc. of Civil Engineers*, 46 (Dec. 1901): 482-550.

Hickson, R.E. "Jetty Maintenance at the Mouth of Columbia." *The Military Engineer*, 25 (Sept.-Oct. 1933): 411-14.

Hurley, John. "Harbor Improvements at Humboldt Bay, California." Unpublished Senior Thesis, Fall Semester, 1964. Humboldt State Univ., Arcata, Cal.

Lillevang, Omar J., and Nickola, Wayne E. "Experimental Studies of Stresses Within the Breakwater Armour Piece, 'Dolos.'" Preprint of a paper prepared for the Fifteenth International Conference on Coastal Engineering, Honolulu, 11-17 July 1976.

Magoon, Orville T.; Sloan, Robert L.; and Shimizu, Nobuyuki. "Design and Construction of Humboldt Jetties, 1880-1975." *Proceedings* of the Fifteenth Coastal Conference, Honolulu, 11-17 July 1976, pp. 2474-98.

Marshall, William L. "River and Harbor Work from a Military Point of View." *Professional Memoirs*, 2 (July-Sept. 1910): 393-96.

Merrifield, Eric M. "Dolos Concrete Armour Protection." *Transactions, Amer. Soc. of Civil Engineers*, 134 (Dec. 1969): 841-43.

Noble, Ronald M. "Shoreline Changes, Humboldt Bay, California." *Journal of the Amer. Shore and Beach Assoc.*, 39 (Oct. 1971): 11-18.

Pearsall, Clarence E. "Scary Crossing of Bar Related by Eyewitnesses." *The Humboldt Historian*, 32 (July-Aug. 1984): 17-18.

Pursell, Carroll W. "Historical and Technological Significance of the Humboldt Bay Jetties, Humboldt, California." Report dated 22 Sept. 1981.

Ripley, Henry Clay. "The Economic Location of Jetties." *Transactions, Amer. Soc. Civil Engineers*, 87D (1924): 979-86.

Symons, Thomas W. "Improving the Entrance to a Bar Harbor by a Single Jetty." *Transactions, Amer. Soc. of Civil Engineers*, 36 (Dec. 1896): 109-24.

Symons, Thomas W. "Jetty Harbors of the Pacific Coast." *Transactions, Amer. Soc. of Civil Engineers*, 27 (March 1893): 155-84.

Taylor, Harry. "Civil Works of the Corps of Engineers." *Military Engineer*, 17 (March-April 1925): 95-103.

Tower, Morton L. "Rebuilding Jetties at Humboldt Bay, California." *Professional Memoirs*, 5 (Sept.-Oct. 1913): 499-518.

Tuttle, Donald C. "Problems of the Sea at Buhne Point. . . ." *The Humboldt Historian*, 30 (July-Aug. 1982): 11-13.

Tuttle, Donald C. "Report on the History of Erosion at King Salmon, — Buhne Point, Humboldt Bay California, from 1850-1985." Department of Public Works, Natural Resources Division, Humboldt County, CA, March 1985.

Whalin, Robert W. "Maritime Works." *Centenary of the Permanent International Assoc. of Navigation Congresses*, 1985, pp. 691-711.

Whittemore, George F. "Construction of Concrete Block at end of South Jetty, Humboldt Bay, California." *Professional Memoirs*, 8 (Jan.-Feb. 1916): 31-41.

Whittemore, George F. "Construction of Humboldt Bay Jetties." *The Military Engineer*, 18 (Jan.-Feb. 1926): 60-63.

Whittemore, George F. "Moving Plant from South Jetty to North Jetty, Humboldt Bay, California." *Military Engineer*, 8 (March-April 1916): 196-210.

Whittemore, George F. "Taking Cross-Sections, Humboldt Jetties, California." *Professional Memoirs*, 9 (Sept.-Oct. 1917): 536-41.

Whittemore, George F., and Finch, Henry A. "Concrete Blocks Replace Stone in Jetties Battered by Sea." *Engineering News-Record*, 115 (8 Aug. 1935): 192-94.

Wisner, George H., *et al.* "Jetty Harbors on the Pacific Coast — Discussion on Paper No. 584." *Transactions, Amer. Soc. of Civil Engineers*, 27 (May 1893): 372-89.

Bibliography:
Oceanside Harbor

Books

California Institute of Technology. *Sedimentation Study of Inland California.* Los Angeles: California Institute of Technology, 1978.

Coletta, Paolo E. *United States Navy and Marine Corps Bases, Domestic.* Westport, CT: Greenwood Press, 1985.

Graves, Gregory, and Simon, Sally, eds. *A History of Environmental Review in Santa Barbara County, California.* Santa Barbara, CA: Graduate Program in Public Historical Studies, 1980.

Herron, William J., Jr. *An Oral History of Coastal Engineering Activities in Southern California, 1932-1981.* Los Angeles: U.S. Army Engineer District, 1986.

Kuhn, Gerald G., and Shepard, Francis P. *Sea Cliffs, Beaches, and Coastal Valleys of San Diego County, California: Some Amazing Histories and Some Horrifying Implications.* Berkeley, CA: University of California Press, 1984.

Leeds, Charles T. *Possible Reconstruction of Entrance of Boat Basin, Camp Joseph H. Pendleton.* Los Angeles: Leeds, Hill and Jewett, Engineers, 1944.

———. *Effects of Shore Erosion and Accretion Adjacent to Camp Pendleton Boat Harbor.* Los Angeles: Leeds, Hill, and Jewett, Engineers, 1949.

Leeds, Hill, and Jewett, Engineers. *Shore Protection and Small Craft Harbor Development in the Oceanside-Camp Pendleton Area, California.* Los Angeles: Leeds, Hill, and Jewett, Engineers, 1955.

———. *Beach Erosion at Oceanside, California, and Compensatory Grant of Federal Land.* Los Angeles: Leeds, Hill, and Jewett, Engineers, 1959.

———. *Oceanside Harbor: The Plan and Its Feasibility.* Los Angeles: Leeds, Hill, and Jewett, Engineers, 1959.

———. *Shoaling Study: Oceanside Small Craft Harbor.* Los Angeles: Leeds, Hill, and Jewett, Engineers, 1968.

Moffatt and Nichol, Engineers. *Experimental Sand Bypass System at Oceanside, California: Phase 1 Report: Data Collection and Analysis.* Los Angeles: Moffatt and Nichol, Engineers, 1983.

―――. *Experimental Sand Bypass System at Oceanside, California: Phase 2: Hydraulic Calculations and Drive System Selection.* Los Angeles: Moffatt and Nichol, Engineers, 1984.

―――. *Experimental Sand Bypass System at Oceanside, California: Phase 3: Final Concept.* Los Angeles: Moffatt and Nichol, Engineers, 1984.

Moss, Elaine, ed. *Land Use Controls in the United States: A Handbook on the Legal Rights of Citizens.* New York: Dial Press, 1977.

Pethick, John. *An Introduction to Coastal Geomorphology.* Somerset, England: Edward Arnold Publishers, Ltd., 1984.

Turhollow, Anthony. *A History of the Los Angeles District: U.S. Army Corps of Engineers, 1898-1965.* Los Angeles: U.S. Army Engineer District, 1975.

U.S. Army. Corps of Engineers. *Annual Reports of the Chief of Engineers, 1958-1980.* Washington, DC: Government Printing Office, 1959-81.

―――. *Beach Erosion Control Report on Cooperative Study of Southern California, Cape St. Martin to Mexican Boundary.* Los Angeles: U.S. Army Engineer District, 1967.

―――. *Coastal Storm Damage, 1983.* Los Angeles: U.S. Army Engineer District, 1984.

―――. *Digest of Water Resources Policies and Authorities.* Washington, DC: Government Printing Office, 1983.

―――. *The Experimental Jet-Pump Sand Bypass System at Oceanside: An Operation and Maintenance Program Under Test by the U.S. Army Corps of Engineers to Solve Some Recurring Problems: Harbor Shoaling, Beach Erosion.* Los Angeles: U.S. Army Engineer District, 1987.

―――. *History of Navigation and Navigation Improvements on the Pacific Coast.* Washington, DC: Government Printing Office, 1983.

―――. *Oceanside Harbor and Beach, California, Design of the Structures for Harbor Improvement and Beach Erosion Control.* Vicksburg, MS: Waterways Experiment Station, 1980.

―――. *Report on a Program for Installation, Monitoring, and Evaluating the Effectiveness of a Sand Bypass System as a Means of Maintenance of the Harbor Channels: Oceanside, California.* Los Angeles: U.S. Army Engineer District, 1982.

―――. *San Diego County, Vicinity of Oceanside, California, Draft Survey Report for Beach Erosion Control, Main Report, Environmental Impact*

Statement, and Appendixes. Los Angeles: U.S. Army Engineer District, 1980.

———. *Water Resources Development by the U.S. Army Corps of Engineers in California, 1977.* Washington, DC: Government Printing Office, 1978.

Articles

Bagley, Larry M., and Whitson, Dana Hield. "Putting the Beach Back at the Oceanside," *Shore and Beach* (Oct. 1982): 24-32.

Heiberg, E.R., III. "Coastal Engineering in the Eighties," *Shore and Beach* (July 1982): 3-7.

Herron, William J., Jr., "Periodic Maintenance Starts at Oceanside Harbor." *Southwest Builder and Contractor* (March 1966). Draft in files of Los Angeles District.

———. "The Influence of Man Upon the Shoreline of Southern California." *Shore and Beach* (July 1983): 17-27.

Government Documents

Federal

First War Powers Act. Statutes at Large. Vol. 55 (1941).

Rivers and Harbors Act of 1945. Statutes at Large. Vol. 59 (1945).

Federal Beach Erosion Participation Act. Statutes at Large, Vol. 60 (1946).

Federal Beach Erosion Participation Amendment Act. Statutes at Large. Vol. 70 (1956).

Omnibus Rivers and Harbors Act of 1965. Statutes at Large. Vol. 79 (1965).

Water Resources Development Act of 1976. Statutes at Large. Vol. 90 (1976).

Energy and Water Development Appropriations Act of 1983. Statutes at Large. Vol. 97 (1983).

U.S. Congress. House. *An Act Authorizing the Construction, Repair, and Preservation of Certain Public Works for Rivers and Harbors and for Other Purposes.* Pub. L. 79-525, 79th Cong., 2d sess., 1946, H.R. 6407.

———, *An Act Authorizing Federal Participation in the Cost of Protecting Shores of Publicly Owned Property.* Pub. L. 79-727, 79th Cong., 2d sess., 1946.

———. *An Act Amending an Act Authorizing Federal Participation in the Cost of Protecting Shores of Publicly Owned Property.* Pub. L. 84-826, 84th Cong., 2d sess., 1956.

———. *Report of the Chief of Engineers on Beach Erosion at Oceanside, California.* 84th Cong., 2d sess., 1956, H.D. 399.

———. *Report of the Chief of Engineers on Beach Erosion at Oceanside California.* 86th Cong., 2d sess., 1961, H.D. 456.

———. *Oceanside Harbor (Camp Pendleton), California: An Interim Survey.* 89th Cong., 1st sess., 1964, H.D. 76.

———. *Oceanside Harbor, Oceanside (Camp Pendleton), California.* H.D. 76, 89th Cong., 1st sess., 1965.

———. *Energy and Water Development Appropriations Bill.* H.R. 177, 97th Cong., 1st sess., 1981.

U.S. Congress. Senate. *An Act Authorizing the Construction, Repair, and Preservation of Certain Public Works for Rivers and Harbors and for Other Purposes.* Pub. L. 85-500, 85th Cong., 2d sess., 1958, S. 3950.

———. *An Act to Authorize Certain Beach Erosion Control of the Shore in San Diego County, CA.* Pub. L. 87-89. 86th Cong., 2d sess., 1961, S. 307.

———. *An Act Authorizing Construction, Repair and Preservation of Certain Public Works for Rivers and Harbors and for Other Purposes.* Pub. L. 90-483, 90th Cong., 1st sess., 1968.

———. *Beach Erosion Control Report, Vicinity of Oceanside, California.* Pub. L. 96-367, 96th Cong., 1st sess., 1980.

State

California State Legislature. *Small Craft Harbor Development Act.* A.B. 2939 (1955).

———. *Environmental Review Process Act.* A.B. 884 (1977-78).

———. *Beach Erosion Appropriation Act.* A.B. 1143 (1979-80).

City

City of Oceanside, California. *Resolution of Necessity and of Intent and Capability of the City of Oceanside to Establish and Operate a Harbor.* (7 Aug. 1958).

———. *Resolution Adopting Schematic Plan of Oceanside Harbor and Directing that a Request be Made to the Federal Government for the Land Necessary Therefore.* (10 Sept. 1958).

———. *Resolution Specifying City Responsibilities in Federal Beach Erosion Control Project.* (1960).

———. *Resolution of the Oceanside Small Craft Harbor District.* (14 Aug. 1962).

———. *Resolution 69-5.* (11 June 1965).

———. *Resolution 81-2.* (10 June 1981).

Newspapers

Los Angeles (California) *Times.* 1964-85.

Oceanside (California) *Blade-Tribune.* 1961-83.

San Diego (California) *Reader.* 1977.

San Diego (California) *Union.* 1961-83.

Vista (California) *Press.* 1969.

Archival

Record Group 77. Records of the U.S. Army Corps of Engineers. National Archives and Records Administration, Laguna Niguel, California.

City of Oceanside. City files.

Interviews

Bagley, Mayor Larry. Interview by the author. Oceanside, CA. 28 Apr. 1986.

Diemer, Douglas. Interview by the author. Los Angeles, CA. 2 Apr. 1986.

Enson, Carl. Interview by the author. Los Angeles, CA. 23 May 1986.

Herron, William J., Jr. Self-interviewed. Questions submitted by author. Sun City, AZ. 8 Apr. 1986.

Joe, Robert. Interview by the author. Los Angeles, CA. 23 Apr. 1986.

Revlett, Charles. Interview by the author. Oceanside, CA. 27 Mar. 1986.

Spencer, Donald. Interview by the author. Los Angeles, CA. 23 Apr. 1986.

Weiss, Ronald. Interview by the author. Los Angeles, CA. 2 Apr. 1986.

Whitson, Dana. Interview by the author. Oceanside, CA. 28 Mar. 1986.

Wong, Claude. Interview by the author. Los Angeles, CA. 2 Apr. 1986.

Index